The Official Rails-to-Trails
Conservancy Guidebook

Rail-Trails
Illinois, Indiana & Ohio

The definitive guide to the region's
top multiuse trails

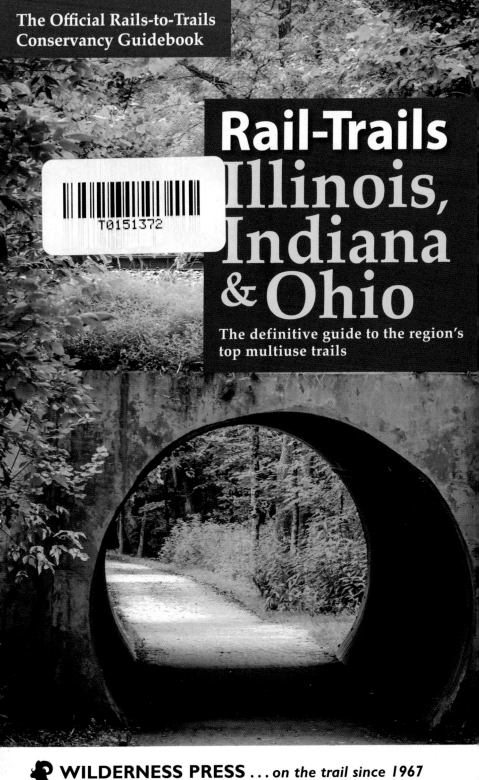

WILDERNESS PRESS ... *on the trail since 1967*

Rail-Trails: Illinois, Indiana, & Ohio

Copyright © 2017 by Rails-to-Trails Conservancy
First edition, seventh printing 2023

Maps: Lohnes+Wright; map data courtesy of Environmental Systems Research Institute
Cover design: Scott McGrew
Book design: Annie Long; book layout: Leslie Shaw

Library of Congress Cataloging-in-Publication Data

Names: Rails-to-Trails Conservancy.
Title: The official Rails-to-Trails Conservancy guidebook : rail-trails Illinois, Indiana, and
    Ohio : the definitive guide to the region's top multiuse trails.
Description: First Edition. | Birmingham, AL : Wilderness Press, [2017] | "Distributed by
    Publishers Group West"—T.p. verso. | Includes index.
Identifiers: LCCN 2016053509| ISBN 9780899978482 (pbk.) | ISBN 9780899978499 (ebook)
Subjects: LCSH: Rail-trails—Illinois—Guidebooks. | Rail-trails—Indiana—Guidebooks. |
    Rail-trails—Ohio—Guidebooks. | Hiking—Illinois—Guidebooks. | Hiking—Indiana—
    Guidebooks. | Hiking—Ohio—Guidebooks. | Bicycle trails—Illinois—Guidebooks.
    | Bicycle trails—Indiana—Guidebooks. | Bicycle trails—Ohio—Guidebooks. | Outdoor
    recreation—Illinois—Guidebooks. | Outdoor recreation—Indiana—Guidebooks. | Out-
    door recreation—Ohio—Guidebooks. | Illinois—Guidebooks. | Indiana—Guidebooks. |
    Ohio—Guidebooks.
Classification: LCC GV191.42.I3 O48 2017 | DDC 796.510977—dc23
LC record available at https://lccn.loc.gov/2016053509

Manufactured in China

Published by:  **WILDERNESS PRESS**
An imprint of AdventureKEEN
2204 First Ave. S, Ste. 102
Birmingham, AL 35233
800-678-7008; fax (877) 374-9016

Visit wildernesspress.com for a complete listing of our books and for ordering information. Contact us at our website, at facebook.com/wildernesspress1967, or at twitter.com
/wilderness1967 with questions or comments. To find out more about who we are and
what we're doing, visit blog.wildernesspress.com.

Distributed by Publishers Group West

Front cover photo: Ohio & Erie Canal Towpath Trail (Trail 57, page 194), photo by Jonathan
VerStrate; *back cover photo*: Great Miami River Trail (Trail 47, page 163), photo by Tom Bilcze

SAFETY NOTICE:: Although Wilderness Press and Rails-to-Trails Conservancy have
made every attempt to ensure that the information in this book is accurate at press time,
they are not responsible for any loss, damage, injury, or inconvenience that may occur to
anyone while using this book. You are responsible for your own safety and health while in
the wilderness. The fact that a trail is described in this book does not mean that it will be
safe for you. Be aware that trail conditions can change from day to day. Always check local
conditions, know your own limitations, and consult a map.

About Rails-to-Trails Conservancy

Headquartered in Washington, D.C., Rails-to-Trails Conservancy (RTC) is a nonprofit organization dedicated to creating a nationwide network of trails from former rail lines and connecting corridors to build healthier places for healthier people.

Railways helped build America. Spanning from coast to coast, these ribbons of steel linked people, communities, and enterprises, spurring commerce and forging a single nation that bridges a continent. But in recent decades, many of these routes have fallen into disuse, severing communal ties that helped bind Americans together.

When RTC opened its doors in 1986, the rail-trail movement was in its infancy. Most projects focused on single, linear routes in rural areas, created for recreation and conservation. RTC sought broader protection for the unused corridors, incorporating rural, suburban, and urban routes.

Year after year, RTC's efforts to protect and align public funding with trail building created an environment that allowed trail advocates in communities across the country to initiate trail projects. These ever-growing ranks of trail professionals, volunteers, and RTC supporters have built momentum for the national rail-trails movement. As the number of supporters multiplied, so did the rail-trails.

Americans now enjoy more than 22,000 miles of open rail-trails, and as they flock to the trails to connect with family members and friends, enjoy nature, and get to places in their local neighborhoods and beyond, their economic prosperity, health, and overall well-being continue to flourish.

A signature endeavor of RTC is **TrailLink.com**, America's portal to these rail-trails, as well as other multiuse trails. When RTC launched **TrailLink.com** in 2000, our organization was one of the first to compile such detailed trail information on a national scale. Today, the website continues to play a critical role in both encouraging and satisfying the country's growing need for opportunities to ride, walk, skate, or run for recreation or transportation. This free trail-finder database—which includes detailed descriptions, interactive maps, photo galleries, and first-hand ratings and reviews—can be used as a companion resource to the trails in this guidebook.

The national voice for more than 160,000 members and supporters, RTC is committed to ensuring a better future for America made possible by trails and the connections they inspire. Learn more at **railstotrails.org**.

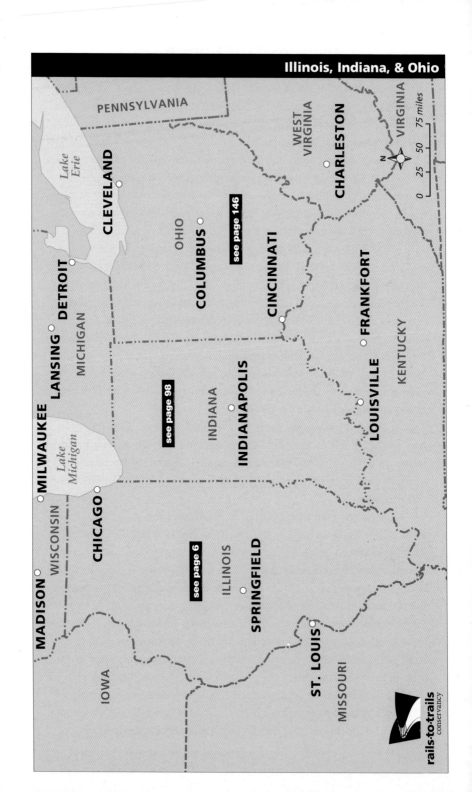

Table of Contents

ILLINOIS 6

INDIANA 98

OHIO 146

For those of you who have already experienced the sheer enjoyment and freedom of riding on a rail-trail, welcome back! You'll find *Rail-Trails: Illinois, Indiana, & Ohio* to be a useful and fun guide to your favorite trails, as well as an introduction to pathways you have yet to travel.

For readers who are discovering for the first time the adventures possible on a rail-trail, thank you for joining the rail-trail movement. Since 1986, Rails-to-Trails Conservancy has been the leading supporter and defender of these priceless public corridors. We are excited to bring you *Rail-Trails: Illinois, Indiana, & Ohio*, so you, too, can enjoy some of the region's premier rail-trails and multiuse trails. These hiking and biking trails are ideal ways to connect with your community, with nature, and with your friends and family.

I've found that trails have a way of bringing people together, and as you'll see from this book, you have opportunities in every state you visit to get on a great trail. Whether you're looking for a place to exercise, explore, commute, or play, there is a trail in this book for you.

So I invite you to sit back, relax, pick a trail that piques your interest—and then get out, get active, and have some fun. I'll be out on the trails too, so be sure to wave as you go by.

Happy trails,

Keith Laughlin, President
Rails-to-Trails Conservancy

Special thanks to writers Gene Bisbee and Debra Eliezer, who contributed a substantial number of trail descriptions for this book.

We are also appreciative of the following contributors and to all the trail managers we called on for assistance to ensure the maps, photographs, and trail descriptions are as accurate as possible.

Aurie Barnes	Milo Bateman
Ken Bryan	Sharon Congdon
Tracy Conoboy	Ryan Cree
Virginia Delaney	Cindy Dickerson
Eli Griffen	Katie McKinney Guerin
Brian Housh	Jake Laughlin
Cam McKinney	Molly McKinney
Margaret Murden	Eric Oberg
Mary O'Connor	Wendy Paulson
Jennifer Sistrunk	Laura Stark
Derek Strout	Liz Thorstensen

Garfield, a character created by a local, waves at visitors from these train cars along the Sweetser Switch Trail (see page 139).

Rail-Trails: Illinois, Indiana, & Ohio highlights 72 of the region's top rail-trails and other multiuse pathways; they offer a broad range of experiences from bucolic Midwestern farmland to woodsy parks and river valleys to vibrant urban centers and friendly small towns.

It was here in the Midwest that the origins of the rail-trail movement began as an intriguing idea that quietly took hold in the 1960s and eventually spread across the country. It was a 1963 *Chicago Tribune* letter to the editor by noted naturalist and writer May Theilgaard Watts that led to the creation of the Illinois Prairie Path. One of the first successful rail-trail conversions in America, it would help create the blueprint for the more than 2,000 rail-trails that exist today, including Chicago's exciting new elevated rail-trail and park system, The 606.

Trail culture continues to thrive in the Midwest as exemplified in the developing Ohio to Erie Trail, which will one day span 320 miles from Cincinnati's Ohio River to the shores of Lake Erie in Cleveland. The monumental task of connecting nearly two dozen trails across the Buckeye State is nearly complete, and 10 of the network's trails are detailed in this book.

Another shining example of trail connectivity is Ohio's Miami Valley network, a hub of interconnected paved trails in the greater Dayton area that spans 340 miles, one of the largest such networks in the country. You'll find two spines of the system—the Little Miami Scenic Trail and Great Miami River Trail—included in these pages, as well as other destination trails in the network.

Indiana is home to a Rail-Trail Hall of Fame star, the Monon Trail, which sets the bar for what an urban rail-trail should be. Newer to the scene is the Indianapolis Cultural Trail; linking five of the city's cultural districts, the trail is flush with museums, theaters, shops, restaurants, public art, and other attractions. Showing off the state's picturesque rural side is the Cardinal Greenway; spanning 61 miles, it is the longest rail-trail in the state.

No matter which routes in *Rail-Trails: Illinois, Indiana, & Ohio* you choose, you'll experience the unique history, culture, and geography of each, as well as the communities that have built and embraced them.

What Is a Rail-Trail?

Rail-trails are multiuse public paths built along former railroad corridors. Most often flat or following a gentle grade, they are suited to walking, running, cycling, mountain biking, in-line skating, cross-country skiing, horseback riding, and wheelchair use. Since the 1960s, Americans have created more than 22,000 miles of rail-trails throughout the country.

These extremely popular recreation and transportation corridors traverse urban, suburban, and rural landscapes. Many preserve historical landmarks, while others serve as wildlife conservation corridors, linking isolated parks and establishing greenways in developed areas. Rail-trails also stimulate local economies by boosting tourism and promoting trailside businesses.

What Is a Rail-with-Trail?

A rail-with-trail is a public path that parallels a still-active rail line. Some run adjacent to high-speed, scheduled trains, often linking public transportation stations, while others follow tourist routes and slow-moving excursion trains. Many share an easement, separated from the rails by extensive fencing. More than 275 rails-with-trails exist in the United States.

*R*ail-Trails: Illinois, Indiana, & Ohio provides the information you'll need to plan a rewarding trek. With words to inspire you and maps to chart your path, it makes choosing the best route a breeze. Following are some of the highlights.

Maps

You'll find three levels of maps in this book: an **overall regional map, state locator maps,** and **detailed trail maps.**

The trails in this book are located in Illinois, Indiana, and Ohio. Each chapter details a particular state's network of trails, marked on locator maps in the chapter introduction. Use these maps to find the trails nearest you, or select several neighboring trails and plan a weekend hiking or biking excursion. Once you find a trail on a state locator map, simply flip to the corresponding page number for a full description. Accompanying trail maps mark each route's access roads, trailheads, parking areas, restrooms, and other defining features.

Key to Map Icons

| Parking | Drinking Water | Restrooms | Featured Trail | Connecting Trail | Active Railroad |

Trail Descriptions

Trails are listed in alphabetical order within each chapter. Each description leads off with a set of summary information, including trail endpoints and mileage, a roughness index, the trail surface, and possible uses.

The map and summary information list the trail endpoints (either a city, street, or more specific location), with suggested points from which to start and finish. Additional access points are marked on the maps and mentioned in the trail descriptions. The maps and descriptions also highlight available amenities, including parking and restrooms, as well as such area attractions as shops, services, museums, parks, and stadiums. Trail length is listed in miles.

Each trail bears a **roughness index** rating from 1 to 3. A rating of 1 indicates a smooth, level surface that is accessible to users of all ages and abilities. A 2 rating means the surface may be loose and/or uneven and could pose a problem for road bikes and wheelchairs. A 3 rating suggests a rough surface that is only recommended for mountain bikers and hikers. Surfaces can range from asphalt or concrete to ballast, boardwalk, cinder, crushed stone, gravel, grass, dirt, sand, and/or wood chips. Where relevant, trail descriptions address alternating surface conditions.

All trails are open to pedestrians, and most allow bicycles, except where noted in the trail summary or description. The summary also indicates wheelchair access. Other possible uses include in-line skating, mountain biking, hiking, horseback riding, fishing, and cross-country skiing. While most trails are off-limits to motor vehicles, some local trail organizations do allow all-terrain vehicles (ATVs) and snowmobiles.

Trail descriptions themselves suggest an ideal itinerary for each route, including the best parking areas and access points, where to begin, your direction of travel, and any highlights along the way. Following each description are directions to the recommended trailheads.

Each trail description also lists a local website for further information. Be sure to visit these websites in advance for updates and current conditions. **TrailLink.com** is another great resource for updated content on the trails in this guidebook.

Trail Use

Rail-trails are popular destinations for a range of users, often making them busy places to enjoy the outdoors. Following basic trail etiquette and safety guidelines will make your experience more pleasant.

➤ **Keep to the right,** except when passing.

➤ **Pass on the left,** and give a clear audible warning: "Passing on your left."

➤ **Be aware** of other trail users, particularly around corners and blind spots, and be especially careful when entering a trail, changing direction, or passing, so that you don't collide with traffic.

➤ **Respect wildlife** and public and private property; leave no trace and take out litter.

➤ **Control your speed,** especially near pedestrians, playgrounds, and heavily congested areas.

➤ **Travel single file.** Cyclists and pedestrians should ride or walk single file in congested areas or areas with reduced visibility.

➤ **Cross carefully** at intersections; always look both ways and yield to through traffic. Pedestrians have the right-of-way.

➤ **Keep one ear open and volume low** on portable listening devices to increase your awareness of your surroundings.

➤ **Wear a helmet** and other safety gear if you're cycling or in-line skating.

➤ **Consider visibility.** Wear reflective clothing, use bicycle lights, or bring flashlights or helmet-mounted lights for tunnel passages or twilight excursions.

➤ **Keep moving,** and don't block the trail. When taking a rest, turn off the trail to the right. Groups should avoid congregating on or blocking the trails. If you have an accident on the trail, move to the right as soon as possible.

➤ **Bicyclists yield** to all other trail users. Pedestrians yield to horses. If in doubt, yield to all other trail users.

➤ **Dogs are permitted** on most trails, but some trails through parks, wildlife refuges, or other sensitive areas may not allow pets; it's best to check the trail website before your visit. If pets are permitted, keep your dog on a short leash and under your control at all times. Remove dog waste in a designated trash receptacle.

➤ **Teach your children** these trail essentials, and be especially diligent to keep them out of faster-moving trail traffic.

➤ **Be prepared,** especially on long-distance rural trails. Bring water, snacks, maps, a light source, matches, and other equipment you may need. Because some areas may not have good reception for cell phones, know where you're going, and tell someone else your plan.

cycling

in-line skating

fishing

wheelchair access

horseback riding

mountain biking

snowmobiling

walking

cross-country skiing

Key to Trail Use

Learn More

To learn about additional multiuse trails in your area or to plan a trip to an area beyond the scope of this book, visit Rails-to-Trails Conservancy's trail-finder website **TrailLink.com**, a free resource with information on more than 30,000 miles of trails nationwide.

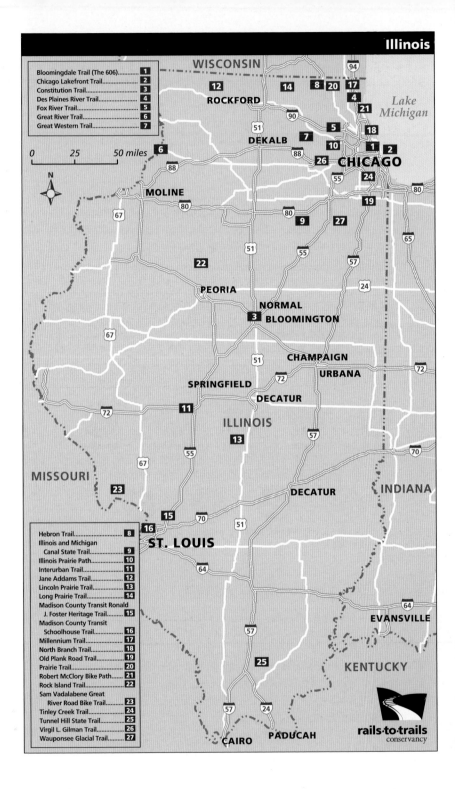

Illinois

WISCONSIN

Lake
Michigan

12   **14**   **8** **20** **17**
4
ROCKFORD
21

90   **5**   **18**

51   **7**
DEKALB   **10**   **1** **2**
88   **26**   CHICAGO
6   **24**

0   25   50 miles   **88**

N   **88**   **19**

MOLINE
80
67   **80**   **80**   **9**   **27**   **65**

51   **55**

57
22

PEORIA   **24**

NORMAL
3 BLOOMINGTON
67

51   CHAMPAIGN
51   **72**   URBANA   **72**
SPRINGFIELD
DECATUR
11
ILLINOIS
13   **57**

MISSOURI   **55**   **70**

67

23   DECATUR   INDIANA

15   **51**
16   **70**
ST. LOUIS

64

EVANSVILLE

57
25   KENTUCKY

57   **24**

CAIRO   PADUCAH

94

rails·to·trails
conservancy

Watch canalboats pass by from the Illinois and Michigan Canal State Trail (see page 35).

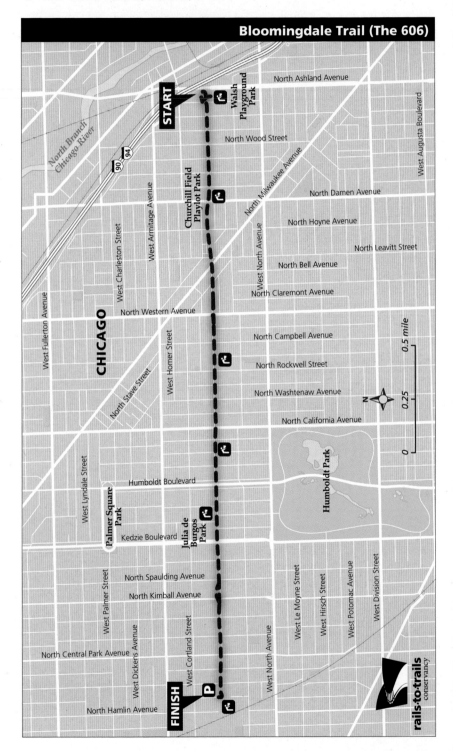

The Bloomingdale Trail, an elevated rail-trail, covers a quick 3 miles just south of Bucktown and Logan Square in Chicago. Plans for this transformation began in the late 1990s, but the freight line remained operational for several more years. By 2003, neighbors and fans of the idea began to gather and advocate, forming the Friends of Bloomingdale Trail (FBT), a nonprofit community involvement group. FBT partnered with the Chicago Park District and The Trust for Public Land, among others, to design and develop ideas for the park. After years of discussions, final plans for the new trail were revealed in 2013, and the trail opened in 2015.

The trail, which sits 17 feet above the roads below, travels through four different neighborhoods in Northwest Chicago; an estimated 80,000-plus people live within a 10-minute walk of the pathway and the parks

The pathway is well integrated into Chicago's northern neighborhoods.

County
Cook

Endpoints
Walsh Playground Park (N. Marshfield Ave. near W. Bloomingdale Ave.) to N. Ridgeway Ave. just south of W. Cortland St. (Chicago)

Mileage
3.0

Type
Rail-Trail

Roughness Index
1

Surface
Asphalt, Concrete

surrounding it. As you travel along the trail among cyclists, strollers, runners, people walking their dogs, and children riding their bikes, you get a very neighborhood feel. Numerous coffee shops, bars, restaurants, and shopping districts are also all within a few blocks of the route. You'll pass five trailside parks, many historical sites, and other points of interest on your journey too.

Twelve ramps down to street level allow for ample neighborhood use. The paved trail is 14 feet wide with a sleek, modern look featuring steel railings, bike parking, benches, and landscaping along its entire length. Currently, there are no restrooms along the trail, but both the eastern and western trailheads have bike repair stations and water fountains.

CONTACT: bloomingdaletrail.org

DIRECTIONS

To reach Walsh Playground Park (the eastern trailhead), take I-90/I-94 to Exit 48A for Armitage Ave. Head east on W. Armitage Ave. and travel about 450 feet before turning right onto N. Ashland Ave. After 0.3 mile, you will see Walsh Playground Park on your right; look for street parking near the park.

To reach the western trailhead, take I-90/I-94 to Exit 47A for Fullerton Ave. Head west on W. Fullerton Ave. and travel along it 1.3 miles. Turn left onto N. Kedzie Blvd., traveling south 0.5 mile. Turn right onto W. Armitage Ave., now traveling west 0.7 mile. Turn left onto N. Ridgeway Ave. and you will see the trail entrance at the cul-de-sac at the end of the road. Look for street parking in this neighborhood.

The Chicago Lakefront Trail is aptly named; it spans 19 miles along the shore of Lake Michigan, going right through downtown Chicago and passing many cultural and tourist attractions throughout the city.

The trail starts at the south end of the South Shore Cultural Center, about 9.5 miles south of downtown Chicago. You begin your ride through Jackson Park and soon pass the Museum of Science and Industry and Promontory Point, a lovely peninsula that provides your first views of the skyline.

You'll pedal through Burnham Park, which maintains a few nature sanctuaries and harbors. A bit farther north, you'll catch a few more interesting sights, such as Soldier Field, Adler Planetarium, and Shedd Aquarium, just before you enter Grant Park in downtown Chicago. You have reached the center of the city—and you

The trail offers outstanding views of Chicago's skyline and Lake Michigan.

County
Cook

Endpoints
E. 71st. St. and S. South Shore Dr. (US 41) to W. Ardmore Ave. and N. Sheridan Road (Chicago)

Mileage
19.0

Type
Greenway/Non-Rail-Trail

Roughness Index
1

Surface
Asphalt, Concrete

Chicago Lakefront Trail

can certainly tell! Tourists and locals flock to this portion of the trail, which provides direct access to Navy Pier, a former navy center that now maintains restaurants, shops, and carnival rides.

As you continue, you'll find yourself surrounded by Lincoln Park, which is home to a zoo, conservatory, and nature museum. To your right, you'll see one of Chicago's most popular beaches, North Avenue Beach, which lines the lake. A few miles farther north, you'll pass a couple more beaches—Montrose Beach and Foster Beach—and your ride will end as you hit Kathy Osterman Beach.

Throughout the trail, you'll find ample amenities, such as restrooms, water fountains, and concessions. Do be wary of traffic as you near the center of downtown; there are a number of intersections to cross, as well as increased foot and bike traffic. And don't forget your bike lock if you plan to stop at any of the numerous attractions along the way, and, of course, bring your camera.

CONTACT: choosechicago.com/articles/view/the-lakefront-trail/454

DIRECTIONS

To access the southern trailhead, take I-55 N to US 41 S/S. Lake Shore Dr. near mile marker 293. Merge onto US 41 S, and go 5.3 miles. Use the left two lanes to turn left onto E. Marquette Dr., which you'll follow 0.5 mile. This will pop you onto S. South Shore Dr. Continue 0.5 mile and use the left two lanes to turn left onto E. 71st St. The trailhead will be on the left, along the wall of the South Shore Cultural Center. Look for street parking in this neighborhood.

To access the northern trailhead, take I-55 N to US 41 N/S. Lake Shore Dr. near mile marker 293. Merge onto US 41 N, and go 9.9 miles. Turn right onto N. Sheridan Road and in 0.1 mile turn right at the first cross street onto W. Ardmore Ave. You will see signage for the trailhead; look for street parking in this neighborhood.

Constitution Trail

East 2100 North Road

Sixmile Creek

East 2000 North Road

39

51

Ziebarth Road

FINISH

North 1500 East Road

North 1600 East Road

North 1700 East Road

North 1800 East Road

55

TOWANDA

Boyd-Wesley Park

East 1800 North Road

Northtown Branch

Northtown Road

Old Route 66

74

P

Heartland Community College

Corn Crib Baseball Stadium

Collegiate Branch

150

North 1200 East Road

Fairview Park

51

Rosa Parks Commons

55

Route 66 Branch

Maxwell Park

55

74

P

Hershey Road

Fort Jesse Road

NORMAL

East College Avenue

Anderson Park

P

Tipton Park

P

Illinois State University

Illinois Central Branch

Clearwater Park

P

Bloomer Line Branch

P

East Empire Street

9

North Mitsubishi Motorway

P

150

Alton Depot Park

P

P

BLOOMINGTON

START

East Empire Street

Central Illinois Regional Airport

Interurban Branch

55

74

P

Miller Park

East Lincoln Street

State Farm Lake

P

Rollingbrook Park

North Towanda Barnes Road

Pepperridge Park

P

State Farm Park

P

P

P

P

Southtown Branch

Morrissey Drive

Pipeline Road

Old Route 66

55

74

51

North 1375 East Road

74

150

74

Route 66 Branch

55

East 800 North Road

rails·to·trails
conservancy

East 700 North Road

51

N

0   1   2   3 miles

The sprawling Constitution Trail covers more than 46 miles throughout the Bloomington-Normal region. The trail was officially named and dedicated in 1987 in celebration of the 200th anniversary of the United States Constitution. The first completed segment opened to the public in 1989, and since then, the trail has grown from the original rail-trail built on the corridor of the Illinois Central Gulf Railroad into an impressive trail network spanning across the region with several small gaps yet to be filled in.

The **Illinois Central Branch**, the main spine of the trail, begins at Croxton Avenue and Indianapolis Street and travels northward through an industrial area. The pathway takes you by the Beer Nuts production plant, where you can visit the company store of the famous Bloomington-produced snack. Shortly after passing through the Washington Street tunnel, you'll come to the Atwood Wayside trailhead with a covered picnic area, water fountain, and parking area.

County
McClean

Endpoints
Croxton Ave. and Indianapolis St. (Bloomington) to W. Ziebarth Road 0.5 mile east of US 51 Bus. (Normal), with several branches extending east and west

Mileage
46.4

Type
Rail-Trail/Rail-with-Trail

Roughness Index
1

Surface
Asphalt, Concrete

The western end of the Southtown Branch has a neighborhood feel.

The tree-lined trail continues through a mix of residential and forested areas. Along the way, be sure to read the historical markers with stories of the rail corridor's past. After passing over Emerson Street and Sugar Creek, you'll pass under the historic Camelback Bridge: its distinctive shape allowed the tall stacks of wood-burning locomotives to pass under it. The wooden bridge is the oldest surviving structure associated with the rail corridor.

Just a few yards farther, you'll come to Allers Shelter Wayside, where the **Bloomer Line Branch** of the trail heads east. This 4-mile section of trail travels through peaceful Bloomington neighborhoods and shopping areas. Along the way, the trail passes by several parks with pleasant side paths to take in the scenery. Three miles in, you'll arrive at Tipton Park, which features an expansive path that takes you through ponds and a lush prairie habitat. About a mile farther, the Bloomer Line Branch comes to an end at the edge of town on Towanda Barnes Road.

Continuing north on the Illinois Central Branch from Allers Shelter Wayside brings you to the town of Normal. Here, the route passes through the center of the trendy Uptown district near Illinois State University (ISU). This neighborhood features several local shops and restaurants just off the path. The **Collegiate Branch** of the trail begins here, heads through the ISU campus, and connects to Heartland Community College. The trail also runs along Fairview Park and an adjacent golf course, making for a tree-canopied mile-long section.

The Illinois Central Branch continues out of the Uptown district along a forested corridor, becoming more and more rural. At the edge of town, you'll pass by Rosa Parks Commons, a vast open field with a playground, restrooms, water, and parking. A mile later, you'll intersect with the **Northtown Branch** of the trail at Northtown Road. This 3-mile section heads east along the roadway and loops around a neighborhood surrounding a large pond.

The **Interurban Branch** is the westernmost section of the trail network. The West Route 9 Wayside trailhead is located on 1400 North Road, just west of the Mitsubishi Motorway (US 150). The trailhead features plenty of parking and a large map to help guide your journey. The first 2 miles of the Interurban Branch are largely rural along the tree-lined path. When you pass under I-74, things begin to change into a more industrial feel. After passing over Goose Creek on the modern trestle, the trail parallels West Washington Street for a stretch, then zigzags across and over railroad tracks into Alton Depot Park. The trail continues alongside an active railroad line for just over a mile before stopping at East Lincoln Street. Turn left (east) here and the trail will pick up as a wide sidewalk on Lincoln Street (just past Bunn Street) until this section ends 0.5 mile later at McGregor Street.

The **Southtown Branch** of the trail begins at the intersection of Fox Creek Road and Historic US Route 66, merging for a time with the Route 66 Branch.

This section continues along Hamilton Road until Bunn Street. After a short gap, the trail picks up again at the intersection of Commerce Parkway and Hamilton Road, but you can access the trail by traveling on Rhodes Lane, then turning left onto Morrissey Drive and continuing on the wide side path at Hamilton Road. The trail briefly shares a boundary with an active railway, forming a rail-with-trail segment. The trail then turns north, passes beneath Hamilton Road, and briefly follows a small creek on its way toward Ireland Grove Road. A loop trail that circles State Farm Lake can extend the trip by roughly a mile. During the day, employees can be seen enjoying the outdoors.

The trail crosses Ireland Grove Road and loosely parallels Arcadia Drive. Like the previous section, it offers a few sweeping turns. A short spur leads back south to parking along North 1200 East Road. When the trail approaches East Lincoln Street, it crosses over to the northern side of the roadway and follows the wide sidewalk along it. At South Hershey Road, you can go north to access parking and facilities at Rollingbrook Park or continue east on the trail. Here, the trail separates from the road and meanders briefly along a small creek and then through nicely kept neighborhoods before it joins White Eagle Drive. It remains a separated trail for another 0.5 mile, where it ends at Streid Drive.

As its name implies, the **Route 66 Branch** follows the famed US highway. Work on this section of the trail network is ongoing, with complete stretches open from the small community of Shirley northeast to Bloomington, and from Normal northeast to the town of Towanda.

CONTACT: constitutiontrail.org

DIRECTIONS

To reach the Atwood Wayside trailhead on the southern end of the Illinois Central Branch: From I-55/I-74, take Exit 160 for US 150. Head east on US 150/W. Market St. In 1.1 miles, turn left onto N. Hinshaw Ave., then take the second right onto W. Locust St. After 1.5 miles, turn right onto N. Robinson St. Four blocks down the street, the trailhead's parking lot will be on your left, just past E. Monroe St.

To reach the northern trailhead of the Illinois Central Branch at Kerrick Road/County Road 1850: From I-55, take Exit 165B for US 51 Bus. N/N. Main St. and head north. In about 1.25 miles, turn right onto Kerrick Road/CR 1850. The parking area will be past three warehouse driveways on the right side.

There are numerous other trailheads for this extensive trail system throughout the Bloomington-Normal area; visit constitutiontrail.org or TrailLink.com for detailed maps and parking directions for those locations.

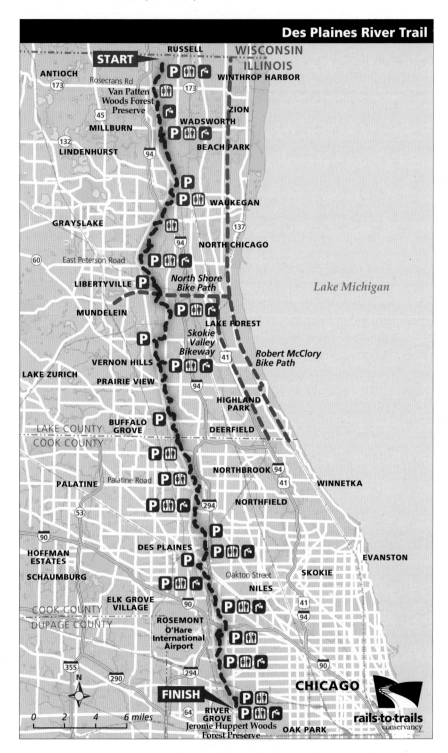

Des Plaines River Trail

The Des Plaines River Trail runs alongside the Des Plaines River for just over 56 miles, protecting watershed habitat and forestland through much of Lake and Cook Counties. The trail is a natural oasis within a short drive of Chicago and its northern suburbs. Having such a long, lush trail just outside of such a densely populated urban area is truly a wonderful asset to the surrounding community.

Traveling from the north end to the south end, you will experience a variety of trail surfaces, from pavement to crushed stone to singletrack forest trail. Be prepared for this terrain to change quickly and often for an exciting adventure at every turn. More novice riders and hikers might wish to start at the northern end and travel south the first 20 miles. Along this segment, users will find that the trail

Counties
Cook, Lake

Endpoints
Van Patten Woods Forest Preserve entrance on Russell Road/County Road 19 (Wadsworth) to Jerome Huppert Woods Forest Preserve near IL 64 and IL 171 (River Grove)

Mileage
56.2

Type
Greenway/Rail-with-Trail

Roughness Index
1–2

Surface
Asphalt, Crushed Stone, Dirt, Gravel

The path closely follows the Des Plaines River for nearly its entire length.

is well maintained and frequented by nearby residents. Keep an eye out for deer, birds, snakes, and turtles, all native to the area and abundant along the path.

Moving farther south, the corridor becomes narrow and filled with roots in certain segments. If the ground is wet, be careful when making turns. Also be cautious at the multiple instances where the trail crosses over several highly trafficked roads. Most of these intersections are well marked and have signals for cars to stop. Additionally, several crossings are by tunnel, which makes it much easier to continue along the trail at these intersections.

Just north of Golf Road in Des Plaines, the trail runs into an active railroad line and continues just on the other side of the tracks. Caution should be used here when crossing the tracks.

Restrooms, picnic areas, and water fountains are frequent throughout this system of connected forest preserves. Several parking lots are also located along the trail's entire length, making it easy to access the route at a variety of points.

CONTACT: fpdcc.com/preserves-and-trails/trail-descriptions/#des-plaines or lcfpd.org/dprt

DIRECTIONS

To reach the Van Patten Woods Forest Preserve at the north end of the trail: From I-94, take Exit 2 for IL 173/Rosecrans Road. Head east on IL 173 E/Rosecrans Road and follow it 1 mile before taking a left into the Van Patten Woods Forest Preserve.

To reach the Jerome Huppert Woods Forest Preserve at the trail's southern end: From I-294, take Exit 39 for Balmoral Ave. Head east on Balmoral Ave. and follow it 0.3 mile, and then turn right onto Des Plaines River Road/N. River Road. After 1.7 miles, turn left onto W. Irving Park Road/IL 19 and travel 1.1 miles before turning right onto N. Cumberland Ave./IL 171. Cumberland turns into Thatcher Ave., which then turns into N. First Ave. Two miles from W. Irving Park Road, turn left onto W. Fullerton Ave. and then turn right at the first cross street onto Thatcher Ave. In 1 mile, you will reach Jerome Huppert Woods Forest Preserve; take a right to enter the park.

tarting from its southern terminus, the Fox River Trail (FRT) originates in the charming village of Oswego, located 50 miles west of Chicago. The trail begins in Hudson Crossing Park, which faces the Fox River and has playgrounds, picnic areas, and benches, as well as a restroom and drinking fountain. At the north end of the park, there's a fork in the trail; veer left to continue on the FRT. For a fun diversion, the right fork takes you on a short pathway along Waubonsie Creek through a small, serene park and leads to downtown.

Leaving Hudson Crossing Park, you'll cross over Waubonsie Creek and parallel the Fox River. After going through another small park, the trail becomes an on-road route for a short distance. Make a left at North Adams Street and travel on the roadway 0.5 mile through a quiet residential area with very little car traffic. At the next bend

For most of its journey, the trail parallels the Fox River.

Counties
Kane, Kendall

Endpoints
Washington St. and S. Harrison St. (Oswego) to Souwanas Trail and Scott St. (Algonquin)

Mileage
44.6

Type
Rail-Trail/Rail-with-Trail

Roughness Index
1

Surface
Asphalt, Concrete, Crushed Stone

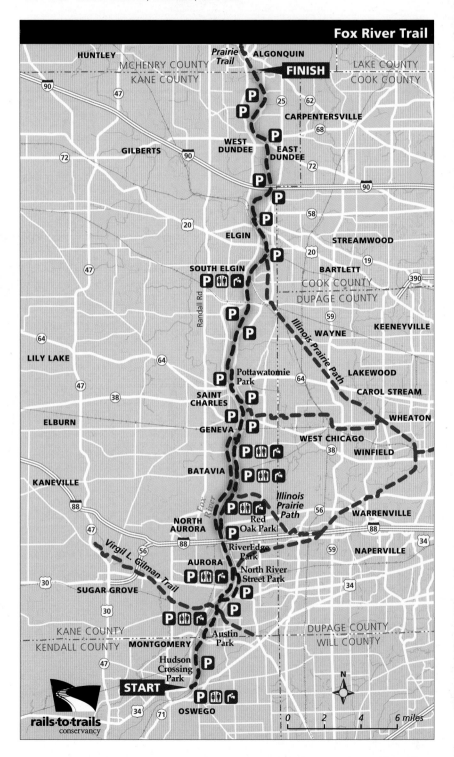

This charming view of the Waubonsie Creek awaits you in Oswego.

in the road, stay to the left, and do not cross the train tracks. The off-road section of the FRT begins again after making a right onto Second Street.

Leaving Oswego, the path is sandwiched between the river and IL 25 for 4.8 miles to the Fox River crossing on the south end of Aurora. The trail initially passes through a mix of commercial districts and neighborhoods, a suburban-urban interface that the FRT weaves in and out of for the entire route.

At mile 4 is Montgomery Dam, a popular fishing spot and 1 of 13 dams along the Fox River. Here, the path traverses a narrow peninsula, then crosses the river back to its east bank. Shortly thereafter, you'll cross to the river's west side on a truss bridge, which is also part of the Virgil L. Gilman Trail (see page 92). Immediately after crossing the bridge, turn right to head north (if you stay straight, you remain on the Virgil L. Gilman Trail) to ride the length of Hurd's Island. Leaving the island, you'll travel 0.5 mile along an on-road protected bike lane.

Aurora (mile 6.5) extends into four counties and features three nationally registered historic districts. The city is actively improving its downtown, including the addition of a riverfront park that the trail passes through north of West Downer Place. Beginning at East New York Street, a mile-long segment of the FRT runs up both the west and east sides of the river. The eastern leg of the trail ends at East Illinois Avenue; on the north side of East Illinois Avenue, you can pick up the Illinois Prairie Path (see page 40) on the far side of a parking lot. If you travel on the west side of the Fox River, you'll cycle through North River Street Park and McCullough Park.

The FRT hugs the river's edge as it carries on toward North Aurora and, for the most part, avoids the hustle and bustle of the city. At the North Aurora Dam, the trail once again splits to run up both sides of the river; the section on the east bank runs through Red Oak Park and Glenwood Park Forest Preserve. The trail merges back into one in Batavia. Make sure to stop in at the Batavia Depot Museum, which houses exhibits about the three railroad corridors that now make up the Fox River Trail, and the Fabyan Villa Museum, redesigned in 1907 by Frank Lloyd Wright.

You'll continue through the communities of Geneva and Saint Charles, as well as several more parks. In South Elgin, you can ride an electric trolley at the Fox River Trolley Museum, which operates a passenger car for a 4-mile round-trip ride along the banks of the river. The FRT runs alongside the rail tracks to the museum. It then crosses the river via a bridge built on the original 1896 piers to stay on the eastern side of the river for the remainder of the ride.

From the bridge crossing, it's 3.5 miles to downtown Elgin. Note that on your way to Elgin, you'll travel through tranquil forest preserves but will also have a couple of short on-road segments to navigate. The FRT goes through East Dundee, a small village established in 1871, and ends at the southern end of Algonquin, where you can pick up the Prairie Trail (see page 71).

CONTACT: oswegolandparkdistrict.org/parks-facilities/trails-parks or foxvalleyparkdistrict.org/trails

DIRECTIONS

There are numerous parking points along the trail's 44-mile length; check the trail websites above or TrailLink.com for details.

The closest parking area to the FRT's southern terminus is at Hudson Crossing Park at Harrison St. in downtown Oswego. To reach it from I-88, take the IL 31 exit near mile marker 117 toward Aurora/Batavia, and head south on IL 31 S/S. Lincolnway St. Stay on IL 31 S 8.4 miles, past Aurora. Immediately after the Oswego Village Hall, make a left onto Washington St. and cross the Fox River. The first street immediately after crossing the Fox River will be S. Harrison St. Make a left onto S. Harrison St. and into the parking lot for Hudson Crossing Park.

On the northern end of the trail, you can park in Algonquin's Riverfront Park (201 N. Harrison St.). To reach the park from I-90, take the exit for IL 31 near mile marker 55. Go north 7.2 miles on IL 31, and turn right onto S. Main St. In 0.1 mile turn right onto Washington St., and then make an immediate left onto S. Harrison St. Riverfront Park is approximately 0.25 mile ahead. From the parking lot, you will need to walk or ride about 0.5 mile southwest on Harrison St. to the Prairie Trail, and then go southeast 1 mile on the pathway to reach the FRT.

The Great River Trail is a breathtaking journey along more than 60 miles of the Mississippi River in northern Illinois. In places, the paved trail follows the former spur route of the Chicago, St. Paul, Milwaukee and Pacific Railroad. Elsewhere, it's a mix of low-traffic rural roads, dedicated bike lanes, and riverfront trails running atop flood levees. It's part of the 500-mile Grand Illinois Trail network in the north; in the south, it traces the American Discovery Trail, which crosses the country with a mixture of trails and on-road routes.

The Great River Trail hugs the Mississippi River as it winds through Port Byron, a charming river town.

Counties
Carroll, Rock Island, Whiteside

Endpoints
Broderick Dr. at US 52 (Savanna) to Sunset Park at 18th Ave. and Mill St. (Rock Island)

Mileage
62.3

Type
Rail-Trail/Rail-with Trail

Roughness Index
1

Surface
Asphalt

Great River Trail

Starting in Savanna, you'll head south through several small towns with traditions still steeped in river culture before reaching the industrial center of the Quad Cities, which includes Rock Island and Moline. Many opportunities exist for browsing antiques, enjoying catfish dinners, and viewing river traffic. Camping and lodging are available for overnight trips. Leaving Savanna, the secluded route rolls across the sand prairie, past nature preserves and farmland to Thomson. Watch for signs that direct you onto quiet local roads from the paved trail.

Farther south, in Fulton, an unusual sight greets you: a Dutch windmill that will make you feel as though you've been transported to the Netherlands. It's no wonder; the structure was originally built there and then transported here to be reassembled by craftsmen.

About 8 miles south in Albany, take a short detour through the Albany Indian Mounds State Historic Site and view dozens of earthen burial mounds that date back more than 2,000 years.

The trail runs alongside IL 84 (Great River Road) most of the way to Cordova, where it meanders through town on local streets. After less than 2 miles, the rail-trail picks up again and closely follows Great River Road for 4 miles into Port Byron, a charming river town visible from the trail's riverbank course. Most of the corridor here is shared with an active rail line, offering a fine example of a safe rail-with-trail relationship.

Three miles downriver is Rapids City, where blue herons, gulls, and other waterfowl are plentiful.

As the Great River Trail crests a levee 4 miles south in Hampton, you get a glimpse of Campbell's Island, the site of the Battle of Rock Island Rapids during the War of 1812. Just ahead on the left, the John Deere manufacturing plant marks the beginning of the trail's urban section. Traveling atop the levee affords majestic vistas of the bridges over the Mississippi River connecting the Quad Cities.

After 5.5 miles, you'll reach Moline. Follow the bike route signs to navigate through the city. Consider stopping at the Quad Cities Convention & Visitors Bureau at Bass Street Landing Plaza on Moline's waterfront. Looking across the slough as you return to the trail, you can see Arsenal Island, home to the historic Rock Island Arsenal, still in operation by the U.S. Army. It also was a prison camp for Confederate soldiers during the Civil War.

Leaving downtown Moline, the route stays up on the riverbank and crosses under the Centennial Bridge as you enter the city of Rock Island. The industrial skyline dominates the landscape for most of the final 7.5 miles to Sunset Park, where a large marina and extensive river views provide a fitting end to this scenic path.

CONTACT: greatrivertrail.org or **qctrails.org/trails/trail/great-river-trail**

DIRECTIONS

To reach the trailhead in Savanna from I-80, take Exit 1 for IL 84. Head north on IL 84 for 41.5 miles, and turn left onto Chicago Ave./US 52. In 1.1 miles, turn left onto Broderick Dr. at the intersection with Main St. Follow signs to Bike Trail Access and Savanna Train Car Museum.

To reach the trailhead at Sunset Park in Rock Island: From I-280, take Exit 11B and merge onto IL 92 E/Centennial Expy. In 1.5 miles, take the 31st Ave. exit and, at the end of the ramp, turn left onto Sunset Lane. Follow the roadway 0.6 mile into the park; look for parking on the right.

A trek on the 17-mile Great Western Trail is a great way to spend the day with family. At the trailhead on Dean Street in Saint Charles, you will find restrooms, water, and a connection to the Randall Road Bike Trail, if you want to extend your trip. The trail surface is primarily crushed stone, but occasional paved sections appear toward its eastern end. The trail surface and adjacent areas are well maintained, and the trail is well integrated within the local community.

This busy section of trail heads northwest toward Wasco and offers opportunities along the way for food and refreshments. A pleasant combination of tree canopy cover and open areas with wildflowers keep the pathway from becoming routine.

A few miles from the west end of the trail, you'll find the Sycamore Speedway and its racing-themed restaurant

A pleasant combination of tree canopy and open areas with wildflowers enrich the trail experience.

Counties
DeKalb, Kane

Endpoints
LeRoy Oakes Forest Preserve at Dean St. 0.25 mile west of Bittersweet Road (Saint Charles) to Old State Road and Ali Dr. (Sycamore)

Mileage
17.0

Type
Rail-Trail

Roughness Index
1–2

Surface
Asphalt, Crushed Stone

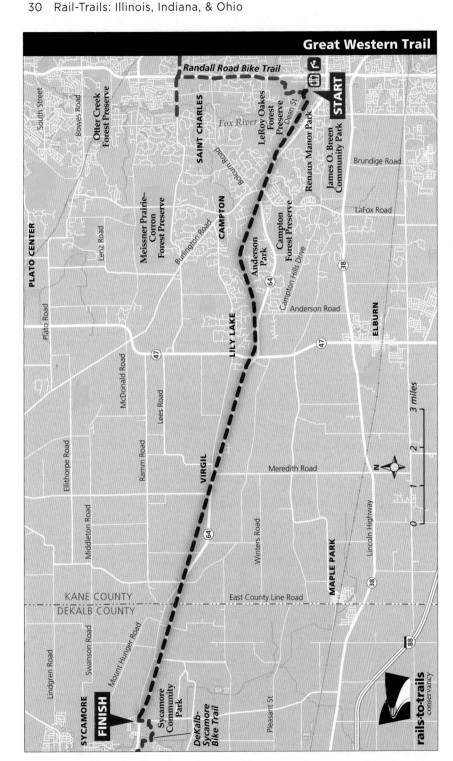

Great Western Trail

Randall Road Bike Trail

START

South Street

Bowes Road

Otter Creek Forest Preserve

SAINT CHARLES

Fox River

LeRoy Oakes Forest Preserve

Dean St

Renaux Manor Park

James O. Breen Community Park

Brundige Road

Boldwin Road

CAMPTON

Meissner Prairie–Corron Forest Preserve

Burlington Road

Lenz Road

Campton Forest Preserve

LaFox Road

PLATO CENTER

Plato Road

Anderson Park

Campton Hills Drive

38

64

Anderson Road

McDonald Road

LILY LAKE

47

ELBURN

47

Lees Road

Ellithorpe Road

Ramm Road

VIRGIL

Meredith Road

3 miles

N

2

Middleton Road

64

1

Lincoln Highway

0

Winters Road

MAPLE PARK

38

KANE COUNTY

DEKALB COUNTY

East County Line Road

Lindgren Road

Swanson Road

Mount Hunger Road

SYCAMORE

FINISH

Sycamore Community Park

DeKalb–Sycamore Bike Trail

Pleasant St

88

rails-to-trails
conservancy

located on the right for all those with a secret interest in stock car racing and demolition derbies. The trail continues about 4 miles more before the rail-trail portion ends at the small parking lot at Old State Road, on the outskirts of Sycamore.

From this location, an on-road route continues mostly along shared roadways through Sycamore Community Park, the Sycamore Community Golf Course, and residential neighborhoods to a connection with the DeKalb-Sycamore Bike Trail (also known as the Peace Road Trail).

CONTACT: kaneforest.com/recreation/trails/greatWestern.aspx

DIRECTIONS

On the east end of the trail in Saint Charles, a trailhead with parking can be found in the LeRoy Oakes Forest Preserve. From I-88, take the exit for IL 31 E near mile marker 117. Head north on IL 31 for 8.8 miles. Turn left onto W. Main St./IL 64. In 0.5 mile, turn right onto N. Ninth St., which becomes Dean St. Take Dean St. 1.2 miles to the forest preserve's parking lot, which will be on your left.

In Sycamore, on the west end of the trail, parking is located off Old State Road. From I-88, take Exit 94 for Peace Road, and head north on Peace Road. Follow the roadway 6.6 miles, then turn right onto W. State St./IL 64. Follow IL 64 for 2.6 miles east to its intersection with Old State Road. Veer left to get onto Old State Road and take this road to the parking lot, which is only about 400 feet farther.

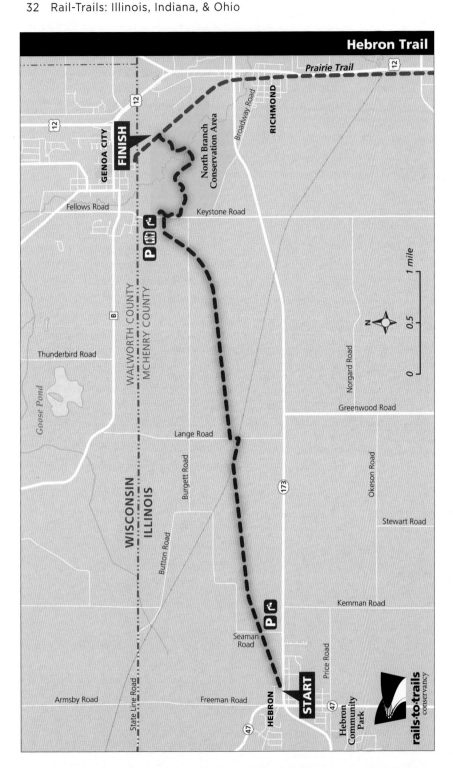

Hebron Trail

The Hebron Trail rolls across the northern Illinois prairie through the former corridor of the Kenosha and Rockford Railroad, known as the Kenosha Division Line at the time of its demise in 1939. Launched in 1861, the railroad boosted economies along its rural route by serving dairy farmers and carrying passengers. Though agriculture still plays a role in the local economy, the railroad closed shop after farmers began hauling their goods to market by truck and passengers turned to the automobile.

Founded 25 years before the railroad arrived, the town of Hebron served as a midpoint stop on the 72-mile-long rail line. Today, it serves as a trailhead for the 6.7-mile Hebron Trail that runs east to the North Branch Conservation Area and a junction with the Prairie Trail (see page

The feeling of the Hebron Trail is undeniably rural.

County
McHenry

Endpoints
Church St. near Maple Ave./IL 173 (Hebron) to Prairie Trail, about a mile north of Kenosha St./ IL 173 and N. Main St. (Richmond)

Mileage
6.7

Type
Rail-Trail

Roughness Index
2

Surface
Crushed Stone, Gravel

71). The crushed-stone path is also part of the 500-mile Grand Illinois Trail that loops around northern Illinois.

To verify that you're in the right town to start your trek, look over the rooftops for a soaring water tower. If the tank is painted to look like a giant basketball, then you're in the right place. The water tower commemorates the state basketball championship won in 1952 by the local high school, the smallest ever to win the statewide honors.

Departing from the trail's parking lot on Seaman Road (about 0.5 mile from the western end of the trail), visitors pass through a shady, wooded corridor that screens the trail from farm fields that border it. The trees disappear after a mile, offering views of cornfields and other crops in a landscape punctuated by red barns and silver silos. A short zag onto a country road at a railroad crossing interrupts the trail after about 2 miles.

The route continues across open farmland and occasional tree-lined corridors until it reaches the North Branch Conservation Area. The preserve is managed by the McHenry County Conservation District, which also oversees the Hebron Trail and more than 115 miles of other trails in the county.

The trail leaves the railroad corridor here and takes a curving route through the 521-acre preserve for about 1.5 miles to the Prairie Trail. Bird-watchers can identify 80 species in the grasslands and forests of the nature preserve. Many species of mussels and fish—some threatened or endangered—live in the clear waters of Nippersink Creek.

The county set aside a small primitive camping area with pit toilets and a drinking fountain in the preserve, where traveling bicyclists can pitch their tents and be lulled to sleep by the croaking of frogs. Note that a permit is required to camp; visit the McHenry County Conservation District website for more information.

CONTACT: mccdistrict.org/rccms/index.php/hebron-trail

DIRECTIONS

To reach the western trailhead in Hebron: From I-94, take Exit 2 for IL 173/Rosecrans Road. Head west on IL 173 for 24.1 miles, then turn right onto Seaman Road. Continue 0.2 mile to a trailhead parking lot on the right. The trailhead is 0.6 mile west in Hebron.

To reach the eastern trailhead at the North Branch Conservation Area from I-94, take Exit 2 for IL 173/Rosecrans Road. Head west on IL 173 for 19.1 miles. Turn right onto Broadway Road, then go another 0.7 mile and turn right onto Keystone Road. The North Branch Conservation Area parking lot is on the right in 0.6 mile. The eastern endpoint at the junction with Prairie Trail is 1.4 miles east via the Hebron Trail.

The Illinois and Michigan (I&M) Canal State Trail follows the eponymous waterway alongside the Illinois River. The trail runs along the old canal towpath from LaSalle to the historical quarry town of Lemont, with a gap in Joliet and a heavily industrial spur through Romeoville. Nearly every mile, you'll find educational markers, so you can learn about the history of the canal and the stories of those who built and traveled the waterway.

The trail surface varies, from well-maintained crushed limestone to grass, asphalt, and gravel. In some sections, the path exists on both sides of the canal. Bicyclists should use thicker tires (hybrids or larger).

The route begins just south of the town of LaSalle at Huse Lake. The trailhead is located at a historical canal lock. Enjoy a mule-powered ride in a replica canalboat or explore Lock 14 and the steel silhouettes that help tell the stories of Abraham Lincoln and his family, "Wild Bill" Hickok, and other personalities associated with the canal.

At the LaSalle trailhead, you'll find this silhouette of Abraham Lincoln and his family.

Counties
Grundy, LaSalle, Will

Endpoints
Huse Lake near Joliet St./ IL 351 and A St. (LaSalle) to near Maley Road and Main St. (Lemont)

Mileage
79.5

Type
Canal/Rail-with-Trail

Roughness Index
2–3

Surface
Asphalt, Crushed Stone, Gravel, Grass

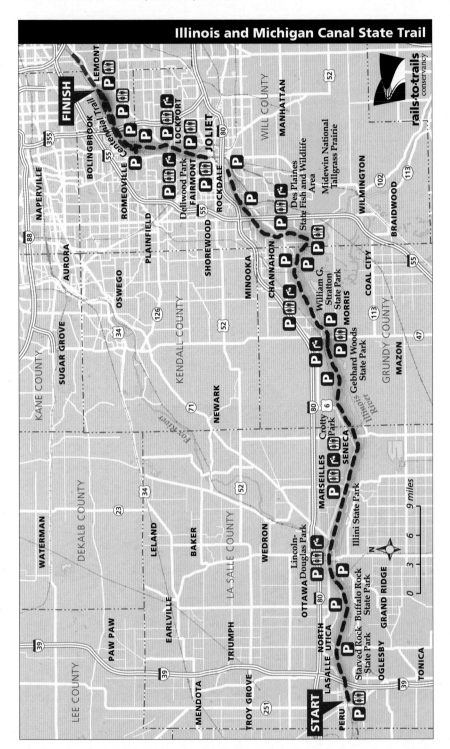

Illinois and Michigan Canal State Trail

The Illinois and Michigan Canal State Trail enters forested canopy on its way into Morris.

From the trailhead, a short segment of trail heads west, while the vast majority of the trail unfurls to the east. You may find that the short jaunt to the west is worth exploring, though, as it offers a nice tree canopy and views. Begin the longer journey by traveling eastward from the trailhead (to the right, as you face the canal).

The towpath surface is primarily compacted gravel and can collect water after heavy showers. Even with some puddles, the trail is widely used on weekends, and many families and groups of riders can be found with smiling faces. The LaSalle County Historical Museum is located in North Utica just across the canal from the trail, and many riders stop for a visit there and at the local cafés.

A small section of trail shares a paved roadway and provides access to private homes as you continue from west to east, but shortly after this section it can get muddy and a water crossing is missing.

As the trail approaches Ottawa, the surface improves and there is a short rail-with-trail section. You will find some options for food or cold beverages in Ottawa. The trail connects with the short but paved Ottawa Riverwalk as it crosses the Fox River. Leaving Ottawa, the path is mostly packed gravel, but depending on seasonal rains, it can get wet in spots.

The trail passes through Marseilles, a former industrial powerhouse on the Illinois River, which once housed one of the state's largest industrial buildings— a cardboard box plant for the National Biscuit Company (NaBisCo). On the other side of the Illinois River, you'll find Illini State Park (take Main Street south to reach it; the park is just past the dam on the far side of the river) with plenty of recreational opportunities, including camping, fishing, and boating. For a closer rest stop, take the bridge between Main Street and Aurora Street to John C. Knudson Park with restrooms, water, and views of the town's historical railroad depot.

The route continues through shaded forest canopy to the town of Seneca, where you'll find the M. J. Hogan Grain Elevator (also known as Armour's Warehouse)—the oldest structure of its kind that still stands along the canalway. This towering structure harkens back to the days when towns like Seneca loaded agricultural goods onto canalboats bound for markets in Chicago and beyond.

As the trail leaves town, it reenters forested canopy on its way to Morris. As you approach the town, you will come across several camping spots right off the trail, offering a great opportunity for a multiday trail excursion. This section of trail travels by Gebhard Woods State Park. With abundant wildlife and amenities, the 30-acre park is one of the most popular state parks in Illinois. Restrooms, water, and parking are right off the trail by way of a bridge over the canal.

The route continues along both banks of the canal, passing over Nettle Creek into the charming town of Morris. Steeped in canal history, the town has a lot to offer to trail visitors, including several small shops. The trail passes right by the Grundy County Historical Museum (on Nettle Street) and over an impressive trestle that crosses Canal Port Park. As you leave Morris, you'll pass through the William G. Stratton State Park with access to the Illinois River.

The trail continues through Aux Sable and into McKinley Woods Forest Preserve in Channahon—a 473-acre state preserve with plenty of camping, fishing spots, and picnic areas. The trail occasionally opens up with large grassy areas along the river.

The McKinley Woods portion is one of the most beautiful parts of the route. Not only are you surrounded by green space and next to the river, but you're also across the river from the Des Plaines State Fish and Wildlife Area. Experience great views of the water, large water birds, and small wildlife of all sorts.

Head north briefly out of the woods, then make your way east up the trail; you can feel yourself slowly getting closer to Chicago. Small towns and recreational areas pop up more frequently. The trail connects via hiking pathways to the vast Community Park in Channahon with various sports fields, forests, and open park areas. The trail comes to an end about 5 miles later in Rockdale, just outside of Joliet.

After a gap, the trail picks up again in the northern end of Joliet at the Joliet Iron Works Historic Site. Here, you can explore the remnants of what was once the second-largest steel mill in the country.

As you approach and enter the town of Lockport, the trail assumes a fun and historical flavor. A nicely paved portion runs through the center of town, where there are some interesting historical signs about the canal and a sculpture of Abraham Lincoln in a small park. As you make your way out of Lockport, the trail begins to feel industrial.

At the Romeo Road underpass, you can connect to the Centennial Trail on the west side of the canal. To continue on the I&M Canal State Trail, proceed to the left under the Romeo Road overpass. The first 0.5 mile is on a shared roadway that passes a U.S. Army Corps of Engineers facility, so be aware of heavy equipment and large vehicles. The pathway continues through an industrial area on a gravel roadway, passing a refinery and other processing plants. After crossing Cico Road, the trail returns to a more traillike condition with crushed-stone surface, but beware that this section of trail can be overgrown in the summer months.

About 1.3 miles after passing the I-355 overpass, you'll leave the industrial refineries behind as you enter the charming town of Lemont, which traces its history to 1833 and is closely tied to the development of the canal. Here, the trail is part of a well-groomed park just off Front Street, with a bridge leading to a parking lot and providing access to restaurants and shops downtown.

The trail ends in the historical limestone quarries that helped place Lemont on the map in the mid-19th century. Stone from the quarry was of the highest quality and used for many of the town's buildings, as well as the stunning Chicago Water Tower building—one of the few buildings to survive the Great Chicago Fire in 1871. The quarries were filled with water and now offer fishing and boating access in the nearly 100-acre Heritage Quarries Recreation Area.

CONTACT: dnr.state.il.us/lands/landmgt/PARKS/I&M/EAST/East.htm or
iandmcanal.org

DIRECTIONS

To reach the westernmost trailhead in LaSalle: From I-39/US 51, take Exit 57 for US 6 toward LaSalle-Peru. Head southwest on US 6 W. In 1.2 miles, turn left onto Joliet St. Continue over the bridge and take the first right, which will take you to the parking lot.

To reach the easternmost access point at the Heritage Quarries Recreation Area: From I-55, take Exit 271A to Lemont Road. Head south on Lemont Road, and in 2.9 miles, turn left onto E. Illinois St. In 0.6 mile make a sharp left onto Main St., then a right onto Talcott Ave. After crossing the railroad tracks, turn right. After you cross a second set of railroad tracks, the entrance to the recreation area will be on your right. Parking is available just beyond the entrance.

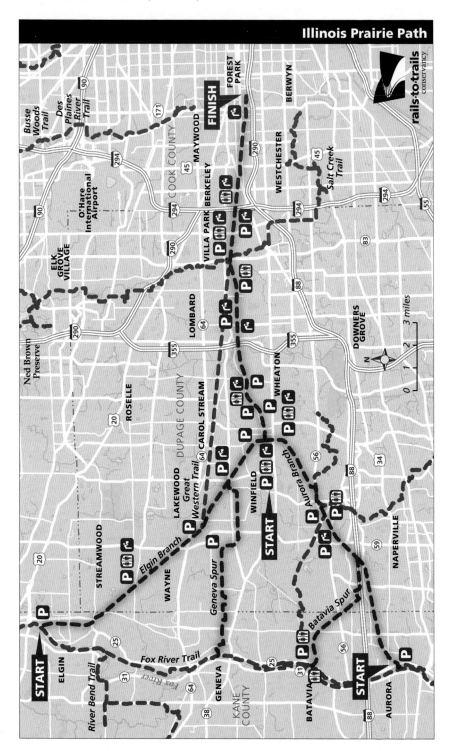

The Illinois Prairie Path (IPP) was one of the nation's first rail-trail conversions. It consists of five connected trail segments with three main branches that converge at Volunteer Park (West Liberty Drive at South Carlton Avenue) in Wheaton.

The 58-mile trail follows the historical path of the Chicago Aurora and Elgin Railroad. Beginning in 1902, the electric railroad provided passenger service from the western suburbs into downtown Chicago. With the railroad in decline, some routes were transferred to bus service. The partial completion of the Eisenhower Expressway (I-290) in 1955 spelled the end for this once mighty railroad: by 1959 passenger and freight service on the line were finished. A letter to the editor by noted naturalist May Theilgaard Watts in the *Chicago Tribune* in September 1963 argued for the novel idea of converting

The Illinois Prairie Path has beauty in all seasons.

Counties
Cook, DuPage, Kane

Endpoints
Forest Park Transit Center at Van Buren St. and Des Plaines Ave. (Forest Park) to W. Liberty Dr. and S. Carlton Ave. (Wheaton), where spurs lead to Aurora, Batavia, Geneva, and Elgin, all ending at points along Fox River Trail

Mileage
58.4

Type
Rail-Trail/Rail-with-Trail

Roughness Index
1–2

Surface
Asphalt, Concrete, Crushed Stone

the former corridor into a footpath. That letter sparked the efforts of a determined group of Chicagoans and ultimately gave rise to the unprecedented conversion of railroad to public trail.

The Illinois Prairie Path's 16-mile **Main Branch** is the most urban of its corridors. Beginning in Wheaton, the IPP's Main Branch follows city streets on extrawide bicycle-friendly sidewalks. Distinct green trail markers shepherd you eastward through the lively shopping district. As you leave downtown Wheaton, Metra commuter rail tracks share the corridor, allowing you about 2 miles of rail-with-trail experience.

The trail maintains a distinct urban ambience, passing through the heart of the western suburbs. In Villa Park, about 8 miles from the trailhead, a restored train depot houses historical displays and offers water and restrooms. As you approach the museum, a short connector trail on the left links with DuPage County's Great Western Trail.

In about 7 miles, the trail crosses First Avenue (IL 171) in Maywood, and a short trek along Maybrook Drive leads to a bicycle-pedestrian bridge over the Des Plaines River. The Main Branch eastern terminus is shortly thereafter in Concordia Cemetery, adjacent to the Forest Park Transit Center. Free parking is spotty at this end, so plan on a return trip along the corridor.

The 13-mile-long **Aurora Branch** begins at the south end of Illinois Avenue Park at a junction with the Fox River Trail (see page 21). The IPP travels north on asphalt along the river through commercial areas and older neighborhoods for a mile; then the surface changes to hard-packed crushed stone that makes up the majority of the branch. In another 5 miles, look for the trail connection on the left; this is the IPP's **Batavia Spur**, which heads 6 miles west to Batavia. Your journey on the Aurora Branch is likely to be quiet, passing through woodlands and fields and beneath high-tension power lines. Wildlife finds refuge on the trail; deer, rabbit, and many bird species are the most common. At 3 miles past the Batavia Spur, pay attention where several trails converge at Winfield and Butterfield Roads in Winfield. Just follow the green IPP markers to stay on course to Wheaton's Volunteer Park.

The **Elgin Branch** of the IPP runs 14 miles between Elgin and Volunteer Park in Wheaton. The surface of the trail is almost entirely hard-packed crushed stone. Heading southeast from the Elgin trailhead, where the IPP again meets the Fox River Trail, you immediately plunge into a lush, rural atmosphere of farms and small forests. About 5 miles from the trailhead, between Army Trail Road and Smith Road in Wayne, a steep hill climb might challenge wheelchair users and youngsters on bikes. Cresting the hill, you'll enjoy a pleasant 4-mile ride through forests and residential developments to the vicinity of Prince Crossing Road, where the IPP joins the 12-mile Great Western Trail for 0.3 mile. (The Great Western also joins the IPP Main Branch in Villa Park.)

Another 2.2 miles along the Elgin Branch through similar terrain brings you to the connection with the **Geneva Spur** of the IPP, on the right side of the trail after crossing Geneva Road. The spur travels 9 miles west to Geneva, where it ends at Fox River Trail in Good Templar Park.

Well-manicured neighborhoods indicate your arrival in Wheaton. Just when you think you have left the trail's remoteness behind, the Lincoln Marsh Natural Area affords a bucolic diversion. With multiple overlooks and interpretive signs, the marsh provides the perfect finishing touch. In less than 1 mile, after spanning a bridge over two city streets and three active rail lines, you arrive at Volunteer Park, named after the countless residents who made May Theilgaard Watts's dream into a reality.

CONTACT: ipp.org

DIRECTIONS

To reach the Main Branch trailhead in Wheaton from I-355, take Exit 24 and go west toward Wheaton on Roosevelt Road/IL 38. Go 3.8 miles and turn right onto S. Carlton Ave. Go 0.4 mile to W. Liberty Dr. and find street parking. All three main branches of the Illinois Prairie Path converge here.

To reach the Forest Park Transit Center (711 Des Plaines Ave.) trailhead by train, take the CTA Blue Line to the end. Bikes are allowed on the train during off-peak hours. The station has limited parking (for a $5 daily fee) and is easily accessible off I-290, if driving. From I-290 E, take Exit 21A for Des Plaines Ave.; turn left onto Des Plaines Ave., and in 0.1 mile you will turn left into the station.

The trail offers several additional trailheads; for details and maps, see ipp.org or visit TrailLink.com.

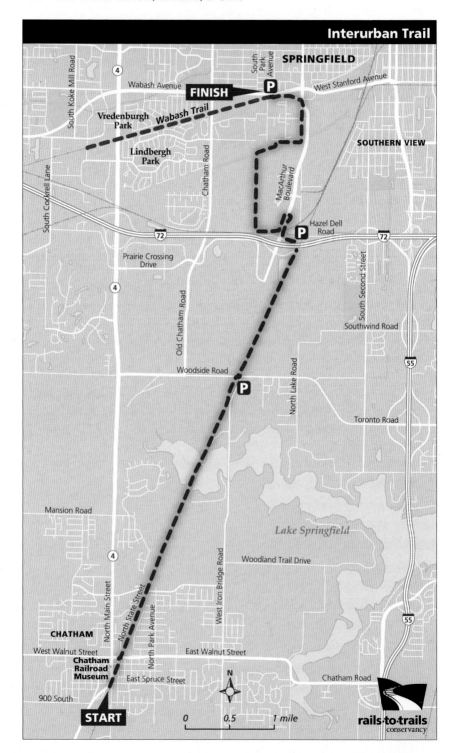

The paved Interurban Trail provides 8.4 miles of suburban and rural scenery for users between Chatham and Springfield. It follows the former route of the electrified Illinois Terminal Railroad (originally Illinois Traction System) that connected St. Louis, Missouri, with towns in central Illinois from the 1890s to 1980s.

Today, bicycle commuters from southwestern Sangamon County aren't the only ones using this transportation corridor. Most of the way, the trail parallels the Union Pacific Railroad tracks that carry Amtrak's high-speed Lincoln Service and Texas Eagle from Chicago to St. Louis.

The trail starts at South Main Street in Chatham, but you'll probably begin 0.2 mile north at the parking lot for the Chatham Railroad Museum, where a plethora of artifacts, photos, and documents are displayed. This vintage 1902 railway station served the adjacent Chicago and

Cross Lake Springfield via a refurbished railroad bridge along the Interurban Trail.

County
Sangamon

Endpoints
S. Main St. near E. Spruce St. (Chatham) to Wabash Ave. and S. Park Ave. (Springfield)

Mileage
8.4

Type
Rail-Trail/Rail-with-Trail

Roughness Index
1

Surface
Asphalt

Alton Railroad, which was eventually acquired (by then operating under a different name) by Union Pacific.

As you leave the museum, be aware that the trail lacks restrooms and water fountains, though facilities are available in communities along the route. Head north on North State Street from the train museum; you will reconnect with the Interurban Trail after crossing East Walnut Street. In 1 mile, the trail skirts along a paved golf cart path as it winds through the manicured greens and fairways of a golf course. Only 0.25 mile beyond the golf course is a highlight of the Interurban Trail: Lake Springfield. The trail uses a refurbished railroad bridge to cross a narrow elbow of the 4,200-acre reservoir that supplies water to residents of Springfield and surrounding areas all year.

Beyond Lake Springfield, the trail passes through farmland for about 2.5 miles until you pass beneath I-72 and the outskirts of Springfield, the state capital. The trail leaves the old rail corridor for the last 3 miles as it maneuvers around busy roads and interchanges to a trailhead parking lot on West North Street. From here, you can follow the Wabash Trail 2.1 miles to a shopping district on the west side of Springfield.

A small oasis from the bustle of suburban and city life, the Interurban Trail is exactly the kind of useful and pleasant link you expect from a rail-trail.

CONTACT: springfieldparks.org/parks/bikeTrails/Interurban.aspx

DIRECTIONS

To reach the southern trailhead in Chatham from I-55, take Exit 88 and follow signs toward Chatham. Head southwest 1 mile on Palm Road and turn right onto Chatham Road. In 1.2 miles, Chatham Road becomes E. Walnut St. Go 1.9 miles to N. State St. and turn left. The parking lot for the Chatham Railroad Museum is on your left in 0.1 mile.

To reach the northern trailhead in Springfield from I-72, take Exit 96 for MacArthur Blvd. Head north 1.6 miles on S. MacArthur Blvd., and turn left onto W. North St. Go 0.4 mile; the Interurban and Wabash Trails parking lot is on your right, just before S. Park Ave.

There's no debating the historical significance of the Jane Addams Trail. Not only is it named for a Nobel Peace Prize–winning social activist who grew up nearby, but the trail also passes the site of the second Abraham Lincoln–Stephen Douglas debate, located in Freeport.

The trail runs nearly 19 miles from historical Tutty's Crossing in Freeport to the Wisconsin border, where it becomes the Badger State Trail. It follows a rail line that the Illinois Central built in 1887 between Freeport, Illinois, and Madison, Wisconsin. The route, which crosses 22 bridges on the way to the border, is part of the 500-mile Grand Illinois Trail. Future plans call for a connection to the Pecatonica Prairie Trail east of Freeport.

Starting at Tutty's Crossing trailhead in Freeport, you'll wind through a historical district on sidewalks and bike paths for about 0.4 mile to a park featuring displays

A covered bridge greets trail goers just south of Orangeville.

County
Stephenson

Endpoints
E. Stephenson St. near Liberty Ave. at Pecatonica River (Freeport) to Wuetrich Road near Imobersteg Road (Orangeville)

Mileage
18.9

Type
Rail-Trail

Roughness Index
1–2

Surface
Asphalt, Crushed Stone

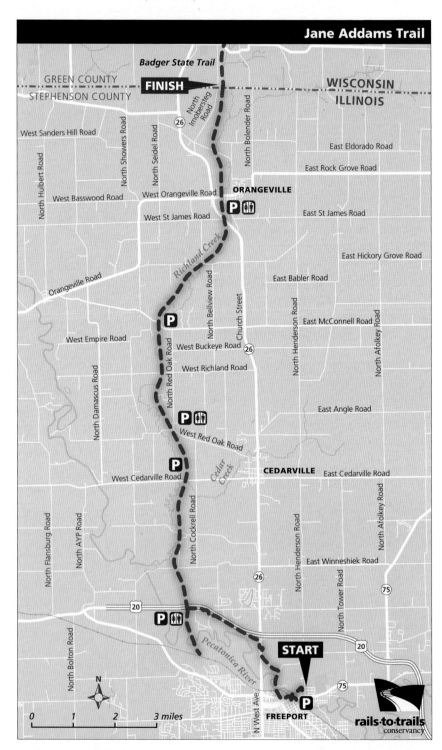

and life-size statues marking the site of the second Lincoln-Douglas debate in 1858. Following on-street bike lanes another 0.4 mile takes you to the original steel truss railroad bridge across the Pecatonica River and the beginning of an off-road paved trail that proceeds 3.5 miles to the Wes Block trailhead. The path is crushed limestone from Wes Block north.

Heading due north, the trail passes through woods that support a wide variety of trees, birds, and other wildlife. During deer-hunting season, it's recommended that trail users wear blaze orange. Bright-colored clothing is also advised for those traveling on foot or skis during winter, as snowmobiling is allowed when at least 4 inches of snow are on the trail.

As you travel from Freeport north to Orangeville, you will see exposed rock embankments as well as creeks and wetlands. Vistas of open prairie and farmland are interspersed among the wooded areas.

You'll cross County Road 5 at 3 miles past the Wes Block trailhead. It's less than 2 miles on a shoulderless road to the childhood home and grave site of Jane Addams in Cedarville. Born here in 1860, she received the Nobel Peace Prize in 1931 for her humanitarian deeds, which included the opening of a settlement house project (Hull House) in Chicago and activism in the social and political movements of her time.

About 7 miles north of CR 5, you'll cross a covered bridge as you arrive in Orangeville, where the Richland Creek trailhead provides a quiet and convenient place to end your trip with a covered shelter and nearby gas station for refreshments. The official end of the trail is at the Illinois-Wisconsin state line, about 2.5 miles north. You'll need a Wisconsin state trail pass if you plan to ride the remaining 40 miles north to Madison on the Badger State Trail.

CONTACT: ci.freeport.il.us/livinginfreeport/Jane%20Addams%20Trail.htm

DIRECTIONS

To reach the southern trailhead in Freeport from I-39, exit onto US 20 W near mile marker 119, and go 32.4 miles. Take the IL 75 exit toward Freeport. Turn left onto IL 75, and go 2.8 miles. Just after crossing the Pecatonica River, turn right into a driveway that heads to Tutty's Crossing trailhead parking lot.

To reach the northern trailhead in Orangeville from I-39, exit onto US 20 W near mile marker 119, and go 35.6 miles. Take the IL 26 exit north toward Monroe, Wisconsin. Turn right onto IL 26, and go 10.3 miles to IL 7/W. Orangeville Road in Orangeville and turn right. The Orangeville trailhead and parking lot is on the left in 0.1 mile.

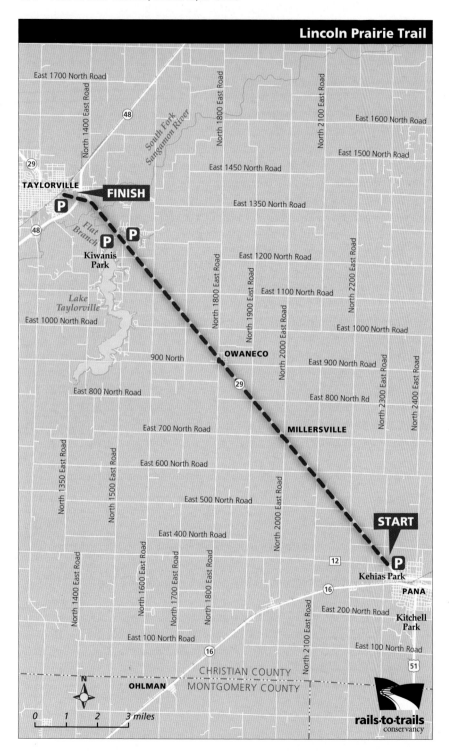

While you're in the land of Lincoln, visit the Lincoln Prairie Trail to make the trip complete. Starting at the trailhead in northwest Pana, leisurely stroll along a paved trail that is nicely separated from the rural highway. The route offers a fairly flat and straight shot to Taylorville with a combination of tree-canopied sections and more open areas.

The trail skirts several active silos via on-road routes as it passes through Millersville and Owaneco, but these short diversions are well marked and located on very lightly traveled small-town roads. The trail is well woven into the local communities and surrounded by the region's many farms. Depending on the time of year, you can find corn, soybean, and sunflower fields for many miles.

One trail highlight is the stretch along Lake Taylorville and the South Fork Sangamon River on the north end

Near Pana, at the southern end of the trail, the experience is quietly rural.

County
Christian

Endpoints
IL 29 at County Road 12/E. 350 North Road (Pana) to S. Paw Paw St. and E. Market St. (Taylorville)

Mileage
14.6

Type
Rail-Trail

Roughness Index
1

Surface
Asphalt

of the route. At the time of this writing, the bridge over Flat Branch was closed; however, this closure doesn't detract too much from the end-to-end experience. As you approach Taylorville, the development patterns become more suburban, and the trail ends unceremoniously at South Paw Paw Street.

CONTACT: panaillinois.org/trail.htm

DIRECTIONS

Parking can be found at the southeastern end of the trail in Pana. From I-70, take Exit 63 for US 51. Head north on US 51 for 29.6 miles. As US 51 N approaches Pana, it becomes Fair Ave. and then Poplar St. Near the center of town, Poplar St. intersects with Washington St.; turn left onto Washington, which is also IL 29. Follow Washington west and then northwest as the road curves 1.1 miles to E. 350 North Road; the trailhead parking lot is located on your left at this intersection.

On the other end of the trail, parking is available in Taylorville. Follow the directions above to IL 29/Washington St. Turn left onto IL 29, and go 15.4 miles. Just after passing IL 48 in Taylorville, turn left onto E. Main Cross St. Go 0.4 mile to S. Paw Paw St., and turn left; in about 280 feet you will see the trail and the unpaved parking area on your left.

The Long Prairie Trail journeys across the width of agricultural Boone County for nearly 14 miles on the railroad corridor previously used by the Kenosha and Rockford Railroad, later known as the Kenosha Division, or KD Line. Formed in the 1860s, the railroad served many small communities in northern Illinois and southern Wisconsin as it connected Rockford, Illinois, and Kenosha, Wisconsin. Offering passenger service and hauling milk and ice from dairies and lakes in the region, the railroad ceased most operations in 1939 due to the growing use of cars and trucks.

The old KD Line still serves the rural communities of Capron, Poplar Grove, and Caledonia in its new life as the paved Long Prairie Trail, part of the 500-mile Grand Illinois Trail. The connecting Stone Bridge Trail in the west and the Stone Mill and Hebron Trails, which lie to the east, also follow the old rail line.

North of Caledonia, the pathway winds through woodlands.

County
Boone

Endpoints
Boone McHenry County Line Road 0.5 mile north of IL 173 (Capron) to McMichael Road 0.25 mile east of The Reserve Dr. (Caledonia)

Mileage
13.9

Type
Rail-Trail

Roughness Index
1

Surface
Asphalt

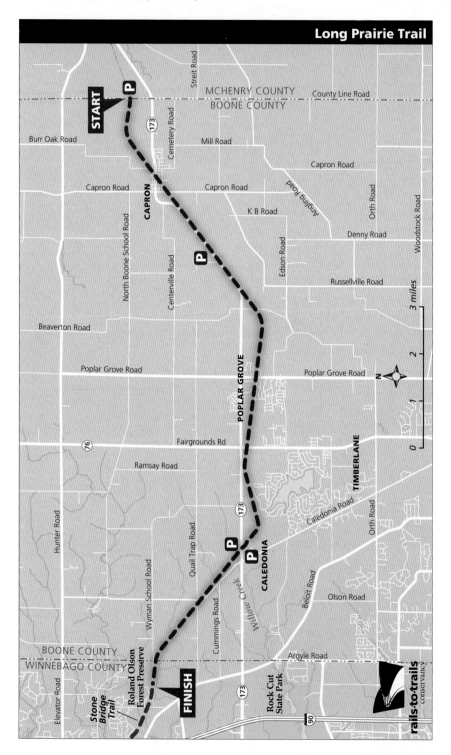

At the trailhead about 2 miles east of Capron, the first of many interpretive signs greets visitors. This one explains the history of the Potawatomi tribe in the area. Other signs inform users about the local flora, fauna, and geology.

Heading toward Capron, you'll likely be thankful on hot summer days for the shady leaf canopy that arches over the trail for miles. You'll see farm crops and cattle ranches through breaks in the trailside growth, though some native prairie survives. Reportedly, rail cars on the KD Line sparked periodic blazes in the adjacent grasslands. Woody species couldn't tolerate the frequent burns, enabling the preservation of some native grasses.

The small town of Capron dates to the same year as the railroad: 1861. Leaving town, you'll parallel IL 173 for 2.5 miles. Gazing across the countryside, you're reminded that this is one of the most rural areas of Boone County.

You'll arrive in Poplar Grove 5 miles past Capron. The small business district offers restaurants and cafés to slake your thirst or curb your appetite. About 2.5 miles west of town, you might be surprised at the sight of mowed fairways and manicured greens. You're passing the golf course for the Candlewick Lake Association, a private community for more than 4,000 residents.

The last village on the Long Prairie Trail is Caledonia, less than a mile from the golf course. While the main KD Line headed west from here through Rock Cut State Park, the trail follows a spur line toward Beloit, Wisconsin. Nearly 4 miles past Caledonia, the trail ends at McMichael Road, where it meets the Stone Bridge Trail, a crushed-stone pathway that continues on into Winnebago County to a shopping district south of Beloit.

CONTACT: bccdil.org/conservation-areas/long-prairie-trail

DIRECTIONS

To reach the eastern trailhead on Boone McHenry County Line Road: From I-90, take Exit 42 and head west on US 20/Grant Hwy. Go 8.8 miles to Marengo and turn right onto State St./IL 23. Go 6.6 miles and turn left onto Dunham Road, then go 4.5 miles and turn right onto Boone McHenry County Line Road. Go another 4.5 miles and look for the trailhead on the left.

To reach parking in Caledonia: From I-90/I-39, take the IL 173 exit near mile marker 9 and go east on IL 173/W. Lane Road. Go 3.6 miles and turn right onto Front St. Go 0.1 mile and turn left onto S. Main St. Parking for the trailhead is immediately on the right. The western endpoint (where Long Prairie Trail meets Stone Bridge Trail) on McMichael Road is 3.7 miles northwest of here.

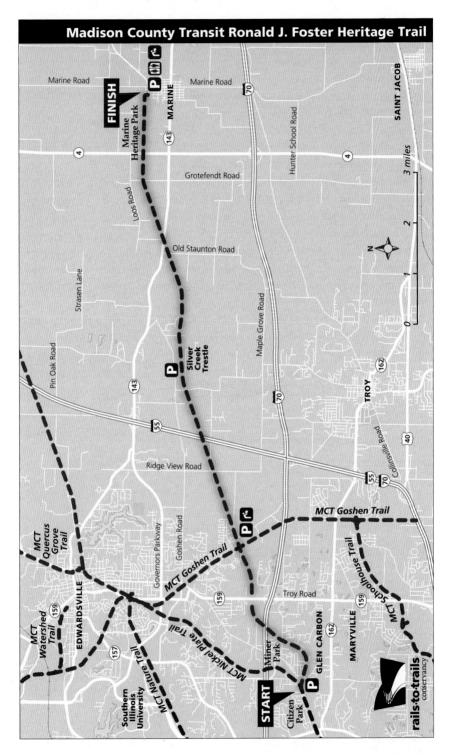

Madison County Transit Ronald J. Foster Heritage Trail

You can make connections all over the countryside from the Madison County Transit (MCT) Ronald J. Foster Heritage Trail. The paved path travels 12.2 miles between the villages of Glen Carbon and Marine and hooks into a 130-mile network of interconnected trails that MCT has been creating since 1993.

The trail is named for a former mayor of Glen Carbon, Illinois; the city originally built the trail on the disused corridor of the Illinois Central Railroad in 1991. Illinois Central was one of three railroads that passed through the coal-rich community from nearby St. Louis, Missouri. In 2012 the village transferred trail ownership to Madison County Transit, which upgraded and extended it.

Today, the trail retains historical markers (that tell about Glen Carbon's coal-mining history) and connects with two other trails, the MCT Nickel Plate Trail (more

An area designated for prairie restoration abuts the pathway.

County
Madison

Endpoints
Citizen Park on S. Main St. near Steiss St. at the MCT Nickel Plate Trail (Glen Carbon) to Marine Heritage Park at N. Verson St. at Lubeck St. (Marine)

Mileage
12.2

Type
Rail-Trail

Roughness Index
1

Surface
Asphalt

than 25 miles long) and the MCT Goshen Trail (which spans about 9 miles). These make off-road connections to other trails in the network: the MCT Nature, Quercus Grove, Schoolhouse (see the next page), and Watershed Trails.

Starting in Glen Carbon at the junction with the MCT Nickel Plate Trail near Citizen Park, you'll enter a wooded area along Judys Branch where the Illinois Central hauled coal from the mines. The area was settled as Goshen in 1801, but the coal boom from the late 1800s to 1930s prompted the name change.

Passing through woods and crossing suburban streets on the way out of town, you'll enter a 150-foot tunnel beneath Troy Road at 2.5 miles. Skirting the Greenspace East Park (bicycling is prohibited in the park), you'll cross the junction with MCT Goshen Trail and reach a trailhead parking lot less than a mile from the tunnel. Just past the trail crossing, there's another tunnel (Old Troy Road) and soon you're out into open farmland.

When there's a break in the trees that border the trail, you'll see that cropland is predominant. Keep your eyes open, however, for areas where biologists are attempting to reestablish grasses and other natural prairie vegetation.

At 4.8 miles past the Goshen Trail junction, you'll find the 340-foot Silver Creek trestle, 1 of 10 spans that MCT rehabilitated when it took over the trail.

In 4 miles, you arrive in Marine. Legend has it that sailors were among the first settlers in the 1800s, and the waving prairie grasses reminded them of the open seas, hence the name. Despite its "marine" history, the village prohibits swimming and wading in the lake at Marine Heritage Park that marks the end of the trail.

CONTACT: mcttrails.org/heritage_trail.aspx

DIRECTIONS

To reach the western trailhead at Citizen Park on S. Main St. in Glen Carbon: From I-270, take Exit 9 for IL 157 toward Glen Carbon and Collinsville. Go approximately 0.9 mile south on IL 157/N. Bluff Road, and turn left onto W. Main St. Go 1 mile (W. Main St. turns into S. Main St.) and turn right onto Daenzer Dr. at the fire station. Enter Citizen Park and take the first right at the baseball field and proceed to the parking lot.

To reach the eastern trailhead at Marine Heritage Park: From I-70, take Exit 21 toward Staunton and head north on IL 4. Go 1.7 miles and turn right onto IL 143/W. Division St. Go 1.1 miles and turn left onto N. Verson St. Go 0.4 mile and turn left onto Mill St., then immediately turn right into Marine Heritage Park.

The Madison County Transit (MCT) Schoolhouse Trail offers a 15.5-mile flat, paved route through the eastern suburbs of greater St. Louis, Missouri, between Madison and Maryville, Illinois. Along the way, it meets two other trails that are part of the MCT's 130-mile network of nine interconnected trails, all of which are linked with public transit. This trail lies along an alignment of the old Illinois Traction System (later the Illinois Terminal Railroad) of electric trains that once connected St. Louis to Springfield. Other rail-trails in the state, such as the Interurban Trail in Sangamon County (see page 44), also use this corridor, which the railroad stopped operating in the 1980s.

The route begins at a trailhead just west of Horseshoe Lake State Park in Madison, Illinois. You'll head south on

The Schoolhouse Trail skirts beautiful Horseshoe Lake.

County
Madison

Endpoints
Harrison St. and Hare St. (Madison) to MCT Goshen Trail near Frey Lane and Vaughn Lane (Maryville)

Mileage
15.5

Type
Rail-Trail

Roughness Index
1

Surface
Asphalt

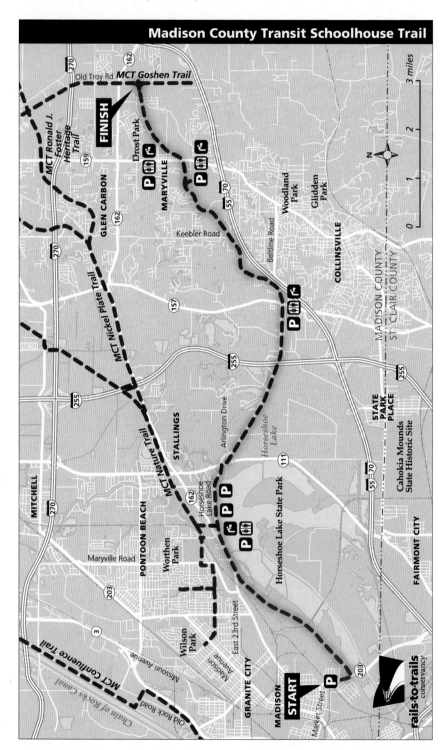

the trail about 0.2 mile until it picks up the old railroad corridor; it then crosses IL 203 on a girder bridge and heads east along the north side of the oxbow lake. For a few miles, the trail shares this route with a utility corridor and passes industrial areas while Horseshoe Lake remains hidden. But be patient. At mile 3, the lake bursts into view when the path emerges from a pocket of trees. The lake offers excellent bird-watching, as nearly 300 species have been spotted here. The state park drains the lake's southern portion in late summer, drawing snowy egrets and great blue herons to feast on clams and snails. Watch for a connection on the left to the MCT Nature Trail, which heads northeast toward Edwardsville.

Leaving the park, you soon cross IL 111, where the trail takes on a more rural feel, with farms on both sides. You'll come upon the trail's namesake, School-house Branch, just before you pass under I-255, roughly the halfway mark for the trail. About 1.1 miles past the interstate, you'll arrive at the Metro East Park and Recreation District (MEPRD) trailhead on the outskirts of Collinsville. Just when it seems like more suburban sprawl will impinge your view, the trail plunges into woodlands behind very tidy neighborhoods. It is quiet through the hardwoods, disguising your proximity to a major interstate. The woods occasionally open up to offer glimpses of farm fields bordered by development.

As you enter the village of Maryville, a trail to the local YMCA joins from the right at 3.4 miles past the MEPRD trailhead. In an additional 1.2 miles, you'll pass Drost Park on the left. Consider stopping here for restrooms and drinking water, as the trail's endpoint has no facilities. It's another 1.2 miles to the MCT Schoolhouse Trail terminus at a junction with the MCT Goshen Trail, which travels north 0.4 mile to parking and another 8 miles to Edwardsville. It connects with the MCT Ronald J. Foster Heritage (see page 56), Nature, Nickel Plate, and Watershed Trails along the way.

CONTACT: mcttrails.org/schoolhouse_trail.aspx

DIRECTIONS

To reach the western trailhead in Madison: From I-55, take Exit 4 or 4B and head north on IL 203. Go 1.9 miles and turn left onto Harrison St. The trailhead and parking are immediately on the left.

To reach the eastern trailhead in Maryville: From I-55, take Exit 18 and head west toward Maryville on IL 162/Edwardsville Road at the end of the ramp. Go 0.8 mile to Old Troy Road and turn right. Parking for the MCT Goshen Trail is about 500 feet ahead on the right. From the parking lot, go south 0.4 mile on the Goshen Trail to the junction with the MCT Schoolhouse Trail.

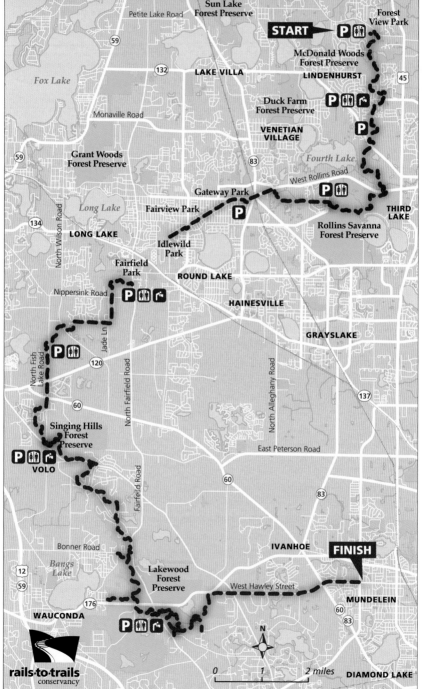

The Millennium Trail currently spans just over 30 miles, but there are plans to extend it to 35 miles and connect it to the Des Plaines River Trail (see page 18). The trail goes through forest, farmland, and the suburban neighborhoods of Lake County with a range of surfaces, including crushed stone, asphalt, and concrete. Though largely well marked with Millennium Trail signs, the route is intertwined with other trails throughout, so pay close attention to the signage.

The trail's northernmost end begins in Lindenhurst's Forest View Park. Early on, the path splits; keep right to stay on the trail and continue through McDonald Woods Forest Preserve. As the path winds southward, you'll travel through farmland, rolling hills, and fields of wildflowers. The trail consists of two disconnected segments with a short gap in the middle. The first segment runs about 10

The path travels through the suburban neighborhoods of Lake County.

County
Lake

Endpoints
Forest View Park at Forest View Road near Waterford Dr. (Lindenhurst) to N. Midlothian Road and W. Hawley St. (Mundelein)

Mileage
30.7

Type
Greenway/Non-Rail-Trail

Roughness Index
1–2

Surface
Asphalt, Concrete, Crushed Stone

miles and takes you on busy town roads past the local school and then back onto the trail. It ends where Sunset Avenue meets Beachview Drive.

Note that there's no off-road connection between the first and second segments of the trail. To pick up the second segment, head to Fairfield Park (part of the Round Lake Area Park District). Along this section of the trail, you'll find prairie land mixed with small shaded sections and a more rugged pathway. The south end travels through Volo and Wauconda and ends in Mundelein. The southern end of the trail provides access to dog parks and areas for picnicking and fishing. Equestrians can also use the trail between Singing Hills Forest Preserve (where horse trailer parking is available) and Lakewood Forest Preserve.

CONTACT: lcfpd.org/millennium-trail

DIRECTIONS

The northern segment of the trail begins at Forest View Park (513 Forest View Road) in Lindenhurst. From I-94, take Exit 2 for IL 173/Rosecrans Road. Head west on IL 173 for 2.8 miles, and turn left onto US 45. In 2.9 miles, turn right onto W. Grass Lake Road and follow the roadway 0.9 mile west to Waterford Dr. Turn left onto Waterford, then make an immediate left onto Forest View Road. It is only a 0.2-mile drive to the park's parking lot on your left.

The southern segment begins in Fairfield Park (350 N. Fairfield Road) in Round Lake. From I-94 W, take Exit 11B for IL 120 W/Belvidere Road. Head 10.3 miles west on IL 120 to N. Fairfield Road. Turn right onto Fairfield and travel north 1.3 miles to the park's parking lot.

Additional access points for the trail are available in the forest preserves through which it passes. See lcfpd.org/millennium-trail or TrailLink.com for maps and directions.

The North Branch Trail follows the North Branch of the Chicago River nearly 20 miles through Cook County. The trail was originally a dirt path often used for horseback riding; though it's now paved, an unpaved equestrian pathway still parallels the main trail.

Near the north end of the trail, the Chicago Botanic Garden, which includes more than two dozen gardens on 385 acres, is worth a short excursion. Nearby, you can also pick up the Green Bay Trail, a busy community route flanked by restaurants, shops, parks, and residential neighborhoods about a mile from the Lake Michigan shoreline.

The north end of the trail features a 4.4-mile loop around Skokie Lagoons and Erickson Woods. Because the loop's west side runs along I-94, you'll find heavy traffic noise; take the eastern side of the loop for a more peaceful experience. After the loop, you'll travel south for more

You'll pass through many parks in the northern suburbs of Chicago along the trail.

County
Cook

Endpoints
Dundee Road and I-94 (Northbrook) to N. Forest Glen Ave. and N. Las Casas Ave. (Chicago)

Mileage
19.7

Type
Greenway/Non-Rail-Trail

Roughness Index
1

Surface
Asphalt

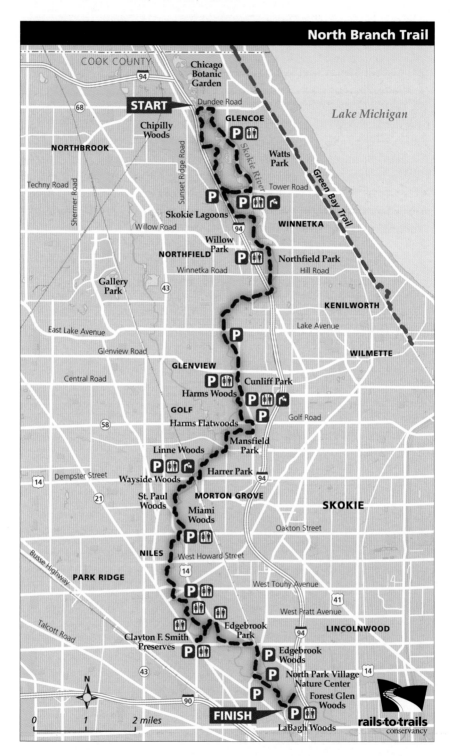

North Branch Trail

COOK COUNTY

94

Chicago
Botanic
Garden

Dundee Road

Lake Michigan

68

START

GLENCOE

Chipilly
Woods

NORTHBROOK

Techny Road

Shermer Road

Sunset Ridge Road

Skokie River

Watts
Park

Tower Road

Green Bay Trail

P

Skokie Lagoons

Willow Road

94

WINNETKA

Willow
Park

NORTHFIELD

Winnetka Road

P

Northfield Park

Hill Road

Gallery
Park

43

KENILWORTH

East Lake Avenue

Lake Avenue

Glenview Road

P

WILMETTE

Central Road

GLENVIEW

P

Cunliff Park

Harms Woods

GOLF

Harms Flatwoods

58

Golf Road

P

P

Mansfield
Park

Linne Woods

P

Harrer Park

94

Wayside Woods

St. Paul
Woods

MORTON GROVE

Miami
Woods

SKOKIE

Oakton Street

14

Dempster Street

21

P

NILES

West Howard Street

14

West Touhy Avenue

PARK RIDGE

Busse Highway

P

West Pratt Avenue

41

Talcott Road

Edgebrook
Park

94

LINCOLNWOOD

Clayton F. Smith
Preserves

P

Edgebrook
Woods

P

North Park Village
Nature Center

14

43

90

FINISH

P

Forest Glen
Woods

P

LaBagh Woods

rails·to·trails
conservancy

N

0   1   2 miles

than a dozen miles through many wooded areas and lagoons and along golf courses. Keep your eyes open for wildlife, especially deer.

Amenities are plentiful, with parking lots, bathrooms, and picnic areas available throughout the route. Though several road crossings occur along the way, they are clearly marked and have electronic buttons for those crossing. Note that the trail ends abruptly at Forest Glen Avenue.

CONTACT: fpdcc.com/preserves-and-trails/trail-descriptions/#north-branch

DIRECTIONS

At the north end of the trail, parking is available at Skokie Lagoons. From I-94 W, take Exit 33B for Willow Road. Travel 0.5 mile east on Willow Road, and turn left (north) onto Forest Way. After 1.3 miles, you'll take another left onto Tower Road. The trail and parking for it will appear on your left, along the south side of the road.

If you want to start on the southern end of the trail, from I-94, take Exit 41A for US 14 W/ Caldwell Ave. Head west on US 14 for 0.9 mile to Central Ave. and turn left. Travel on Central Ave. 0.2 mile until you see the entrance and parking lot for Edgebrook Woods on your left.

You'll find additional trail access and parking within the many recreational areas along the route; see the link above or visit TrailLink.com for a map and directions.

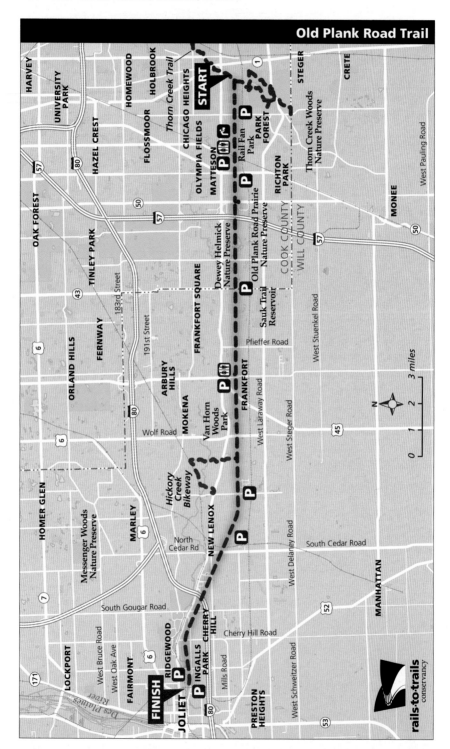

Old Plank Road Trail

The Old Plank Road Trail travels nearly 22 miles between Chicago Heights and Joliet across a densely populated suburban landscape, where you're never far from a café or espresso stand. Still, you might be surprised at the richness of the natural areas that border this historical pathway.

The trail follows an American Indian track around Lake Michigan that was later used by fur trappers and early settlers. Business interests later acquired the corridor for a plank road. Before they started laying lumber, however, they decided that a railroad was a better idea. The old Michigan Central Railroad (MCRR) line fired up in the mid-1850s and ran through here between East Gary (now known as Lake Station), Indiana, and Joliet, Illinois, until the 1970s. Observers nicknamed it the Joliet Cut-Off because it enabled trains headed west to bypass Chicago. Remaining mileage markers still tell the distance to East Gary.

An unusual bridge adorns the route in Frankfort.

Counties
Cook, Will

Endpoints
Campbell Ave. just south of W. Hickory St. (Chicago Heights) to E. Washington St. near Logan Ave. (Joliet)

Mileage
21.7

Type
Rail-Trail

Roughness Index
1

Surface
Asphalt

When the line went out of service, trail supporters realized that the railroad had unintentionally preserved swaths of natural prairie that had never been cultivated. That prairie growth survives along the trail in many places today.

Beginning in Chicago Heights where the Old Plank Road Trail meets the Thorn Creek Trail, you'll head 2.5 miles west to the village of Park Forest's Rail Fan Park, a railroad aficionado's dream. The park features a raised viewing platform, where you can watch north-south and east-west trains on the Canadian National Railway change direction on an elevated interchange that's described as a giant cloverleaf, while Metra commuter trains whiz past.

Look for wildlife in about 3 miles as you pass through the Dewey Helmick and Old Plank Road Prairie Nature Preserves at the headwaters of Butterfield Creek. More than 200 species of prairie plants thrive here, attracting 170 bird species, such as bald eagles and herons. Mammals include muskrats, coyotes, and beavers.

Frankfort, the trail's physical and spiritual center, comes into view in about 5 miles. You're welcomed by an archway overhead that's emblazoned with the trail's name. The pathway runs through the community's historical downtown with many shops and restaurants within easy reach. A bustling Sunday farmers' market offers locally grown produce and homemade baked goods May–October. On the western side of town, the trail reaches an award-winning arrowhead-shaped suspension bridge, which takes you over US 45.

A side trip 2.2 miles past US 45 picks up the Hickory Creek Bikeway (its west branch) that winds through a forest preserve for 3.6 miles. It ends at a trailhead and site of a 1930s-era one-room schoolhouse in New Lenox.

Returning to the Old Plank Road Trail, the terrain slopes slightly downhill for the next 8 miles to the outskirts of Joliet. Though you're passing through a developing residential and commercial area, a forested buffer screens much of it.

CONTACT: oprt.org

DIRECTIONS

To reach the eastern endpoint on Campbell Ave. in Chicago Heights: From I-57, take Exit 340 for US 30/Lincoln Hwy. Go 4.6 miles east and turn right onto Campbell Ave. Go 0.5 mile to the Old Plank Road Trail crossing and look for parking on side streets.

To reach the western trailhead on E. Washington St. in Joliet: From I-80, take Exit 134 and go north on S. Briggs St. Go 0.6 mile and turn left onto E. Washington St. Go 0.5 mile and look for trailhead parking on the right.

The Prairie Trail runs the length of McHenry County, spanning just over 26 miles from the Wisconsin border and the farms and woodlands along its northern half to the far-flung Chicago suburbs in the south. Along the way, it upgrades from gravel to asphalt and passes through eight communities, where you'll find food and drink, as well as numerous parks and conservation areas.

Built on the Fox River Valley alignment of the old Chicago and North Western Railway, the Prairie Trail meets the Hebron Trail (see page 32) in the north and seamlessly joins the Fox River Trail (see page 21) after crossing into Kane County. It's part of the 500-mile Grand Illinois Trail for its entire length.

Four Chicago and North Western Railroad lines began serving McHenry County in the 1850s, about 20 years after the first prairie settlements took root. At first benefiting the dairy farmers and cheese makers, the railroad later carried vacationers anxious to escape Chicago's

The rail-trail traverses scenic natural areas in northeastern Illinois.

County
McHenry

Endpoints
Southeastern Court near Gideon Court (Genoa City, WI) to Souwanas Trail at Scott St. (Algonquin, IL)

Mileage
26.5

Type
Rail-Trail/Rail-with-Trail

Roughness Index
1–2

Surface
Asphalt, Crushed Stone, Dirt, Gravel

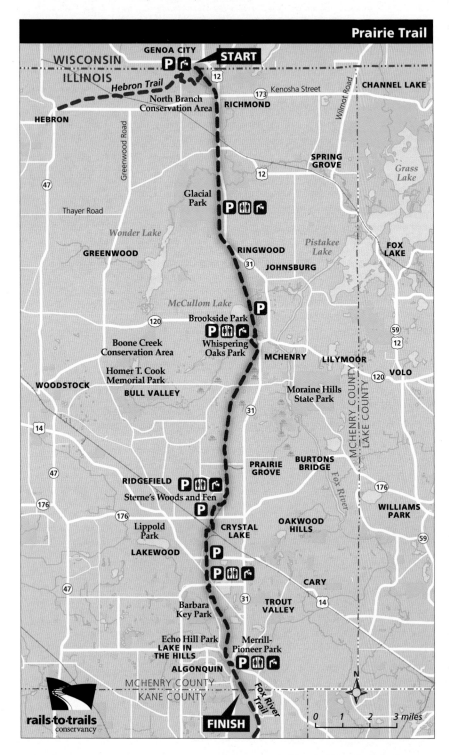

Prairie Trail

WISCONSIN

ILLINOIS

GENOA CITY

START

Hebron Trail

HEBRON

North Branch
Conservation Area

RICHMOND

Kenosha Street

CHANNEL LAKE

Greenwood Road

SPRING
GROVE

Grass
Lake

Thayer Road

Glacial
Park

Wonder Lake

*Pistakee
Lake*

FOX
LAKE

GREENWOOD

RINGWOOD

JOHNSBURG

McCullom Lake

Brookside Park

MCHENRY

LILYMOOR

VOLO

Boone Creek
Conservation Area

Whispering
Oaks Park

WOODSTOCK

Homer T. Cook
Memorial Park

BULL VALLEY

Moraine Hills
State Park

PRAIRIE
GROVE

BURTONS
BRIDGE

RIDGEFIELD

Sterne's Woods and Fen

Lippold
Park

CRYSTAL
LAKE

OAKWOOD
HILLS

WILLIAMS
PARK

LAKEWOOD

CARY

Barbara
Key Park

TROUT
VALLEY

Echo Hill Park

LAKE IN
THE HILLS

ALGONQUIN

Merrill-
Pioneer Park

Fox River

MCHENRY COUNTY

KANE COUNTY

Fox River
Trail

FINISH

rails·to·trails
conservancy

N

0   1   2   3 miles

sweltering heat. After World War II, the railroad helped spur growth in towns like Crystal Lake, McHenry, and Algonquin by offering commuters a way into the city. Today, the Metra commuter rail line shares the corridor with the Prairie Trail between McHenry and Crystal Lake.

Starting at the rural Wisconsin-Illinois border, you'll find the trail is a rough and sometimes muddy mix of dirt and gravel. The junction with Hebron Trail comes up in 0.3 mile as you pass the North Branch Conservation Area, where there's parking, drinking water, and primitive camping.

In 1.3 miles, the trail passes through the village of Richmond, partly below grade with street bridges overhead. The trail surface improves to crushed rock as it passes farmlands and a 2.5-mile section of the 3,400-acre Glacial Park. The trail improves once again a mile after leaving the park when it turns to asphalt in Ringwood.

Entering suburbia, the Prairie Trail leaves the corridor and shifts onto local bike paths and bike lanes for about 1 mile in McHenry. Six miles later, just north of Crystal Lake, the trail again leaves the corridor for a 2-mile section through rugged Sterne's Woods, the most forested part of the trail. The hills are short and very steep; cautionary signs warn bikers to dismount and walk down treacherous slopes.

Rejoining the corridor, the Prairie Trail takes a 6-mile downhill grade to Algonquin and the Fox River bridge that sits atop original limestone pillars. The Prairie Trail ends in 0.6 mile at the McHenry-Kane county line, where it becomes the Fox River Trail.

CONTACT: mccdistrict.org/rccms/bicycling

DIRECTIONS

There is no parking at the two trail endpoints, only trail access. The closest parking locations to the north and south endpoints are outlined below.

To reach the northern trailhead at the North Branch Conservation Area: From I-94, take Exit 2 for IL 173/Rosecrans Road. Head west on IL 173 for 19.1 miles. Turn right onto Broadway Road, then go another 0.7 mile and turn right onto Keystone Road. The North Branch Conservation Area parking lot is on the right in 0.6 mile. Go 1.4 miles east on the Hebron Trail through the conservation area to the Prairie Trail. The trailhead is 0.3 mile north, just across the border in Genoa City, Wisconsin.

To reach the southern trailhead in Algonquin: From I-90, take the exit for IL 59 near mile marker 60. Go 3.3 miles north on IL 59, and turn left onto Algonquin Road. In 7.6 miles turn right onto Meyer Dr. In about 300 feet, turn left at the first entrance marked with the sign MCCD PRAIRIE TRAIL parking lot. The parking lot is at the end of a 0.1-mile-long driveway. A 0.1-mile trail joins the Prairie Trail.

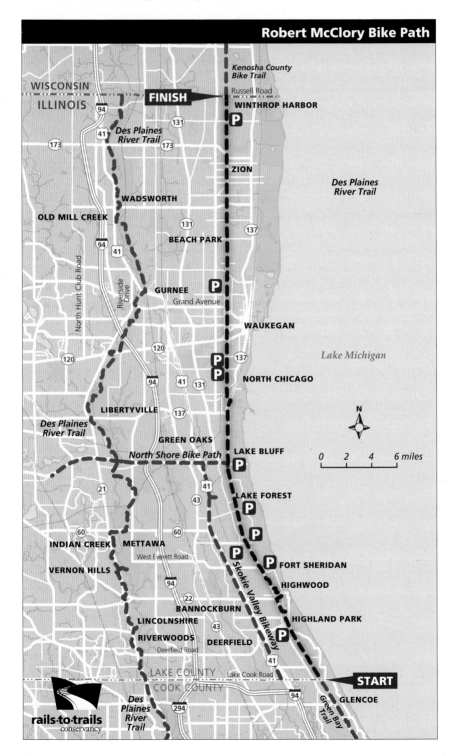

Robert McClory Bike Path

Kenosha County
Bike Trail

Russell Road

FINISH

WISCONSIN

ILLINOIS

94

131

WINTHROP HARBOR

P

41

*Des Plaines
River Trail*

173

173

ZION

173

*Des Plaines
River Trail*

WADSWORTH

OLD MILL CREEK

131

BEACH PARK

94

41

137

North Hunt Club Road

Riverside Drive

P

GURNEE
Grand Avenue

WAUKEGAN

120

Lake Michigan

120

P

137

120

94

41

131

P
P

NORTH CHICAGO

LIBERTYVILLE

137

*Des Plaines
River Trail*

GREEN OAKS

North Shore Bike Path

LAKE BLUFF

P

21

41

43

LAKE FOREST

P

N

0   2   4   6 miles

60

60

INDIAN CREEK   **METTAWA**
West Everett Road

P

VERNON HILLS

94

P

FORT SHERIDAN

HIGHWOOD

22

BANNOCKBURN

Skokie Valley Bikeway

LINCOLNSHIRE

43

HIGHLAND PARK

RIVERWOODS   **DEERFIELD**
Deerfield Road

P

LAKE COUNTY   Lake Cook Road
COOK COUNTY

START

*Des
Plaines
River
Trail*

294

94

Green Bay Trail

GLENCOE

rails·to·trails
conservancy

The Robert McClory Bike Path runs the length of Lake County, knitting together a string of communities on the north shore of Chicago all the way to the Wisconsin border. In 1997 the trail was named after a Republican congressman who served the area for 20 years.

The 25-mile bike path primarily follows the route of the Chicago North Shore and Milwaukee Railroad, which expanded all the way to Milwaukee in 1919 as an electric interurban freight and passenger railroad. It ceased operations in 1963 after ridership declined. The trail also uses low-traffic city streets. A Metra commuter railway connects Chicago to Kenosha, Wisconsin, on Union Pacific Railroad tracks that parallel much of the trail.

The route knits together neighborhoods, commercial districts, parks, and forest preserves north of Chicago.

County
Lake

Endpoints
Green Bay Trail at Lake Cook Road and St. Johns Ave. (Highland Park) to Kenosha County Bike Trail at Russell Road, 0.1 mile west of Old Darby Lane (Winthrop Harbor)

Mileage
25.4

Type
Rail-Trail/Rail-with-Trail

Roughness Index
1–2

Surface
Asphalt, Concrete, Crushed Stone

The trail surface consists of asphalt in the south; concrete where the path leaves the rail corridor and follows city streets; and a finely screened limestone that offers a good, hard base for most trail uses in the north. It's hemmed in by residential and commercial districts, though it does pass some parks and forest preserves. In the south, the trail connects with the Green Bay Trail at the county line, while in the north it meets the Kenosha County Bike Trail at the state line. US Bicycle Route 37 and the Grand Illinois Trail both occupy parts of the trail.

Beginning in the south at the Braeside Metra Station, you'll ride 2.5 miles through a wooded linear park alongside the tracks until you reach a commuter parking lot in central Highland Park. You'll then have to take St. Johns Avenue (there are sidewalks) 0.7 mile to Vine Avenue, turn left, and go one block to a ramp to return to the trail.

You'll return to a parklike corridor for another 0.6 mile, then take a slight detour by turning right onto Bloom Street. Go 0.2 mile, turn left onto St. Johns Avenue, and go another 0.2 mile to return to the Robert McClory Bike Path adjacent to Walker Avenue.

For the next 1.5 miles, the trail skirts old Fort Sheridan, a historical garrison decommissioned by the U.S. Army and transformed into a fashionable neighborhood. You'll find hiking and biking trails within the 230-acre historic district; another 250 acres is in forest preserve.

Crossing Sheridan Road, you'll return to the old railroad right-of-way that runs through a wooded corridor next to Metra through Lake Forest and Lake Bluff (the junction for the east-west North Shore Bike Path is here) for the next 7.2 miles to North Chicago. Here the trail takes a ramp over a highway, loses Metra, and enters a warehouse and light-industrial district for a few blocks.

For the next 12 miles to the Wisconsin border, the bike path corridor is pleasantly wide. Mile markers are visible north of Waukegan. Another unique feature is the number of community gardens that appear mile after mile, adding a charming country touch to the urban atmosphere.

Parks and open spaces become more prevalent farther north. The trail meets the Kenosha County Bike Trail on a pedestrian bridge spanning Russell Road at the state line. That trail continues another 4.5 miles into Kenosha.

CONTACT: lakecountyil.gov/441/Bikeways

DIRECTIONS

To reach the southern end of the Robert McClory Bike Path: From I-94 W, take Exit 29 for US 41/Skokie Hwy. In 0.7 mile, take the Lake Cook Road exit and head east. Go 1.3 miles, and turn left onto Blackhawk Road or St. Johns Ave. Look for parking at the Braeside Metra Station. (Parking is extremely limited and expensive; consider taking your bicycle on board a Metra train.)

   To reach the northern end of the Robert McClory Bike Path at the state line: From I-94, take Exit 1 for Russell Road, and head east. Go 4.9 miles and turn right onto N. Lewis Ave. Go 1 mile and turn left onto W. Ninth St. In 0.4 mile turn right onto W. Broadway Ave. Look for parking on the left side of the road. The bike path crosses W. Ninth St. just around the corner; the state line is 1 mile north.

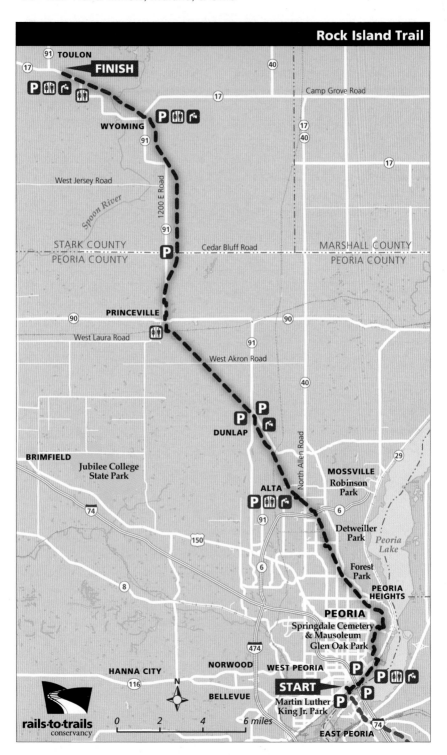

The Rock Island Trail offers both a town and a country experience. At its southern end, the trail begins at the vibrant Peoria waterfront. Here, the trail runs along an active Tazewell & Peoria Railroad line, forming an example of a successful rail-with-trail. As the well-maintained asphalt-and-brick trail makes its way through town, it passes a nicely refurbished depot that has been converted for commercial use, as well as restaurants along the route.

The trail follows Peoria Lake a short distance and then heads up through Glen Oak Park, which dates to the late 1800s and houses a zoo, botanical garden, fishing lagoon, and other recreational amenities. Adjacent to the park is the historical Springdale Cemetery, founded in 1855; a couple of short, but steep, hills lead up to it.

This trestle crosses the Spoon River near Wyoming on the north end of the rail-trail.

County
Peoria, Stark

Endpoints
Bob Michel Bridge at IL 40/N. William Kumpf Blvd. and SW Water St. (Peoria) to Downend St. at E. Main St./IL 17 (Toulon)

Mileage
38.2

Type
Rail-Trail/Rail-with-Trail

Roughness Index
1–2

Surface
Crushed Stone, Asphalt

Leaving Peoria, the trail does include several lightly traveled roadways along its route, but signs keep you pointed in the right direction. The urban feel begins to change to suburban, and you may pass residents exercising on the trail. The corridor here shares space with a power line and another adjacent railroad. After about 13 miles of riding, you'll approach Alta, where the trail begins to turn more rural.

The northern section of the pathway connects the friendly small towns of Alta, Dunlap, Princeville, Wyoming, and Toulon. This crushed-rock section, stretching about 26 miles, travels through classic Midwestern farmland, woodlands, prairie grasses, and wildflowers.

In Wyoming, look for the restored Chicago, Burlington & Quincy Depot, a barn-red building that houses a visitor center and railroad museum. Leaving the town, you'll enjoy the trestle bridge that spans Spoon River. The bridge has observation bump-outs that offer a convenient rest stop, with the lush river valley as a backdrop.

CONTACT: **dnr.state.il.us/lands/Landmgt/parks/r1/rockisle.htm** or
peoriaparks-planning.org/ppd-rock-island-greenway

DIRECTIONS

To access parking at the south end of the trail: From I-74, take Exit 93 for Adams St. and Downtown Peoria. Head northeast on Adams St. and almost immediately make a hard right onto Eaton St. Follow the brown signs that point to the Riverfront District. Continue on Eaton 0.2 mile to the waterfront on your left, where you'll find a large parking lot and the trail paralleling the railroad tracks.

To reach the northern end of the trail: From I-74, take Exit 71 for IL 78. Head north, first on N. Bell School Road, then US 150, then IL 78, for a total of 17.3 miles to IL 17. Turn right onto IL 17 and follow the roadway 4.7 miles through Toulon to the trailside parking lot on the east end of town; it will be on your left.

Sandwiched between towering limestone bluffs and the confluence of two mighty rivers, the Sam Vadalabene Great River Road Bike Trail offers scenery once enjoyed by riverboat captains. Today, you can experience the views from an asphalt trail and bike lane that runs just over 20 miles between Pere Marquette State Park and the outskirts of Alton.

Much of the trail that hugs the Illinois shoreline follows the Alton-Grafton section of the Illinois Terminal Railroad, which ran interurban lines in western and central Illinois. This section served residents along the river from 1896 to the 1950s.

The state Department of Transportation opened the eastern 15.5-mile segment in the late 1970s, and the Department of Natural Resources extended the trail to Pere Marquette State Park in the early 1990s. It was named for a state senator who was remembered as a champion of bicycling resources.

Counties
Jersey, Madison

Endpoints
Pere Marquette State Park at Scenic Dr. and IL 100 (Grafton) to Piasa Park at IL 100/Great River Road, 0.9 mile northwest of US 67 (Alton)

Mileage
20.6

Type
Rail-Trail

Roughness Index
1

Surface
Asphalt

The bike trail parallels two scenic rivers, the Mississippi and the Illinois.

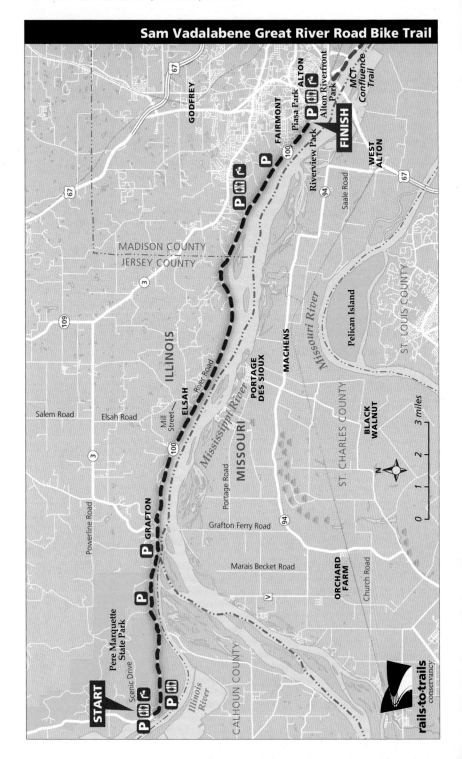

Visit Pere Marquette State Park, the largest park in the state's system, before setting out. Named for the first European to set foot on Illinois soil, the park is known for its scenic overlooks, American Indian burial mounds, autumn colors, and winter population of bald eagles.

Leaving the park, you might be challenged by some short hills until the trail settles in comfortably alongside IL 100 after 3 or 4 miles. You can catch fleeting glimpses of the Illinois River through the woods here and visit a stone monument commemorating Jacques Marquette's arrival in 1673 at 4.5 miles into your ride.

You'll roll into the historical river town of Grafton in another 0.5 mile as the Illinois and Mississippi Rivers meet. The trail traces the waterfront for a mile, where you'll see turtles and waterfowl, then it shares a street, where it passes a marina and ferry landing within a block of shops and cafés on Main Street.

At the east end of downtown Grafton, the trail merges onto IL 100 as a 3- to 4-foot-wide bike lane separated from traffic by rumble strips. While traffic whizzes past on your left, barges make their way up and down the wide river that's flowing just beyond your right shoulder. Adding to this spectacle, towering limestone bluffs soar above the trees across the road. You'll ride next to the Mississippi River for the next 8.3 miles on this highway that's part of the Great River Road, which runs from Minnesota to Louisiana and is designated as a National Scenic Byway.

Four miles from Grafton, you'll find a pleasant detour in the town of Elsah. A spin through the hamlet on LaSalle and Mill Streets reveals pre-1860 stone buildings still in use, lending Elsah a step-back-in-time quality that earned it a spot on the National Register of Historic Places in 1973.

Four miles past Elsah, the Sam Vadalabene Great River Road Bike Trail crosses IL 100 and finishes the last 5.6 miles as a bike path with a sometimes rough surface at the foot of the bluffs on the northeast side of the highway.

Arriving at the trailhead about 1 mile upstream from Alton, you'll see the Piasa Bird overlooking the parking lot. The giant painting on a limestone bluff is a reproduction of an American Indian petroglyph that settlers discovered nearby. Bicyclists looking to extend their journey can pick up the Madison County Transit Confluence Trail in Alton.

CONTACT: greatriverroad.com/vadalabene.htm

DIRECTIONS

To reach the trailhead at Pere Marquette State Park from I-55, take Exit 52 toward Litchfield and Gillespie and head west on IL 16. Go 8.4 miles and turn right onto Broadway St., remaining on IL 16. Go 8.0 miles and turn right to remain on IL 16. Continue 33.2 miles, pass through Jerseyville, and turn left onto IL 100. Go 9.7 miles and turn left into the park. Parking is straight ahead; follow signs for the trail.

To reach the trailhead at Piasa Park from I-270, take Exit 3 or 3B toward Alton on IL 3/ Lewis and Clark Blvd. Head north on IL 3 for 6.7 miles and turn left onto IL 143 W/Great River Road. Then go another 4.3 miles and continue straight on US 67 N/Broadway Connector. Go 0.8 mile and take the left lanes onto W. Broadway, which becomes Great River Road/McAdams Pkwy. In 0.9 mile turn right into the parking lot at Piasa Park.

The northern section of the Tinley Creek Trail is a series of color-coded connected loops and spurs that weave through several forest preserves in Cook County. The 24-mile trail system is paved, making it a paradise for all types of trail users.

After parking near Turtlehead Lake at the northern end of the red trail loop, get your bearings at the first of a series of trailside maps. Decide whether to take the loop north or south, and enjoy the scenic, rural 9.4-mile trip around a series of small lakes and through beautiful prairie grassland. Along the way you will see many different species of birds, including sparrows and orioles, flying back and forth across the trail.

At the north end of the trail, you also have the opportunity to connect to the Orland Park Bikeway system at 139th Street, which heads west and southwest to

On its way to Midlothian Reservoir, the path travels through St. Mihiel Woods.

County
Cook

Endpoints
Turtlehead Lake, 0.3 mile southwest of IL 43 and 135th St. (Orland Township), to Midlothian Meadows near W. 155th St. and Crawford Ave. (Midlothian)

Mileage
24.0

Type
Greenway/Non-Rail-Trail

Roughness Index
1

Surface
Asphalt

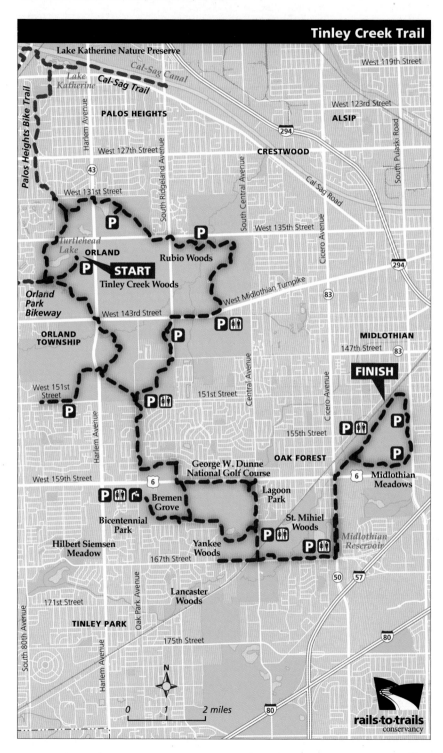

Tinley Creek Trail

downtown Orland Park, as well as the Palos Heights Bike Trail at 131st Street, which heads north to the Lake Katherine Nature Preserve and the Cal-Sag Trail.

Not quite ready to return back to your car? At mile marker 0, take a left onto the green trail, which cuts along Oak Park Avenue to the 3-mile purple loop, which will take you through Yankee Woods and the George W. Dunne National Golf Course. Use this opportunity to stop at the excellent trailside picnic facilities in Yankee Woods. A short yellow spur leads to Bremen Grove, which is also a great spot to have a snack and take in a bit more of the forest preserve.

The trail continues along the 3-mile blue leg of the network through St. Mihiel Woods and around the Midlothian Reservoir. Feed the local geese or hop off the trail and cast a line in the reservoir, where fishing is allowed. After passing the reservoir on your left, use the crosswalk to traverse Cicero Avenue at 167th Street. Follow the trail along Cicero Avenue for about a mile. You may feel like you're traveling on a wide sidewalk, but you will soon reenter the forest preserve at Midlothian Meadows. There's another scenic 3-mile loop through the meadow, as well as two options for parking at the eastern end of the park.

CONTACT: fpdcc.com/preserves-and-trails/trail-descriptions/#tinley-creek

---

DIRECTIONS

To reach Turtlehead Lake: From I-294, take the exit for 127th St. and Cicero Ave. near mile marker 12. From I-294 S, head south on Cicero Ave. From I-294 N, turn left onto W. 127th St. and take the very next left onto S. Cicero Ave. After 1.5 miles on Cicero, turn right onto 135th St. and follow it 3 miles. Turn left onto IL 43 S., and in 0.2 mile take a right at the Turtlehead Lake sign. Parking will be visible immediately once you enter the park.

To reach Midlothian Meadows: From I-57, take Exit 348 for US 6 W/W. 159th St. Head 0.2 mile west on W. 159th St., and turn right onto Crawford Ave./Pulaski Road. Take the very next left at W. 155th St. into Midlothian Meadows. Parking is ahead in 0.5 mile.

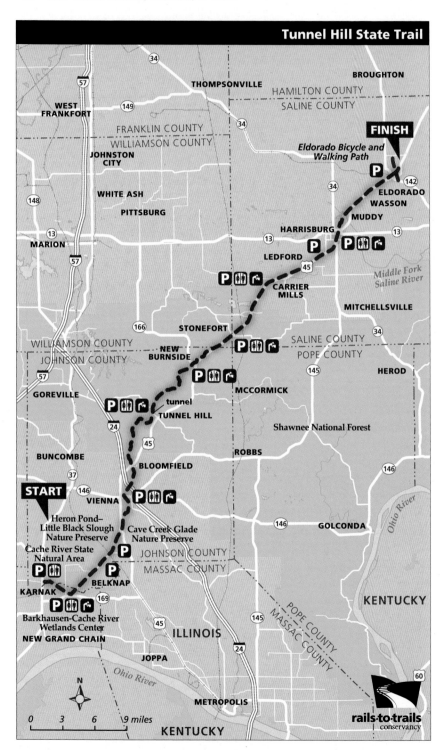

Tunnel Hill State Trail

THOMPSONVILLE

BROUGHTON

HAMILTON COUNTY
SALINE COUNTY

WEST
FRANKFORT

FRANKLIN COUNTY
WILLIAMSON COUNTY

JOHNSTON
CITY

WHITE ASH

PITTSBURG

FINISH

*Eldorado Bicycle and
Walking Path*

ELDORADO
WASSON

MUDDY

MARION

HARRISBURG

LEDFORD

CARRIER
MILLS

MITCHELLSVILLE

WILLIAMSON COUNTY
JOHNSON COUNTY

STONEFORT

NEW
BURNSIDE

SALINE COUNTY
POPE COUNTY

HEROD

GOREVILLE

MCCORMICK

*Middle Fork
Saline River*

tunnel
TUNNEL HILL

Shawnee National Forest

BUNCOMBE

ROBBS

BLOOMFIELD

START

VIENNA

Heron Pond–
Little Black Slough
Nature Preserve

Cave Creek Glade
Nature Preserve

Cache River State
Natural Area

JOHNSON COUNTY
MASSAC COUNTY

GOLCONDA

Ohio River

KARNAK

BELKNAP

Barkhausen-Cache River
Wetlands Center

NEW GRAND CHAIN

KENTUCKY

JOPPA

ILLINOIS

POPE COUNTY
MASSAC COUNTY

N

Ohio River

0   3   6   9 miles

METROPOLIS

KENTUCKY

rails·to·trails
conservancy

A dark railroad tunnel and two dozen trestles crossing streams and rocky ravines welcome visitors to the scenic Tunnel Hill State Trail as it travels 55 miles through forests and farmland in sparsely populated southern Illinois.

This gem of Illinois rail-trails was built on the former Cairo and Vincennes Railroad, which was completed in 1874 and hauled coal from southern Illinois mines, as well as produce and timber. Over the years, the railroad went through a series of ownership changes, and the tracks last belonged to Norfolk Southern Railroad, which turned the corridor over to the state in 1991. The first sections of trail opened in 1998.

Beginning at the Barkhausen-Cache River Wetlands Center, you'll encounter a gentle, uphill slope for 22.5 miles to the tunnel, where the trail crests and begins a downhill run toward Eldorado. Several small towns and

Though best known for its tunnel, the route also features nearly two dozen bridges.

Counties
Johnson, Pulaski, Saline, Williamson

Endpoints
Barkhausen-Cache River Wetlands Center at IL 37, 0.15 mile north of Perks Road (Cypress), to Eldorado High School athletic fields at N. Main St., just south of University St. (Eldorado)

Mileage
55.3

Type
Rail-Trail

Roughness Index
1–2

Surface
Concrete, Crushed Stone

Between New Burnside and Tunnel Hill, dense forest shades trail users.

ghost towns are on this route, but services aren't always available. It's a good idea to refill water bottles when you can.

The first 2.7 miles to Karnak run on a former spur line of the Chicago and Eastern Illinois Railroad. It passes through the swampy Cache River State Natural Area, which is home to giant cypress trees, some 1,000 years old. In Karnak, where a trailside campground opened in 2016, the Tunnel Hill State Trail bears left and picks up the railroad corridor.

You'll pass the Heron Pond–Little Black Slough and Cave Creek Glade Nature Preserves. About halfway to Vienna, look for the ghost town of Forman to your left. A trailside park in Vienna, 10.5 miles past Karnak, is a good stop, and cafés and groceries are available in town.

In 3 miles, you'll probably notice the grade steepen just outside Bloomfield. The railroaders tried to keep these slopes as gentle as possible to save fuel and time. That's why they dug a tunnel, originally 800 feet long, through the hill here, 6.7 miles past Bloomfield, instead of going over the top. A section of the tunnel collapsed in 1929. The remaining 543-foot tunnel is pitch-black inside, so be sure to carry a flashlight or bike light so you don't scrape the wall or run into another visitor.

Back out into the light, you'll find a fully stocked trailhead on your right in the town of Tunnel Hill, where the remaining 33-mile ride to Eldorado begins. Entering the Shawnee National Forest, you'll find a stunning landscape, with a high tree canopy that shades a trickling brook on the right. You're more likely to hear the birds here than you are to see them, but the local rabbit population is everywhere. Users often report seeing deer and turkeys along the length of the trail.

After 6 miles, you arrive in the town of New Burnside. Looming bluffs mark the terrain here, providing a dramatic contrast to the forest you traveled through earlier. Another 4.4 miles takes you along a flat section along US 45 to Stonefort, whose trailhead includes a well-restored railroad depot. The next 6.7-mile stretch remains within sight of US 45 most of the way to Carrier Mills. Keep an eye out for turtles and snakes, which also like to use this trail. The next 7.5 miles meander past farm fields and the outskirts of Harrisburg, the largest town on the trail. You'll spot restaurants, grocery stores, and motels as you pass through.

From the trailhead on the north side of town, it's another 8.2 miles to the endpoint in Eldorado. The trail crosses IL 13, spans a bridge over the Middle Fork of Saline River in Muddy, and continues alongside US 45. Near your destination, you cross the 2-mile crosstown Eldorado Bicycle and Walking Path, another rail-trail.

CONTACT: dnr.state.il.us/lands/Landmgt/PARKS/R5/tunnel.htm

DIRECTIONS

To reach the Barkhausen-Cache River Wetlands Center near Cypress: From I-57, take Exit 24 and go east on Cypress Road/Dongola Road. Go 8.3 miles and turn right onto IL 37, following signs to the WETLANDS CENTER. Go 2.5 miles and turn left into the Barkhausen-Cache River Wetlands Center, traveling a short distance to trail parking.

To reach the Eldorado High School trailhead: From I-64, take Exit 110 and head south on US 45 toward Norris City. Go 21.4 miles, and turn right to remain on US 45. In another 11.2 miles, turn right onto Alexander St. in Eldorado. Go 0.5 mile and turn left onto N. Main St. Go 0.4 mile and turn left into an unmarked drive that heads into the Eldorado High School sports complex. The Tunnel Hill State Trail begins 0.2 mile ahead.

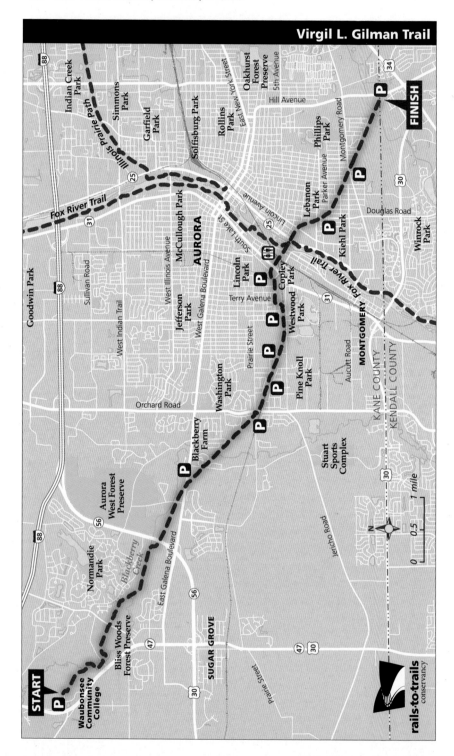

The Virgil L. Gilman Trail travels from quiet forest and prairie lands to bustling neighborhoods in just 11 miles, linking a woodsy community college campus with the eastern Chicago suburb of Montgomery. The trail's namesake, Virgil Gilman, served as administrator of the Fox Valley Park District for 30 years and successfully championed public access to Fox River, as the public shoreline grew from 66 feet in 1946 to 20 miles during his tenure.

The rail-trail is built along the routes of two former railroads. In the west, the corridor of the Chicago, Aurora & DeKalb Railroad was utilized; it ran as an interurban route 1906–1923, though it never reached Chicago. East of Copley Park, trail builders used the Elgin, Joliet & Eastern Railway's Aurora Branch, which survived as a railroad until the late 1970s.

Beginning at Waubonsee Community College, you'll head across native prairie for the first mile on asphalt, then travel on a short section of crushed stone (for 0.3 mile) before returning to a paved surface for the remainder of the trail. Back on pavement, you'll head into the Bliss Woods Forest Preserve, where you'll find large white and

A highlight of the trail is its suspension bridge over Blackberry Creek.

Counties
Kane, Kendall

Endpoints
Circle Dr., 0.1 mile west of Waubonsee Dr. (Sugar Grove), to Hill Ave., 0.1 mile north of Goodwin Dr. (Montgomery)

Mileage
11.4

Type
Rail-Trail/Rail-with-Trail

Roughness Index
1

Surface
Asphalt

black oaks, as well as sycamore, white poplar, and cottonwood. Birders enjoy spotting downy woodpeckers, cardinals, and blue jays along the path.

Leaving Bliss Woods, the route follows Blackberry Creek and crosses IL 56 on a pedestrian bridge 3.2 miles past the college. In 0.2 mile, a trail heads north into the 715-acre Aurora West Forest Preserve, an old farming area that's being restored to its natural state.

In another 1.3 miles, look for a path on the left that heads into Blackberry Farm. This living history replica of 19th-century pioneer life was created by Virgil Gilman as Pioneer Park and continues to be popular today.

Past the park, the trail rolls in between housing subdivisions and alongside an active railroad corridor, though thick vegetation screens both from your sight. Arriving at Terry Avenue, the trail continues 0.5 mile on quiet side streets that are very easy to navigate. Take a left onto Terry Avenue, followed quickly by a right onto Rathbone Avenue. Follow Rathbone, and turn left immediately after an at-grade railroad crossing to regain the trail as you enter Copley Park.

Leaving the park, you pass beneath two railroad overpasses in quick succession and arrive at a circa 1897 railroad trestle across the Fox River in 0.4 mile. This is also a junction for the north-south Fox River Trail (see page 21) that runs 44 miles from Algonquin to Oswego.

After crossing the bridge and the riverside commercial district, the trail ends with a 2.7-mile run through established Aurora neighborhoods with frequent street crossings. There's a little bit of wildness in the remaining 0.3 mile before the trail ends, however, as the trail crosses Waubonsie Creek, whose wetlands host migratory birds in season.

CONTACT: kaneforest.com/recreation/trails/virgilLGilman.aspx

DIRECTIONS

To reach the western trailhead at Waubonsee Community College: From I-88 W, take Exit 113 for IL 56 W. Continue south on IL 56 for 2.3 miles and turn right onto E. Galena Blvd. In 1.3 miles, turn right onto IL 47, and in 1.5 miles, turn right onto Waubonsee Dr. at the entrance of Waubonsee Community College. Go 0.4 mile, turn right onto Circle Dr., and look for parking. From I-88 E, take Exit 109 for IL 47. Head south on IL 47 for 2.1 miles, and turn left onto Waubonsee Dr. at the entrance of Waubonsee Community College. Go 0.4 mile, turn right onto Circle Dr., and look for parking.

To reach the eastern trailhead on Hill Ave.: From I-88, take the exit for N. Farnsworth Ave. near mile marker 119. Head south on N. Farnsworth Ave. 4.5 miles, and turn right onto Montgomery Road. In 0.3 mile, turn left onto Hill Ave. The trailhead parking lot is 0.6 mile ahead on the left.

In just a few short miles, the Wauponsee Glacial Trail leaves the urban confines of Joliet to bask in open farmland and reclaimed tallgrass prairie where the bison roam again. Named for a glacial lake that covered the area 13,000 years ago, the Wauponsee Glacial Trail sports a mastodon logo on its trail signs. The surface is paved through Joliet but is crushed stone the rest of the way. The route passes through areas where towns are few and far between and shade is a rare commodity.

The 22-mile-long path follows the route of two historical railroad lines: the Illinois, Iowa & Minnesota Railway (later acquired by the Chicago Milwaukee St. Paul and Pacific) from Joliet to Manhattan, and the Wabash Railroad (eventually sold to Norfolk Southern Railway) from Manhattan to Custer Park.

Trees line the southern end of the path as the Wauponsee Glacial Trail traverses Forked Creek Preserve.

County
Will

Endpoints
Rowell Ave., just south of the I-80 overpass (Joliet), to Washington St. and IL 113 (Custer Park)

Mileage
22.3

Type
Rail-Trail/Rail-with-Trail

Roughness Index
1

Surface
Asphalt, Crushed Stone

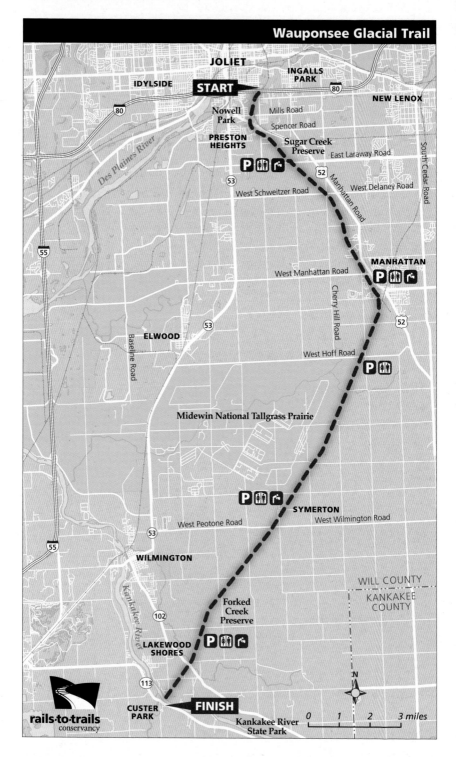

Wauponsee Glacial Trail

JOLIET

INGALLS PARK

IDYLSIDE

80

START

NEW LENOX

80

Nowell Park

Mills Road

Spencer Road

PRESTON HEIGHTS

Sugar Creek Preserve

East Laraway Road

South Cedar Road

52

53

West Schweitzer Road

Manhattan Road

West Delaney Road

55

MANHATTAN

West Manhattan Road

Des Plaines River

Cherry Hill Road

52

53

ELWOOD

West Hoff Road

Baseline Road

Midewin National Tallgrass Prairie

SYMERTON

West Peotone Road

West Wilmington Road

53

WILMINGTON

55

Forked Creek Preserve

Kankakee River

102

LAKEWOOD SHORES

WILL COUNTY

KANKAKEE COUNTY

113

CUSTER PARK

FINISH

Kankakee River State Park

0   1   2   3 miles

N

rails·to·trails
conservancy

Beginning near the I-80 overpass in Joliet, the trail leaves an industrial area as it briefly runs alongside the Metra commuter railway and then passes through woodsy neighborhoods. Leaving the city behind, you might consider stopping at the Sugar Creek Administration Center to get more information on forest preserve trails and camping permits or to fill your water bottles.

After the center, you'll notice that the path becomes crushed stone, on which horseback riding is permitted. Vast fields of corn and soybean stretch to the horizon along this 5-mile stretch that aims southeast toward Manhattan, where a trailhead with restrooms and water greets you. Restaurants and an ice cream parlor are a couple of blocks away in town.

In 1.5 miles, the trail transitions away from Manhattan in a southwesterly direction on the old Wabash Railroad spur. (The corridor heads northward as a Metra line between Manhattan and Chicago.) You'll find another trailhead (parking entrance on West Hoff Road) 1.8 miles south of Manhattan as you begin to pass the 18,500-acre Midewin National Tallgrass Prairie. You can gain access to the prairie reserve's 33 miles of trail on a path that's another 0.8 mile south on the right. The Joliet Arsenal controlled this land from World War II until its decommissioning in the 1970s, and many ammo bunkers are still visible. The U.S. Forest Service introduced a bison herd on the west side of the property in 2015.

After passing nearly 5 miles of reclaimed prairie on the right, you'll come to a trailhead in the farming community of Symerton, and another trailhead is 4.6 miles south in Wilmington township. Another 2.3 miles brings you to a circa 1902 trestle, originally a four-truss bridge, that stretches 600 feet across the Kankakee River. A pony plate girder span replaced the easternmost truss after a railroad accident.

The trail ends just across the river in unincorporated Custer Park.

CONTACT: reconnectwithnature.org/preserves-trails/Wauponsee-Glacial-Trail

DIRECTIONS

Only on-street parking is available at the trail terminus southeast of downtown Joliet. To reach this endpoint, from I-80, take Exit 134 and go south on S. Briggs St. Take the first right onto W. Haven Ave. (which becomes New Lenox Road) and go 1 mile before turning right onto Rowell Ave. In 0.2 mile, the Wauponsee Glacial Trail begins on the left, though there is no parking lot.

To reach the southern trailhead in Custer Park: From I-55, take Exit 240 for Lorenzo Road. Head southeast on Lorenzo Road 0.2 mile, and then turn right onto SE Frontage Road. Go 2.5 miles and turn left onto IL 129/Washington St. In 0.2 mile, turn left at the first cross street onto W. Strip Mine Road/County Road 29. In 1.6 miles, turn left onto Baltimore St. and make an immediate right onto W. River Road. Go 3 miles and turn left onto IL 113. Continue 1.8 miles and turn right onto Washington St. The parking lot is immediately on the right.

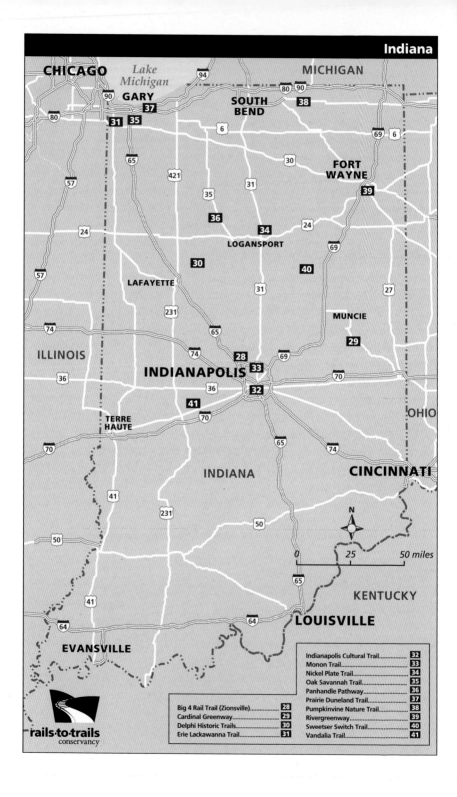

CHICAGO

Lake Michigan

MICHIGAN

94

80 90

GARY

37

SOUTH BEND

80

6

31 35

69 6

65

421

30

FORT WAYNE

57

35

31

39

36

24

LOGANSPORT

34

69

30

40

24

LAFAYETTE

231

57

31

27

65

MUNCIE

74

74

28

29

ILLINOIS

36

INDIANAPOLIS

33

69

70

36

32

TERRE HAUTE

41

70

OHIO

70

65

74

CINCINNATI

41

INDIANA

231

50

50

N

50

50 miles

0   25

65

KENTUCKY

41

65

64

LOUISVILLE

EVANSVILLE

64

rails·to·trails
conservancy

Just north of Wicker Park, the Erie Lackawanna Trail is lush and green in spring and summer (see page 110).

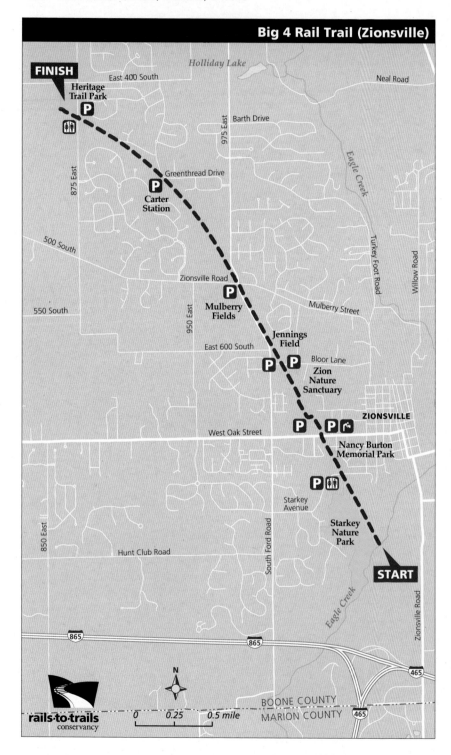

Big 4 Rail Trail (Zionsville)

FINISH
Heritage Trail Park
East 400 South
Holliday Lake
Neal Road
975 East
Barth Drive
Eagle Creek
875 East
Greenthread Drive
Carter Station
500 South
Turkey Foot Road
Willow Road
Zionsville Road
550 South
950 East
Mulberry Fields
Mulberry Street
East 600 South
Jennings Field
Bloor Lane
Zion Nature Sanctuary
ZIONSVILLE
West Oak Street
Nancy Burton Memorial Park
850 East
Starkey Avenue
Starkey Nature Park
Hunt Club Road
South Ford Road
START
Zionsville Road
865
865
465
N
BOONE COUNTY
MARION COUNTY
465

rails-to-trails
conservancy

0   0.25   0.5 mile

The Big 4 Rail Trail will one day stretch 50-plus miles across Boone County, from the northern suburbs of Indianapolis to Lafayette. The *Big 4* in the trail name refers to the old Cleveland, Cincinnati, Chicago and St. Louis Railway corridor. It could just as easily refer to the four communities pushing this long-term project: Zionsville, Whitestown, Lebanon, and Thorntown. The description here details the portion of this regional network that runs through Zionsville, which was formerly known as the Zionsville Rail Trail. Another 9.5 miles of the Big 4 Rail Trail are open to the northwest between Lebanon and Thorntown.

A number of railroads operated trains on those tracks, starting with the Lafayette and Indianapolis Railroad in 1850 and ending with Conrail in 1976. The tracks carried newly elected President Abraham Lincoln through

Deep woodlands frame the southern end of the paved trail.

County
Boone

Endpoints
Bridge over Eagle Creek 0.5 mile south of Starkey Ave. and 0.25 mile east of Sugarbush Dr. to Heritage Trail Park at County Road 875 E, 0.2 mile south of CR 400 S (Zionsville)

Mileage
3.7

Type
Rail-Trail

Roughness Index
1

Surface
Asphalt, Crushed Stone

this area in 1861 and carried his body home four years later. The "Big 4" Railroad operated the longest period, 1889–1930. Zionsville installed a trail along the corridor in the 1990s.

At the south end of the path, you'll begin your adventure on a bridge 60 feet above Eagle Creek. A side trip down a boardwalk to the floodplain leads to paths in Starkey Nature Park. The first 0.8-mile stretch of the trail, known as the Nancy Burton Corridor, travels through woods on a hard-packed limestone surface. The last 1.5-mile section is known as the Dave Brown Corridor.

At 0.6 mile turn right onto a short path and take residential streets for a visit into downtown Zionsville. Founded in 1852, the town draws tourists to its brick-paved Main Street, where you'll see a progression of architectural styles from previous eras. Dining and shopping are popular pursuits, and the town offers a full calendar of events.

The trail emerges from the woods onto asphalt in less than a mile. The route is somewhat unusual in that it passes all the way through town before encountering the first at-grade crossing, located at County Road 875 on the north side of Zionsville. The trail passes beneath all other streets via tunnels as it goes through much of town below street level. Numerous parks in town—including Jennings Field, Carter Station, and Heritage Trail Park, as well as the Rail Trail Gardens Event Center at the north end of the route—have connections to the trail.

CONTACT: zionsville-in.gov/Facilities/Facility/Details/The-Big4-Rail-Trail-8

DIRECTIONS

To reach parking at the south end of the trail: From I-465, take Exit 27 onto US 421 N toward Zionsville. Go 0.1 mile north on US 421, and turn left onto W. 96th St. Go 2.6 miles and turn right onto Ford Road. Go 1.3 miles and turn right onto Starkey Ave. Go 0.6 mile and look for parking on the left. The trail endpoint is 0.6 mile south.

To reach the northern end of the trail: From I-65, take Exit 133 onto Albert S. White Blvd. Head east 3 miles (the road becomes County Road 400 S), and follow the road as it curves right onto CR 700 E, then left onto CR 425 S. Go 0.5 mile on CR 425 S, and turn left onto Zionsville Road. Follow it as it curves right onto CR 400 S. Go 1.3 miles and turn right into Heritage Trail Park. The park path connects to the trail.

The Cardinal Greenway, the longest rail-trail in Indiana, stretches just over 61 miles from Marion to Richmond along a former CSX railroad corridor. The trail takes its name from the Cardinal, the passenger train that once regularly ran the route. The long greenway connects Marion, Muncie, Losantville, Richmond, and a host of smaller towns in rural Indiana. The trail is open sunrise–sunset, and it's well maintained and mostly flat for its entire length. The design elements along the path are consistent throughout, with arched steel embellishments on bridge crossings and stone mile markers every 0.5 mile.

Starting just north of Marion, the Cardinal Greenway seamlessly connects to the Sweetser Switch Trail (see page 139), which heads north, while the Cardinal Greenway runs south back into downtown Marion. For a stretch at the beginning of the Cardinal Greenway into

Muncie's depot has been beautifully restored to its 1901 condition.

Counties
Delaware, Grant, Henry, Randolph, Wayne

Endpoints
County Road 400 W just south of IN 18 (Marion) to E. 10th St. just east of Boyd St. (Jonesboro) and W. CR 850 N, 0.1 mile west of Broad St. (Gaston), to the intersection of N. Third St. and N. D St. (Richmond)

Mileage
61.2

Type
Rail-Trail/Rail-with-Trail

Roughness Index
1

Surface
Asphalt

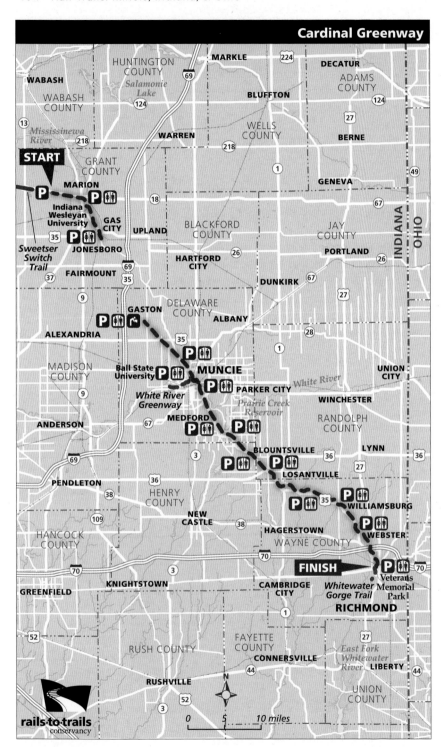

Cardinal Greenway

Marion, the path runs adjacent to and then crosses an active Norfolk Southern line as the greenway passes through a flat, rural landscape that highlights industrial and farmland scenery.

Heading southwest out of Marion, you will pass trailheads at Miller Avenue and Hogin Park, both featuring information kiosks and ample parking. After the park, you will cross the first of nine bridges in rapid succession. Once the trail winds its way into Jonesboro, you will cross US 35; the trailhead is on the left. A slight uphill climb takes you to a bridge that overlooks the Mississinewa River.

An 11.3-mile gap in the Cardinal Greenway currently exists from Jonesboro to Gaston due to private landowners acquiring the former rail corridor. An on-road route has been designated between the two towns and can be found on the official trail website listed (see page 106).

Wildflowers flank the Gaston section of the greenway during the spring and summer. As you reach the County Road 400 trailhead, the urban fingers of Muncie start to reach out. An influx of runners, walkers, and in-line skaters—many of them students at nearby Ball State University—hit the trail. Farther south, the McCulloch Boulevard trailhead allows for a connection to Muncie's White River Greenway, which follows the trail's eponymous river. Here, you will also be faced with two bridges: to the right, a historical trestle bridge; to the left, the bicycle and pedestrian bridge that takes you across the White River. Another 0.3 mile south is the beautifully restored Wysor Street Depot, listed on the National Register of Historic Places, which serves as the main office of Cardinal Greenways, Inc.

Heading south from the depot, you will find yourself in the quiet residential neighborhoods of Muncie. Passing under US 35, you will reenter the sun-drenched Indiana countryside, where the trail meanders along the highway through Medford and Blountsville. At the Medford trailhead (County Road 500 South), equestrians can access the 3.5-mile Cardinal Greenway Horse Trail that parallels the paved Cardinal Greenway and extends to South County Road 534 East. The Medford trailhead features a circular gravel lot with hitching rails and room for horse trailers.

The newest section of the Cardinal Greenway runs from Losantville south to Richmond, continually changing from open, sunny stretches to shady sections under a wooded tree canopy. From Losantville to Williamsburg, much of the trail runs adjacent to the road, but your eye is instead drawn to scenic wood bridges and farmlands with rustic barns and silos around every corner. This stretch of the route has light traffic, giving it a remote feeling, and is relatively flat with a slight downhill grade.

From Williamsburg to Richmond the path shows its rail roots with a stretch on an elevated railbed. As you pass through Webster, the trail begins a slight uphill grade through woodlands; this is a good spot for birding. As the greenway approaches the outskirts of Richmond, you will pass under I-70 and through local parks and woodlands. This section of trail is no longer elevated as it makes its way through residential areas.

Along the final mile of the Cardinal Greenway, the trail features a trestle bridge over the East Fork Whitewater River before its official end at the D Street trailhead. From the trailhead, the greenway seamlessly connects to the 3.5-mile Whitewater Gorge Trail, which heads southwest to Test Road. The Whitewater Gorge Trail features geological landmarks, such as vertical cliffs and waterfalls, that are accessible by foot on side paths off the main trail.

CONTACT: cardinalgreenways.org

DIRECTIONS

To access the northernmost trailhead just outside of Marion: From I-69, take Exit 264 for IN 18. Head west on IN 18, and go 10.8 miles. Turn left onto County Road 400 W. The trailhead and parking lot for the Sweetser Switch Trail (which serves both the Sweetser Switch Trail and the Cardinal Greenway) will be on your right. Cross the railroad tracks to access the Cardinal Greenway on the opposite side of the street.

To reach the trailhead in Gaston, take I-69 to Exit 255 for IN 26 toward Hartford. Head east on IN 26, and travel 1.5 miles. Turn right onto S. Wheeling Pike. In 3 miles, turn right onto S. CR 900 E, which becomes N. CR 600 W. In 4.9 miles, turn right onto CR 850 N/W. Elm St. In 0.3 mile turn left onto Broad St. to find the trailhead.

To access the southernmost trailhead near Veterans Memorial Park: From I-70, take Exit 149 or 149A, and head south on Williamsburg Pike. In 2.4 miles, turn left onto Richmond Ave. In 0.6 mile, cross the East Fork Whitewater River, and Richmond Ave. becomes N. D St. Go 0.1 mile after crossing the river, and turn right onto N. Fifth St. Immediately turn right onto N. D St. The parking lot is 0.1 mile straight ahead. The trailhead will be on your right and is located just under the Richmond Ave. Bridge.

Visitors to the Delphi Historic Trails network can tour the historical town of Delphi in north-central Indiana by foot or bicycle—or skis in the winter—on old canal towpaths and former railroad corridors. Nearly 10 miles of trail follow the routes of the Monon Railroad and the Wabash and Erie Canal, as well as city streets that pass houses and public buildings that are on the National Register of Historic Places.

Laid out in 1828, Delphi became a canal boomtown when the 468-mile cross-state Wabash and Erie Canal arrived in 1840. That era of commercial success ended some 30 years later when the canal became obsolete and railroads became the primary mode of transporting passengers and freight.

Beginning at Canal Park northwest of downtown, you can visit an interpretive museum and a canal-era village with historical structures or experience replica canalboat tours. Tent camping and a few RV sites are also available.

County
Carroll

Endpoints
Canal Park at N. Washington St. near N. Charles St. to Trailhead Park at Old IN 25, 0.8 mile south of IN 39, and from City Park at N. Walnut St. and Samuel Millroy Road to County Road 300 N, 0.5 mile west of CR 575 W (Delphi)

Mileage
9.8

Type
Rail-Trail/Canal

Roughness Index
1

Surface
Boardwalk, Concrete, Crushed Stone

Part of Delphi's trail network runs through Canal Park.

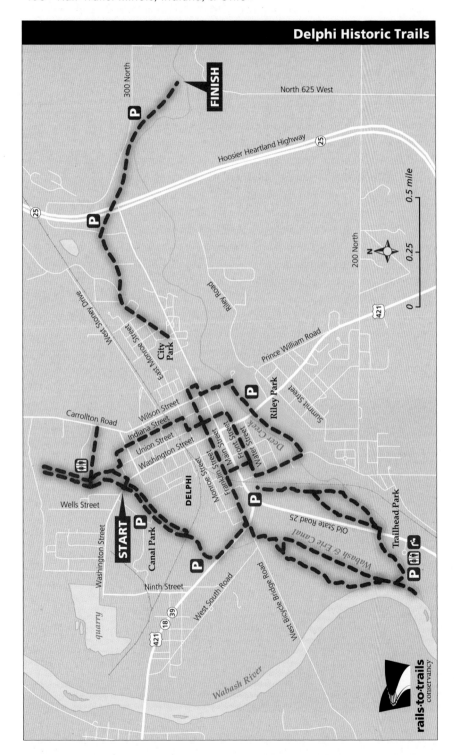

Delphi Historic Trails

A section of the network called the **Underhill Towpath Trail** is a good place to start; follow the 1-mile trail north across Washington Street to another section called the **Founders Towpath Trail**. This 0.5-mile trail loops around to the 0.5-mile **Draper North End Trail** and passes the restored iron bridge (from 1873) on its way to Founders Point and the "tumble," where fresh groundwater feeds the canal. Draper Trail swings back past the cutoff to **Belt Railroad Trail**, a 0.3-mile section of trail along a former railroad that served local merchants and connected to Monon Railroad.

Draper Trail also runs past a replica limekiln from the 1850s canal heydays, as well as a replica warehouse and boathouse, and then back to Washington Street. Picking up the Underhill Towpath Trail heading south, you'll pass a replica guard lock and a historical railroad baggage depot station.

You'll pass through a tunnel under a railroad on the way out of town and then another tunnel under US 421. Follow the trail across the Blue Bridge, a 78-foot iron bridge built in 1905 and moved here in 2007. Now you're on the mile-long **VanScoy Towpath Trail**, where historical markers provide information on an Irish work camp, the site of Lock #33, and paper mill sites.

At the end of the VanScoy Trail is Sunset Point, featuring a view of Deer Creek, the canal, and the Wabash River. A spur from the river goes to **Robbins Trail**, a 0.5-mile section along Deer Creek that offers access to Trailhead Park and Deer Creek Falls.

The Robbins Trail turns into **Happy Jack's Loop** with a spur to the site of Smith Dairy Farm along the **Interurban Trail**, a 0.8-mile route. The interconnecting trail system also includes routes along city streets and paths along **Campbell Ridge Trail** (a 1-mile loop at the south end of VanScoy) and the **Monon High Bridge Trail** (1.5 miles) beginning at City Park at the corner of East Monroe and North Walnut Streets. The Monon High Bridge Trail stops just short of a circa 1890 railroad bridge that soars some 60 feet over the creek.

CONTACT: cityofdelphi.org

DIRECTIONS

To reach the trailhead at Canal Park: From I-65, take Exit 175 toward Delphi on IN 25. Head northeast on IN 25, and go 10.9 miles. Turn left onto Old St. Road 25, and go 2.7 miles. Turn left onto W. Monroe St./US 421. In 0.6 mile turn right onto N. Ninth St. Go 0.2 mile and turn right into the driveway one block past New York St. Take that 0.4 mile to parking at Canal Park.

To find the Monon High Bridge Trail from Canal Park, leave the northeast entrance of the parking lot and turn right onto N. Washington St. Go 0.5 mile and turn left onto Monroe St. In another 0.5 mile turn right onto N. Walnut St. Go about 100 feet and look for parking on your right.

The Erie Lackawanna Trail rolls nearly 18 miles between Crown Point and Hammond, two former rail junctions whose early fortunes were tied to the tracks carrying people and goods to and from Chicago. Despite traveling through the densely populated Chicago metropolitan area, the trail is bordered by green space and visits wetlands and parks along the way.

The paved path follows a railroad corridor that had been in use since the late 1800s. Conrail was the last owner, ending the line in 1986, 10 years after acquiring it from the Erie Lackawanna Railway. The oldest parts of the trail date to the 1990s in Hammond, which was first to jump aboard the idea of a rail-trail on this corridor.

Beginning in Crown Point, your trailhead is less than a mile from the city's most famous landmark, the jail (226

This charming shelter offers a nice respite at the trailhead near Crown Point.

County
Lake

Endpoints
W. Summit St. at N. West St. (Crown Point) to Sibley St. near State St. (Hammond)

Mileage
17.7

Type
Rail-Trail

Roughness Index
1

Surface
Asphalt

S. Main St.) from which 1930s bank robber John Dillinger escaped just months before he was cut down in a hail of gunfire by Chicago lawmen. Heading north from the trailhead, your first 2 miles pass mostly wood lots, a farm field, and a golf course before you arrive at the first street crossing.

Nearly 5 miles from Crown Point, you'll cross Burr Street and reach another trailhead with facilities. The route enters unincorporated Lake County here, where the parks department mows only 10 feet on either side of the trail surface to ensure wildlife habitat farther out from the path. Less than 2 miles up the trail, you'll come to another trailhead and cross South Arbogast Avenue, which links to the Oak Savannah Trail (see page 123) 1.7 miles northeast on the other side of Oak Ridge Prairie Park.

In another mile, you'll arrive at the Griffith junction, where you'll use South Broad Street to cross several sets of tracks. Before regaining the trail, look right to find Griffith Historical Park. The circa 1911 Grand Trunk Western Railroad depot and the 1924 brick tower that oversaw operations at the Broad Street crossing were relocated to the park. From here, the path enters the denser residential and commercial areas of the near-Chicago suburbs. Expect more street crossings.

At 3.7 miles past the Griffith interchange, you'll arrive at a trail junction; a 0.7-mile, one-way spur to the right leads to the Indiana Welcome Center, while the main trail stays left and skirts a shopping district. Taking the underpass beneath I-94, you'll be traveling on the older part of the trail that passes through the city of Hammond and ends in 3.8 miles.

The Hammond Civic Center is 2.9 miles past the interstate underpass. In 0.6 mile the trail meets Lake County's 4-mile Monon Trail, which heads south to Munster. The Erie Lackawanna Trail ends at Sibley Street, but a connection north is being considered.

CONTACT: lakecountyparks.com/info_and_fees/info/trails.html

DIRECTIONS

To reach the southern trailhead in Crown Point: From I-65, take Exit 249 to E. 109th Ave. toward Crown Point. Head west on E. 109th Ave., and go 0.7 mile. Turn right onto Broadway, and go 0.5 mile. Turn left onto E. Summit St. The trailhead is 1.6 miles ahead on the right.

To reach parking at the northern endpoint: From I-94, take Exit 71B for IN 83/Sibley Blvd. Head east on Sibley Blvd., and go 3.1 miles, crossing Hohman Ave. Look for parking on the right for the Towle Community Theatre. The trail starts east of the parking lot.

Located in the heart of vibrant downtown Indianapolis, the Indianapolis Cultural Trail is an ideal way to experience all the city has to offer. The trail links five cultural districts flush with museums, theaters, shops, restaurants, hotels, and parks. It also features engaging public art specially commissioned for each of the neighborhoods through which it passes.

The route is comprised of a core downtown loop with a northeast spur that heads out along Massachusetts Avenue, where it connects to the south entrance of the famed Monon Trail (see page 116). Another spur takes off from the southeast corner along Virginia Avenue through the Fountain Square Historic District, where it connects to the Pleasant Run Trail. This section of trail, from the intersection with Pleasant Run Trail north to Prospect Street, is an on-road separated bike route. A small spur

The Canal Loop section of trail provides scenic views of the water and Indianapolis's skyline.

County
Marion

Endpoints
White River State Park at W. Washington St. and N. California St. to Monon Trail at E. 10th St. and Lewis St. (Indianapolis)

Mileage
9.1

Type
Greenway/Non-Rail-Trail

Roughness Index
1

Surface
Asphalt

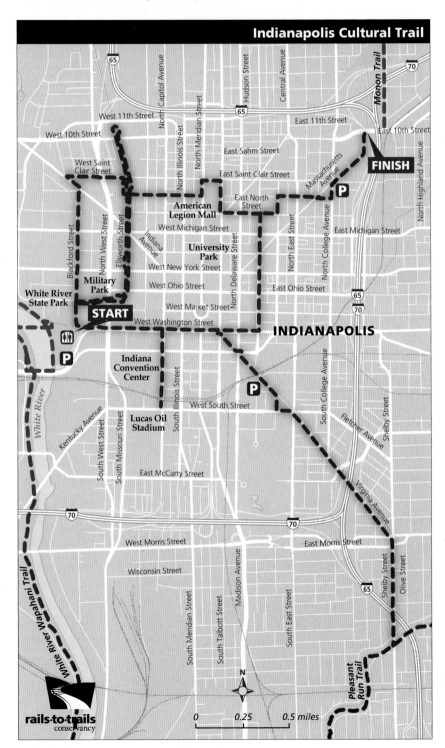

Indianapolis Cultural Trail

FINISH

INDIANAPOLIS

American Legion Mall

University Park

Military Park

White River State Park

START

Indiana Convention Center

Lucas Oil Stadium

Moron Trail

White River

White River Wapahani Trail

Pleasant Run Trail

rails·to·trails
conservancy

0   0.25   0.5 miles

N

from the southern midpoint of the downtown loop leads to the Indiana Convention Center and Lucas Oil Stadium, home of the Indianapolis Colts football team. The southwestern section of the trail includes a connection to White River State Park and the White River Wapahani Trail. The Eiteljorg Museum of American Indians and Western Art, NCAA Hall of Champions, and Indiana State Museum can all be found in this southwest section.

Turning north from the southwest end of the downtown loop, visitors will come to a bridge overlooking a scenic 1-mile canal. Wide ramps from the bridge lead to the canal loop. The canal path is heavily used by pedestrians and is therefore not recommended for bicyclists. The northern section of the loop features a stunning combination of the Indianapolis Central Library, American Legion Mall, and University Park. Artful signage and seating document history along this stretch of the trail. The canal can also be accessed from the northern end of the loop.

Throughout, the trail is clearly identifiable with tinted concrete pavers, providing visual continuity. There is no official start or end point to the trail, increasing its utility, as it is fully accessible along its entire route. Visitors will also find bike-share stations located along the trail. During winter, snow is removed, allowing year-round use of the path.

The Indianapolis Cultural Trail is a great example of an urban trail network that offers residents and visitors biking and walking options for work or play.

CONTACT: indyculturaltrail.org

DIRECTIONS

Parking is available in White River State Park (801 W. Washington St.) on the western end of the trail, where you will also find a visitor center with restrooms. Note that there are parking fees. From I-70 take Exit 79A for West St. Head north on S. Missouri St. Go 0.8 mile and continue onto S. West St. In 0.2 mile turn left onto W. Washington St. In another 0.2 mile turn right at the traffic light onto Schumacher Way to enter the parking lot for White River State Park. The visitor center and trail access are to the right in the parking lot.

Metered on-street parking and garage parking are also available throughout the city.

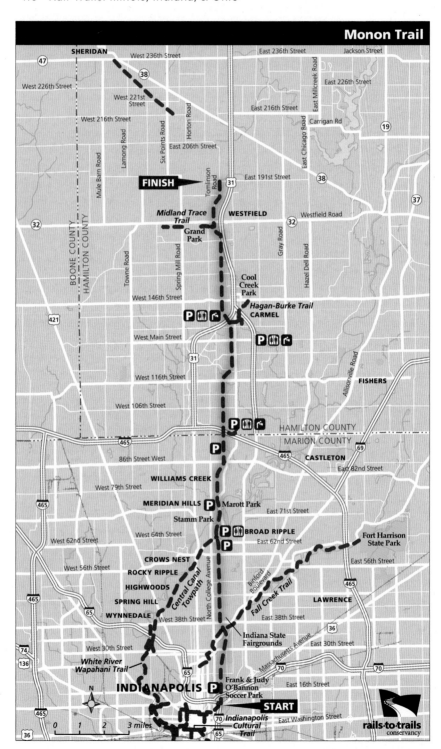

Railroads helped Indianapolis grow into a transportation hub and manufacturing center beginning in the 1850s. One of those early railways that shaped the city's future is remembered today along the Monon Trail, which follows a line whose tracks are long gone. It serves as a transportation corridor that stitches together Indianapolis neighborhoods, Carmel, and the northern suburbs of Westfield and Sheridan.

The 23-mile paved path follows a former section of the Chicago, Indianapolis & Louisville Railway, whose lines formed an X as they crossed in Monon. The railroad adopted the train's popular nickname, the Monon, as its official name in the 1950s. The Louisville & Nashville Railroad acquired the railroad in 1971, but by 1987 parts of the line were no longer used, including a section that

The Monon Trail features several scenic bridge crossings.

Counties
Hamilton, Marion

Endpoints
E. 10th St. and Lewis St. (Indianapolis) to 191st St. between Tomlinson Road and Grand Park (Westfield), and from OH 47/E. 236th St. and Opel St. to W. 216th St., 0.25 mile west of Six Points Road (Sheridan)

Mileage
23.1

Type
Rail-Trail

Roughness Index
1

Surface
Asphalt

The trail serves as a popular transportation corridor between Indianapolis and Westfield.

launched the Monon Trail in 1999. The town of Monon itself, located 90 miles northwest of Indianapolis, is not part of the route.

Beginning in Indianapolis, the Monon Trail is undeniably urban. You will travel beneath the ramps of I-70 and I-65, passing residential areas and light industrial zones. The 10th Street trailhead is a block from the Indianapolis Cultural Trail (see page 113), which spans five downtown cultural districts with museums, theaters, shops, and restaurants.

Local artwork along this stretch adds a unique flavor, with pieces ranging from bright community murals to a network of pipes painted on the side of a utility substation. After 2.7 miles, you cross Fall Creek on a bright-red former railroad trestle. In another 0.5 mile you'll arrive at the Indiana State Fairgrounds, a destination for many via the trail. Beyond the fairgrounds, the route travels along the backyards of suburban Indianapolis through a corridor lined with a ribbon of trees and green space.

At mile 6.2, you reach the gateway to Broad Ripple, a community that practically vibrates with culture, offering eateries, galleries, breweries, and shops.

After crossing two bridges, one over a canal and one over White River (the original bridge collapsed as a train crossed in 1884), the trail meanders through quiet neighborhoods before crossing busy 86th Street. From here, it's another mile to the trailhead at 96th Street (mile 10.3) and the border of Carmel.

In 3 miles, you'll see the Palladium, based on a grand 16th-century Italian villa and the focal point of the gardens and theaters of Carmel's Center for the Performing Arts. It's also where you'll find a farmers' market on Saturday mornings in season. In 0.5 mile, you'll pass the relocated Carmel Monon Depot, built in 1883. The side streets are chock-full of places where travelers can eat, drink, and shop.

A pedestrian bridge over 146th Street (mile 15.7) marks your entrance to the city of Westfield. Here you'll find a junction with the Midland Trace Trail; many other community trails are also located nearby. Though you're still not out of the Indianapolis metro area, the trail passes wood lots and farms on the north side of town before it ends just past the Grand Park soccer fields on 191st Street.

Plans call for extending the Monon Trail 7 miles farther north to the town of Sheridan by the end of 2017. A 2.2-mile segment of this route—disconnected from the main spine of the trail—opened in the summer of 2016 between Lamong Road and 216th Street on the southern outskirts of Sheridan and connects to a previously opened 0.9-mile section to East 236th Street.

CONTACT: greenwaysfoundation.org

DIRECTIONS

To reach parking for the southern end of the trail at Frank & Judy O'Bannon Old Northside Soccer Park: From I-65/I-70, take Exit 111 for Washington St. Head west on Washington, and go 0.2 mile. Turn right onto N. College Ave., and go 1.5 miles. Turn right onto E. 16th St. In 0.2 mile look for parking on the right at the soccer park. The trail runs along the east side of the park and ends 0.5 mile south of the park.

To reach parking for the northern end of the trail at Grand Park soccer fields: From I-465, take Exit 33 for Keystone Ave. Head north on Keystone 5.4 miles and merge onto northbound US 31. Then go 4.5 miles and take the exit for 191st St. Head 0.8 mile west on 191st St., and turn left into a parking lot at the soccer fields. The trail crosses 191st St. here.

Nickel Plate Trail

ndiana's Nickel Plate Trail runs along the former corridor of the Peru & Indianapolis Railroad chartered in 1846. The line offered passenger and freight service under various names, including the nickname Nickel Plate Road. The last trains ran on the tracks in 1992, and the corridor was railbanked in 1999. Remnants of the railroad can still be seen at the trailhead gazebo in Rochester, where the trail takes off to the south and the unused tracks remain visible to the north.

The Nickel Plate Trail traverses rural Indiana from Rochester south to the outskirts of Kokomo, with a 3.6-mile gap in the middle in Peru. Beginning in Rochester, the northern segment runs 21 miles through a shifting landscape of trees, cultivated fields, and small-town neighborhoods. The route passes through the communities of Macy, Birmingham, Deedsville, Denver, and Courter

The path showcases picturesque views of northern Indiana farmland.

Counties
Fulton, Howard, Miami

Endpoints
Mitchell Dr. and Wabash Ave. (Rochester) to US 35 and N. Reed Road (Kokomo)

Mileage
36.9

Type
Rail-Trail

Roughness Index
1

Surface
Asphalt

before entering the outskirts of Peru, home to the International Circus Hall of Fame, which hosts a Circus City Festival every summer. The segment ends at the small country road Lovers Lane.

The official Nickel Plate Trail website provides a recommended on-road route to connect to the southern section from Lovers Lane. After the gap, the southern section, spanning more than 15 miles, picks up in Peru at Walnut Street, just north of downtown. However, the more convenient way to access the trail is at one of the various parking lots off Main Street, where a trailside gazebo and signage can be seen from the road.

From Main Street heading south along the path, you will immediately cross the trail's iconic trestle bridge over the Wabash River. The original bridge structure, embellished with bright-blue guardrails, offers scenic views of the river rock formations that comprise the bed of Little Pipe Creek. Historical markers on either side of the bridge share some of the history along this former rail corridor, including a tragic train accident in January 1893 when the train jumped the tracks at the bridge, plunging passengers and crew 30 feet off the bridge into the icy waters below.

From the bridge, the trail passes through the towns of Bunker Hill, Miami, and Cassville, offering a bounty of dense forests, water views, and wildlife. You will find yourself in a forest thick with willows and maple trees. It may seem quiet here in the forest, but you are not alone: deer, rabbits, squirrels, and chipmunks are likely to cross your path. Many different species of birds make their homes in these trees. If you're cross-country skiing here in winter, this path is nothing short of a snowy wonderland.

The trail continues through the forest canopy, passing small farms and rural homesteads that periodically pop into view as it passes through the small farming community of Cassville and ends at a trailhead with parking at the intersection of IN 931 and US 35.

CONTACT: nickelplatetrail.org

DIRECTIONS

To access the northern trailhead in Rochester: From Indianapolis, take US 31 N approximately 80 miles, and turn right onto Wabash Ave. in Rochester. In 0.5 mile turn left to stay on Wabash, and go another 1.1 miles. The trailhead and parking lot will be immediately on your left just after crossing Mitchell Dr.

To access the southern trailhead in Kokomo: From Indianapolis, take US 31 N approximately 44 miles to Exit 166 for US 35. Bear left onto US 35 and travel 0.8 mile. Turn left into the parking lot as you approach the traffic light at the intersection with IN 931.

First-time visitors to the Oak Savannah Trail might be surprised at the profusion of natural areas they'll encounter as they travel the 8 miles between Hobart and Griffith in northern Indiana's Chicago metropolitan area.

The paved path follows the old Porter Branch of the Elgin, Joliet and Eastern Railway, whose main line made a semicircle around Chicago to avoid that city's congested rail yards. The Griffith to Hobart line, first opened in 1888, later pushed out to Porter. In its prime, the railroad carried grain, meat, fruit, vegetables, and coal. Rail service in the corridor ended in 1984.

The trail, together with the Prairie Duneland Trail (see page 129) in the east, serves as a backbone in northwestern Indiana's trail network. US Bicycle Route 36 runs the length of the two trails on its way between Chicago and the Michigan border.

County
Lake

Endpoints
E. Fifth St., 0.1 mile west of Center St. (Hobart), to Oak Ridge Prairie Park near S. Colfax St., 0.2 mile south of Gatlin Dr. (Griffith)

Mileage
8.4

Type
Rail-Trail

Roughness Index
1

Surface
Asphalt

A lovely viewing area on the trail overlooks Lake George.

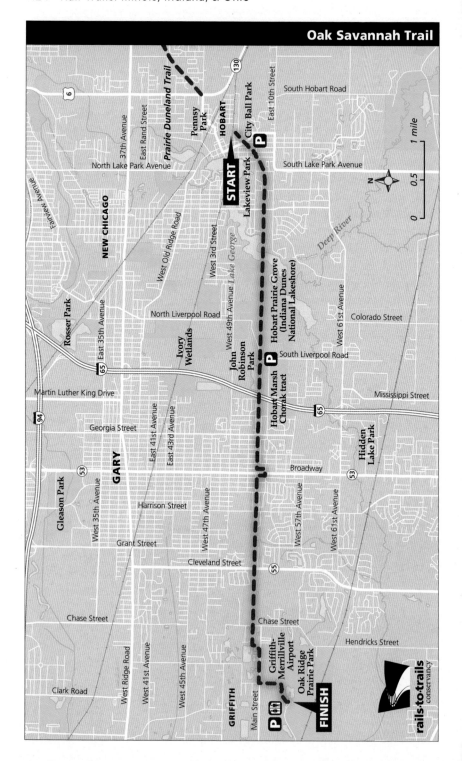

Oak Savannah Trail

Beginning on East Fifth Street in Hobart, you'll soon pass through the 300-acre Hobart Prairie Grove section of the Indiana Dunes National Lakeshore. The route takes you to the edge of Lake George here, an excellent fishing spot for bass and crappie. The lake is also home to a permanent population of geese, ducks, and ring-billed gulls. From the trail bridge, you can walk onto platforms overlooking the lily pad–covered neck of the lake between the lake's larger main bodies.

The next few miles of trail beyond the lake travel west through oak savanna ecosystems. Shortly, you emerge at another lake at John Robinson Park, where you may want to take a rest in the small field of grass along the lakefront.

After the I-65 underpass, the path enters a more urban setting with several road crossings; an underpass below busy Broadway in Gary makes that crossing much easier. In a couple of blocks, you return to the quiet forest and prairie that dominate the trail. After passing a large private fishing club, you will see the end of the county airport runway, just west of the corridor.

Here, a very dense forest marks the entrance of Oak Ridge Prairie Park and the trail's end. At more than 200 acres, most of the park represents former farmland that has been restored to oak savanna prairie.

Future plans include a connection to the Erie Lackawanna Trail (see page 110), which rolls between Crown Point and Hammond, as well as a connection to the nearby Chesapeake and Ohio Greenway.

CONTACT: lakecountyparks.com/parks/oak_ridge_prairie_and_oak_savannah _trail.html

DIRECTIONS

To reach the eastern trailhead in Hobart: From I-94, take Exit 15 or 15A and merge onto southbound US 6/Ripley St. Travel 3.5 miles, continuing south as US 6 becomes N. Hobart Ave. At E. Cleveland Ave., turn right, traveling west on Cleveland 0.6 mile until you reach a fork in the road. Veer left, toward the railroad tracks, onto Front St. In 0.2 mile, turn left onto Main St. and continue heading southeast on Main 0.5 mile until E. Seventh St. Turn right onto Seventh St. and travel two blocks, then take a left onto Lake St. A parking lot will appear on your left in a small city park; the trail runs right through the park.

To reach the parking in Oak Ridge Prairie Park on the west end of the trail: From I-94, take Exit 6 for Burr St. Head south on Burr 1.4 miles, and turn right onto W. Ridge Road. Go 0.5 mile and turn left onto N. Colfax St. Go 2.2 miles and turn left into the entrance for Oak Ridge Prairie Park and look for parking, or go 2.9 miles (Colfax becomes S. Arbogast Ave.) and look for parking on the right.

Indiana's Panhandle Pathway follows a former Pennsylvania Railroad corridor out of Winamac south to Kenneth. Along the way, the trail links the communities of Star City, Thornhope, and Royal Center along its 22 miles of paved and well-maintained surface.

Heading south out of Winamac, this spectacular rail-trail passes through bucolic Midwestern farmland, which seems to stretch across the horizon. Trail users will experience a unique and dramatic vista less than 1.5 miles south of the Winamac trailhead: a long concrete bridge with metal-screened fencing affixed to wood posts offers unfettered views of the Tippecanoe River. Take a seat along one of the benches on the bridge and soak it all in.

On the section of trail from Winamac to just south of Royal Center, the pathway runs adjacent to US 35, with many well-marked road crossings that offer access to the

You'll find these towering silos as you ride through the community of Thornhope.

Counties
Cass, Pulaski

Endpoints
IN 14/W. 11th St. at Logan St. (Winamac) to US 24, 0.5 mile west of France Park and 1 mile east of S. County Road 600W (Kenneth)

Mileage
22.0

Type
Rail-Trail

Roughness Index
1

Surface
Asphalt

trail along the way. The scenery consists of farmlands, barns, and silos stretching into the endless Indiana blue sky. Abundant wildlife, including birds, rabbits, woodchucks, and deer, is active along the trail. Several interpretative signs along the route tell the story of the region's agriculture and history. The trail passes Pond View Golf Course and Little Indian Creek as it approaches Royal Center.

South of Royal Center, the pathway veers away from the highway along an elevated rail corridor. This section of trail passes through woodlands with heavy tree canopy and offers a feeling of isolation from nearby communities. About halfway through this section, the trail crosses Crooked Creek.

There is an official trailhead and parking area as the path approaches Kenneth. The route extends past the Kenneth trailhead, and there are plans to extend it all the way to France Park. However, for now there is no vehicle access to the trail's southern endpoint, so it is experienced as an out-and-back trip from the Kenneth trailhead parking lot.

Benches are provided all along the trail, and at its trailhead in Kenneth, you'll find benches, picnic tables, and a bike rack. Note that, with the exception of a portable toilet at the Kenneth trailhead, there are no restrooms or drinking fountains on the trail itself.

CONTACT: panhandlepathway.org

DIRECTIONS

To access the northern trailhead, park at the Winamac train depot (200 W. Main St.). From I-65, take Exit 220 for IN 14, and head east. Go 1.9 miles, and turn left to stay on IN 14. In 19 miles, turn left onto US 421. Go 2 miles, and turn right onto IN 14 again. In 14.8 miles turn right onto N. Logan St. Go 0.4 mile, and you'll see the depot and the parking lot at the corner of Main and Logan Sts.

To access the southern end of the trail at the Kenneth parking lot: From I-65, take Exit 201 for US 24/US 231. Head east on US 24/US 231, and go 5 miles. Turn left onto US 24, and go 14.7 miles. Turn left onto N. Railroad St. and immediately turn right onto US 24/W. Washington St. In 14.9 miles turn left onto County Road 600 W. Proceed north on CR 600W 0.5 mile to the first stop sign; turn right onto CR 50 N. Travel 0.3 mile to the trailside parking lot on your left.

Prairies and dunes are just two of the natural features you'll experience on the Prairie Duneland Trail, located just a few miles south of the Lake Michigan shoreline and the Indiana Dunes National Lakeshore. You will have views of ponds and wood lots but will also see some pockets of suburban sprawl, which become more frequent and dense as you travel westward from Chesterton to Hobart.

The flat, 10.3-mile rail-trail follows a straight branch of the former Elgin, Joliet and Eastern Railway that served as a bypass around the busy Chicago rail yards between Gary, Indiana, and Waukegan, Illinois, for more than 100 years. The first section of the rail-trail opened in 1996. Chesterton still gets its share of railroad traffic, however, and you can watch trains pass from the vintage 1914 New York Central Railroad passenger depot and freight terminal a mile off-trail at 220 Broadway.

A dense tree canopy shades part of the route.

County
Porter

Endpoints
S. 15th St. between Broadway and W. Indiana Ave. (Chesterton) to N. Hobart Road and E. Cleveland Ave. (Hobart)

Mileage
10.3

Type
Rail-Trail

Roughness Index
1

Surface
Asphalt

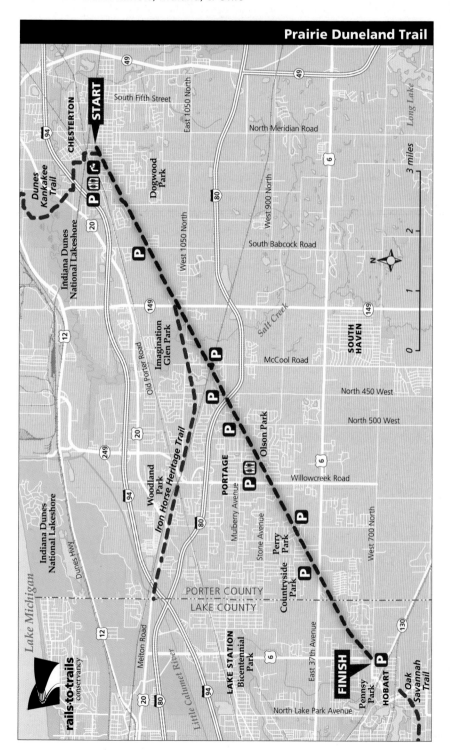

Prairie Duneland Trail

Beginning at the Chesterton trailhead, you'll pass a trailside skate park and cross South Jackson Boulevard. A wide sidewalk on the right serves as a junction with the Dunes Kankakee Trail, which runs on- and off-street through the town of Porter to Indiana Dunes State Park.

Continuing southwest on the Prairie Duneland Trail, you'll leave behind the sights and sounds of town life in less than 2 miles. It's lightly forested here, interspersed with farm fields. You'll also encounter remnants of tallgrass prairie that at one time dominated the landscape. Elsewhere, a dense forest canopy creates a lush passageway.

A trail junction at 3.5 miles marks the Iron Horse Heritage Trail that leads into the town of Portage, a former farming community that underwent explosive growth in the second half of the 20th century. The 5-mile trail passes just south of Imagination Glen, a 276-acre park that's popular with mountain bikers for its 10 miles of dirt trails.

After you cross the CSX railroad tracks at 4.4 miles and pass beneath I-80, you'll begin to see backyards and residential subdivisions. Numerous side paths connect these neighborhoods, often screened from the path by trees, to the trail.

The route goes beneath two busy streets, Willowcreek Road and West 37th Avenue/US 6, before you arrive at a trailhead on County Line Road. The trail's end is just a little farther at North Hobart Road. From here, you can travel a short distance on-road to reach the beginning of the Oak Savannah Trail (see page 123), which heads west from Hobart to Hammond. If you travel both trails, you'll understand why these two are considered the backbone of the Northwest Indiana regional trail network.

CONTACT: chestertonin.org/156/Bike-Trails

DIRECTIONS

To reach the eastern trailhead in Chesterton: From I-94, take Exit 26A onto IN 49 headed south. Go 0.5 mile and turn right onto Indian Boundary Road, which changes to Woodlawn Ave. Go 1.6 miles and turn left onto N. 15th St., then go 0.2 mile and turn right onto Broadway. Go 0.1 mile, turn left onto S. Jackson Blvd., and look for trail parking on the left.

To reach the western trailhead: From I-94, take Exit 15A and merge onto southbound US 6/Ripley St. Go 2.3 miles and turn left onto E. 37th Ave., and then go 1.5 miles and turn left at the sign for Countryside Park (5250 US 6). Parking is 0.1 mile down that entrance road.

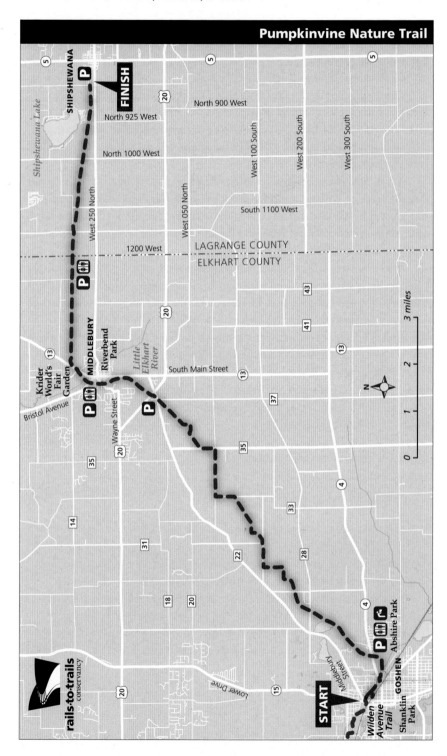

The Pumpkinvine Nature Trail covers just over 17 miles between the towns of Goshen, Middlebury, and Shipshewana. The railroad line between Goshen and Middlebury served as a popular passenger and mail service route at the turn of the 20th century. Because of its numerous curves and turns, the railroad received its "pumpkin vine" nickname. All service on the line ended in 1980, and the Friends of the Pumpkinvine Nature Trail acquired the corridor in 1993.

This premier rail-trail offers an incredible scenic landscape and a step back in time with sights from Indiana's large Amish communities in Goshen, Middlebury, and Shipshewana. Glimpses of Amish people tending fields with horse-drawn plows, hand-cutting fields of flowers, biking down the trail in old-fashioned clothing, and riding in buggies offer a unique experience. The trail itself is well maintained and includes mile markers. The route is paved, with the exception of a short section of crushed limestone on the leg between Goshen and Middlebury.

In Shipshewana, you'll see the local Amish riding bicycles or traveling by horse and buggy.

Counties
Elkhart, Lagrange

Endpoints
N. Fifth St. just south of Crescent St. (Goshen) to N. County Road 850 S just north of W. CR 250 N (Shipshewana)

Mileage
17.6

Type
Rail-Trail

Roughness Index
1

Surface
Asphalt, Crushed Stone

The path begins in downtown Goshen, close to the existing active rail line, and seamlessly connects at North Fifth Street to Wilden Avenue Trail, which runs west 3.2 miles and connects to the MapleHeart Trail, which goes all the way into Elkhart.

As you head east out of Goshen, interpretive signage explains the railroad history of the area through which you're traveling. A restored railroad viaduct carries you across a small creek and into a quaint neighborhood. A second bridge, equally well preserved, is a short distance ahead. After the trail crosses IN 4 at a crosswalk, it immediately rolls into a wooded area on its way to Abshire Park, which makes for a nice rest area. When the path crosses IN 4 again, the surface changes to hard-packed crushed limestone for 1.75 miles to County Road 28.

At milepost 5, from CR 33 stretching to CR 35, there is a 1.7-mile on-road segment. This hilly stretch of road has limited vehicular traffic. The remaining miles toward Middlebury are beautiful, enveloped in a thick forest of maple and oak trees. More than 30 species of wildflowers bloom along the trail in spring.

In Middlebury, the route runs north through a tunnel under US 20 and runs behind businesses along Main Street as it approaches spectacular Krider World's Fair Garden, a replica of a world's fair exhibit that ran 1933–1934. This lovely trailhead includes a pavilion and picnic tables, bike rack, and signage. Leaving the gardens, you pass over a 160-foot wooden trestle across the Little Elkhart River before reaching Main Street, where you cross the road and follow the sidewalk north (left) for a short while to reconnect with the trail on your right.

The remaining 5 miles to Shipshewana can only be described as breathtaking. You'll enjoy the wooded tree canopy with glimpses of farms beyond; horses are nose to nose with you along the trail, and rustic barns complement the scenery. This remarkable experience is one for the bucket list.

Extend your stay and visit one of the Midwest's largest auctions and flea markets in Shipshewana, open May–September, Tuesday–Wednesday.

CONTACT: pumpkinvine.org

DIRECTIONS

To access the Goshen trailhead from I-80, take Exit 96, and head south on County Road 17. In 8.7 miles turn right to stay on CR 17, go 0.2 mile, and turn right onto CR 45, which becomes W. Wilden Ave. In 2.6 miles turn right onto N. Fifth St. Go 0.4 mile to reach the trailhead just after crossing Crescent St.

To access the Middlebury trailhead at Krider World's Fair Garden, from I-90 take Exit 107, and head south on IN 13. Go 5.3 miles, and turn right onto Pleasant St. Go 600 yards and turn right onto Bristol Ave. Take an immediate right onto the access road to the parking lot for Krider World's Fair Garden.

The Rivergreenway is an impressive 30-mile linear park that is part of a growing network of trails in the cities of Fort Wayne and New Haven. The Rivergreenway connects neighborhoods, historical attractions, waterways, and 15 city parks. The trail consists of three main pathways, named for the rivers they parallel. With portions of the route directly beside rivers, flooding is possible, so check the official trail website for updates.

The northern branch of the Rivergreenway runs from Shoaff Park south to downtown Fort Wayne along the St. Joseph River (**St. Joseph Pathway**). The southern branch starts just past Tillman Park at Southtown Centre and runs along St. Marys River (**St. Marys Pathway**) heading north to meet the St. Joseph Pathway. The St. Joseph and St. Marys Rivers converge in downtown Fort Wayne to form the Maumee River that runs east alongside the third

This scenic overlook can be found at the historical filtration plant and Three Rivers trailhead.

County
Allen

Endpoints
Shoaff Park near St. Joe Road just north of Hike Ln. to US 27/Spy Run Ave. just south of Baltes Ave. to S. Phoenix Pkwy. and Bridgeway Blvd. (Fort Wayne) and to Moser Park at Main St. and State St. (New Haven)

Mileage
30.1

Type
Greenway/Non-Rail-Trail

Roughness Index
1

Surface
Asphalt, Concrete, Gravel, Dirt

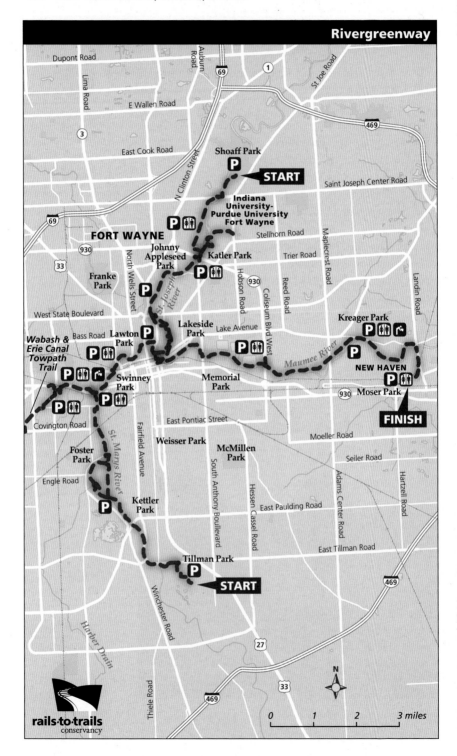

Rivergreenway

A suspension bridge over the St. Joseph River brings the trail to the Indiana University–Purdue University campus.

segment of trail (**Maumee Pathway**) into New Haven. This natural river corridor and trail system provides an unlimited opportunity for recreation, fitness, and conservation. The trail network connects residential and downtown business districts, linking residents with their places of work.

The northern St. Joseph Pathway starts at Shoaff Park. At the 2-mile mark, the trail travels along an unfinished, rutted, gravel-and-dirt section for the next 1.6 miles. The paved surface resumes and continues east to the Indiana University–Purdue University Fort Wayne campus across an expansive suspension bridge over the St. Joseph River. The trail goes north through the campus to St. Joe Road. It also continues south over Coliseum Boulevard and connects to Johnny Appleseed Park across the river. The path continues south adjacent to the river to a scenic overlook at the convergence of the rivers.

The southern St. Marys Pathway starts in Southtown Centre and nearby Tillman Park. The trail runs along the east side of the river to Foster Park, a large community park with its own 2-mile loop. From Foster Park, the path crosses over St. Marys River and includes some lovely wood platforms that extend over the river. Some of these are narrow, so pay attention for cyclists or other users coming from the opposite direction. The route travels to Swinney Park with an option to go west to connect to the Wabash & Erie Canal Towpath Trail that runs southwest to the Lutheran Hospital of Indiana.

As you continue north out of Swinney Park, a short on-road section passes through a lightly trafficked residential street, resumes on a separated trail to Lawton Park, comes up behind the Historic Old Fort, and connects to the St. Joseph Pathway.

From the Historic Old Fort, travel along the trail on Spy Run Avenue (US 27) to connect to the Maumee Pathway, which heads to New Haven. This also connects to a different segment of the St. Joseph Pathway that mirrors the first on the other side of the St. Joseph River. Heading east on the Maumee Pathway, the trail passes through pretty residences along a raised levee for a mile. It then drops into woodlands away from the river to a scenic overlook of the Hosey Dam.

The route continues along the Maumee River through woodlands to Memorial Park (accessible off a spur). The remainder of the trail, from Memorial Park to Moser Park, is wooded and runs along the Maumee River and creekbeds with heavy tree canopy. This parklike section includes four wood ramps and passes Kreager Park, which can be accessed by a road crossing. Kreager Park has its own trail loop to extend your ride. The path ends after crossing over active rail lines and dropping back down a series of wood ramps into a final wooded stretch to a small fishing pond at Moser Park.

CONTACT: fortwayneparks.org

DIRECTIONS

To reach the Shoaff Park trailhead, take I-69 S to Exit 312A or I-69 N to Exit 312B, and head south on Coldwater Road. In 0.3 mile turn left onto E. Washington Center Road, which becomes St. Joe Center Road. Go 1.8 miles, and turn left onto St. Joe Road. Continue 0.6 mile and turn left into Shoaff Park to find the trailhead next to the parking lot.

To reach the trailhead in New Haven's Moser Park, from I-469 take Exit 19, and head northwest on Lincoln Hwy./IN 930. In 1.3 miles turn right onto Green St. Go 0.2 mile and turn left onto Lincoln Hwy. again. Go 0.6 mile and turn right onto State St. In 0.2 mile continue straight to enter the parking lot at Moser Park and find the trailhead next to the parking lot.

To reach the Tillman Park trailhead from I-469, take Exit 11 and head north on US 27. In 3.5 miles turn left onto S. Hanna St., go 0.3 mile, and turn right into Tillman Park after crossing E. Tillman Road.

Parking for the Rivergreenway can also be found on city streets and in a number of parks along the trail's route.

The Sweetser Switch Trail is a "sweet" paved rail-trail and an important regional connector in spite of its short 4-mile length. The trail joins the 2-mile Converse Junction Trail in the west and a segment of the Cardinal Greenway (see page 103) in the east, making it a key piece of north-central Indiana's trail system.

The path runs from the community of Mier in the west to the east end of the small town of Sweetser. It follows the original corridor of the Pittsburgh, Cincinnati, Chicago and St. Louis Railroad branch line built through here between Columbus, Ohio, and Chicago in the 1860s. Conrail took over the corridor in 1976 before service ended in the 1980s.

Local lore says Sweetser's unusual name is derived from the installation of a 0.5-mile railroad switch in 1869

The Sweetser Switch Trail meets the Cardinal Greenway outside of Marion.

County
Grant

Endpoints
County Road 800W just south of W. Mier 27 (Mier) to CR 400W 0.2 mile south of IN 18 (Sweetser)

Mileage
4.0

Type
Rail-Trail/Rail-with-Trail

Roughness Index
1

Surface
Asphalt

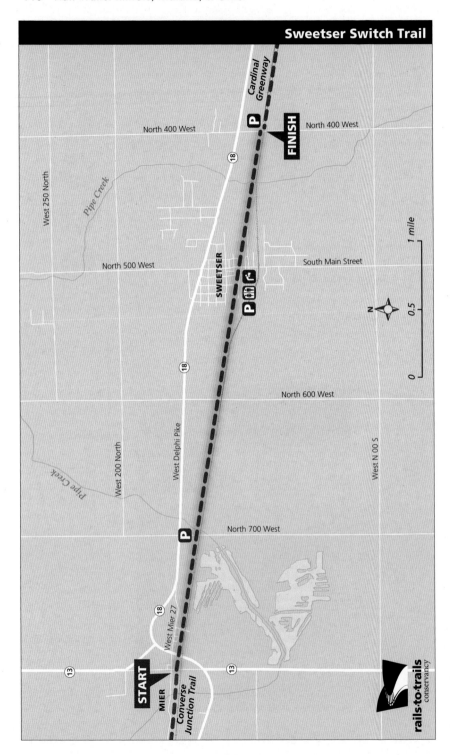

that spawned the community, which the railroaders first called Switch, then Switzer, and then Sweetser. At one time, the town's depot served eight passenger trains daily between two different railroads.

The history of the trail itself is a little uncommon. When residents explored the possibility of turning the right-of-way into a trail, they first had to create a park board because the small town didn't have a parks and recreation department. Then the residents chipped in with donations and volunteer labor to complete the path's first mile. Maybe that's why the trail is so beloved locally.

The route expanded to 3 paved miles in 2003, and by 2011 the Cardinal Greenway met it on the east side. In 2016 the Sweetser Switch Trail extended another mile to the community of Mier, this time using federal and state grants in addition to private donations.

Beginning at the Converse Junction Trail terminus in the west, the path parallels the short-line Central Railroad of Indianapolis, primarily a grain hauler. You'll cross a covered bridge in a mile, then continue down a path bordered by trees, with wildflowers in the clearings, until you reach Sweetser.

Two restored railcars and a caboose, outfitted with restrooms and water, sit at the Main Street trailhead, making this a worthwhile stop. Food is available in town. You'll also find a 5-foot statue of Garfield the comic strip cat in Sweetser; it's one of almost a dozen such statues scattered around Grant County to acknowledge the cartoon's creator and area native Jim Davis.

Heading east for the final mile, you'll pass more railroad artifacts and notice more clearings along the route. The Sweetser Switch Trail ends at a trailhead shortly after another covered bridge. Cross the railroad tracks here to pick up the Cardinal Greenway heading east toward Marion.

CONTACT: sweetserin.us/switch_trail.html

DIRECTIONS

To access the eastern trailhead in Sweetser: From I-69, take Exit 264 to IN 18 toward Marion. Head west 10.7 miles and turn left onto County Road 400 W. Go 0.2 mile and find the trailhead on the right.

To access the main trailhead in Sweetser: From I-69, take Exit 264 to IN 18 toward Marion. Head west 11.7 miles and turn left onto Main St. Go 0.4 mile to the trailhead on Main St.

To access the western trailhead: From I-69, take Exit 264 to IN 18 toward Marion. Head west 13.7 miles and turn left onto CR 700 W. Go 0.1 mile and find the trailhead on the left. Take the trail 1 mile west to the endpoint.

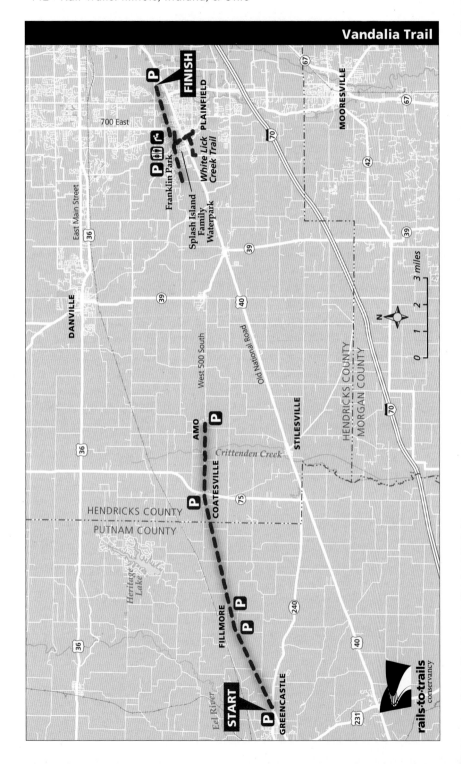

Vandalia Trail

The Vandalia Trail is the longest open component of the National Road Heritage Trail (NRHT), a proposed border-to-border trail stretching between Terre Haute and Richmond, a span of more than 150 miles. Much of the NRHT occupies part of a former Pennsylvania Railroad corridor—the successor to the Vandalia Railroad—which closely parallels the Historic National Road.

The Vandalia Trail consists of two disconnected segments. The first segment runs nearly 12 miles from Greencastle to Amo. The second segment runs about 4 miles through the suburban neighborhoods and parks of Plainfield.

As you travel through Fillmore and into Coatesville, you'll come across wildflowers and an abundance of birds and butterflies.

Counties
Hendricks, Putnam

Endpoints
N. Calbert Way and Indianapolis Road/IN 240 (Greencastle) to Township Line Road and Hunt St. (Plainfield)

Mileage
16.0

Type
Rail-Trail

Roughness Index
2

Surface
Asphalt, Crushed Stone, Dirt, Grass, Gravel

Starting in Greencastle, visitors will find trailhead parking and a gazebo. However, the route goes 0.6 mile on lightly traveled North Calbert Way until the official separated trail begins. The trail surface is packed crushed stone into Coatesville. The path includes several covered shelters along the way, but there are no restroom facilities other than the public library in Coatesville on this segment of the trail.

This section of trail, through Fillmore and into Coatesville, is largely uninterrupted by road crossings and offers trailside wildflowers with an abundance of birds and butterflies and farm fields. Bluebirds, finches, and herons frequent this corridor, offering excellent birding opportunities. In both Fillmore and Coatesville, trailside businesses provide a place to rest and get a bite to eat. A separate bridle trail parallels much of the path and occasionally joins the main trail, but horses are required to remain on the grass in these combined stretches.

For the remaining 3 miles, from Coatesville to Amo, the Vandalia Trail traverses enchanted woodlands along an elevated railbed leading up to the trestle 30 feet above Crittenden Creek. A separate horse trail follows beside the main path, and there is a hitch rail at Crittenden Creek. This well-maintained stretch into Amo changes periodically from grass to gravel but is easily navigable with a hybrid bike. Plans are underway to pave this section in 2017.

The 4.6-mile Plainfield segment begins with a trailhead at its western end on Vandalia Boulevard. For now, this paved section is the only portion of the trail appropriate for in-line skating and wheelchairs. Heading east from the starting point, the route travels through woodlands behind residential communities and then through a tunnel under the Saratoga Parkway to the Splash Island Family Waterpark.

Immediately past the water park, the path intersects with the White Lick Creek Trail, which heads south at the circular intersection. Go left over the bridge to stay on the Vandalia Trail as it navigates past the ballparks and playgrounds of Franklin Park. The trail continues into the neighborhood and takes a sharp left onto North East Street, heading up a short hill. At the top of the hill, the scenery changes as you wind your way out of the neighborhood. The trail takes on a more remote feeling as it passes through woodlands to the parking lot at the trail's end.

The Plainfield trail is heavily used by the local community; expect to see walkers, runners, dog walkers, and cyclists.

CONTACT: nrht.org/vandalia

DIRECTIONS

On the west end of the trail in Greencastle, a trailhead with parking can be found at the intersection of N. Calbert Way and Indianapolis Road/IN 240. Take I-70 to Exit 59 for IN 39. Head north toward Belleville. Go 4.3 miles and turn left onto US 40. Go 9.9 miles and turn right onto County Road 200 S./IN 240. Go 8.6 miles and turn right onto N. Calbert Way to find the trailhead 200 feet on your left.

On the east end of the trail in Plainfield, parking is available at the trailhead at the end of Township Line Road, at Franklin Park, and at Splash Island Family Waterpark. To reach the parking lot at Township Line Road, take I-70 to Exit 68 for Ronald Reagan Pkwy. N. Go 3 miles on the exit ramp, veering right for the northbound parkway, and continue onto Ronald Reagan Pkwy. an additional 1.3 miles. Turn left onto Stout Heritage Pkwy. Go 1 mile and turn right onto Perry Road. Go 1 mile to the traffic circle and take the third exit (heading left, south) onto Smith Road. Take an immediate right onto Township Line Road to the trailside parking lot.

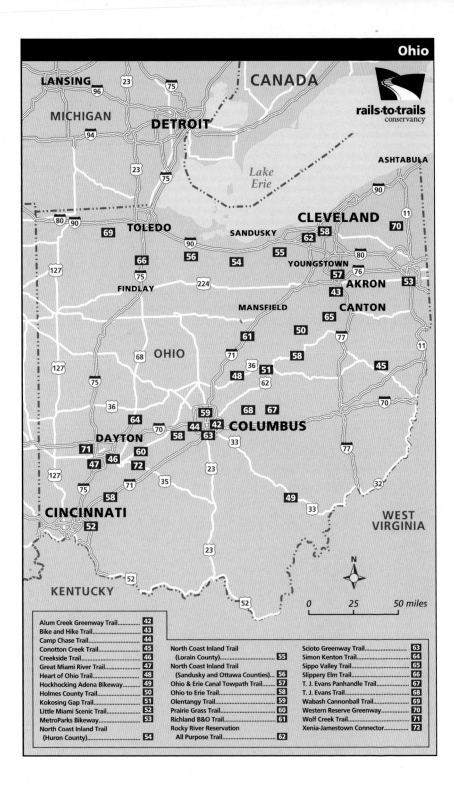

Ohio

rails·to·trails conservancy

LANSING
96
23
75

CANADA

MICHIGAN

94

DETROIT

Lake Erie

ASHTABULA

23

75

80 90

90

TOLEDO
69

SANDUSKY

CLEVELAND

11

70

62 58

90
66
75

56

54

55

YOUNGSTOWN

80

FINDLAY

224

57 76

AKRON

53

43

MANSFIELD

CANTON

65

OHIO
68

61

50

77

71

58

11

127

36

48 51

45

62

75

70

36

64

68 67

127
70

59

COLUMBUS

DAYTON

44 42

58

63

77

71

60

33

47 46

72

23

75

71

35

32

58

49

WEST VIRGINIA

CINCINNATI

33

52

23

KENTUCKY

52

23

N

0   25   50 miles

52

52

The Holmes County Trail meanders in and out of dense tree canopies and open farmland (see page 172).

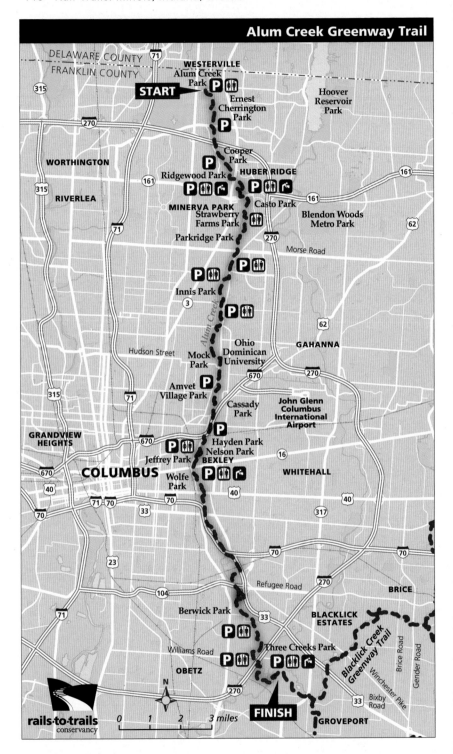

Alum Creek Greenway Trail

DELAWARE COUNTY
FRANKLIN COUNTY

71

315

270

WESTERVILLE
Alum Creek Park

START

Ernest Cherrington Park

Hoover Reservoir Park

WORTHINGTON

Cooper Park

Ridgewood Park

161

HUBER RIDGE

161

315

RIVERLEA

MINERVA PARK
Strawberry Farms Park

Casto Park

Blendon Woods Metro Park

62

71

Parkridge Park

270

Morse Road

Innis Park

3

Alum Creek

Hudson Street

Mock Park

Ohio Dominican University

GAHANNA

62

Amvet Village Park

670

John Glenn Columbus International Airport

270

315

71

Cassady Park

GRANDVIEW HEIGHTS

670

COLUMBUS

Jeffrey Park

BEXLEY

Hayden Park
Nelson Park

16

WHITEHALL

Wolfe Park

670

40

40

40

70

71 70

70

40

317

70

33

Refugee Road

270

BRICE

23

104

70

70

Berwick Park

33

BLACKLICK ESTATES

71

Williams Road

OBETZ

Three Creeks Park

Blacklick Creek Greenway Trail

Winchester Pike

Brice Road

Gender Road

N

270

FINISH

33

GROVEPORT

Bixby Road

rails-to-trails
conservancy

0   1   2   3 miles

The Alum Creek Greenway Trail takes you through a scenic landscape from Westerville through Columbus to Groveport, with easy access to adjoining neighborhoods and a multitude of public parks to enjoy. While the trail crosses busy suburban areas, your proximity to the winding and picturesque Alum Creek—with its many bridges in a range of architectural styles—physically and mentally removes you from the hustle and bustle.

The paved path is appropriate for all levels of users, and it provides great signage and enough amenities to facilitate a smooth biking or walking experience. As you ride along, you'll appreciate the continuity maintained by several underpasses beneath major roadways; in fact, there is only one short section (at approximately the midpoint of the trail) where you are briefly routed onto a sidewalk to cross a busy intersection.

South of Wolfe Park, you'll pass over a bridge built in 1922.

Counties
Franklin

Endpoints
W. Main St. just west of Alum Park Dr. (Westerville) to Three Creeks Park near Spangler Road, 0.1 mile south of Watkins Road (Groveport)

Mileage
23.1

Type
Greenway/Non-Rail-Trail

Roughness Index
1

Surface
Asphalt, Concrete

The trail's first 7 miles, from its northern end in Westerville to Easton Town Center in Columbus, offers a plethora of dining and shopping options. This section also traverses Strawberry Farms Park, where you cross the creek on a lovely double-arch bridge.

About midway, the trail skirts the Ohio Dominican University campus. From there, the southern end of the greenway takes you through Bexley, which has a charming arts district. You'll continue on through the preserved natural areas of Three Creeks Park, a perfect location for some rest and relaxation with picnic areas, boat access, and walking trails, as well as a connection to the nearly 18-mile Blacklick Creek Greenway Trail.

As you travel on the Alum Creek Greenway Trail, you can also learn about the incredible history of active transportation, celebrated with plaques and bridges along the path, honoring such important figures as African American bike racer Marshall "Major" Taylor and Ohio to Erie Trail project founder Ed Honton. The greenway is part of the statewide Ohio to Erie Trail (see page 198), which will eventually span more than 300 miles as it continues north to Cleveland and south to Cincinnati from Columbus.

CONTACT: columbus.gov/recreationandparks/trails/Alum-Creek-Trail or centralohiogreenways.com/index.php/site/full_trail/15

DIRECTIONS

At the northern end of the trail, you can park in Alum Creek Park North (221 W. Main St., Westerville) and take a short connector trail across Alum Creek to the start of the Alum Creek Greenway Trail. From I-270, take Exit 27 and head north on Cleveland Ave. In 1.2 miles turn right onto Main St., traveling east about 0.3 mile to reach the park, which will be on your right. Find parking along Alum Park Dr.

At the southern end of the trail, park in Three Creeks Park (3860 Bixby Road, Groveport). From I-70, take Exit 103B and head south on Alum Creek Dr. about 3.1 miles; then turn left onto Watkins Road. The road heads east, then curves south after a short distance; when you come to an intersection in 0.6 mile, continue straight onto Spangler Road for another 0.1 mile. Turn left at the THREE CREEKS PARK sign and follow this park entrance road past a series of parking lots; park at the third parking lot as it's closest to the Alum Creek Greenway Trail. From the corner of the parking lot, pick up the paved connector trail that heads east, past the playground, to Alum Creek; cross the creek and you'll be on the Alum Creek Greenway Trail.

Additional parking can be found within many of the parks along the Alum Creek Greenway Trail.

Though not far from two of Ohio's largest cities, Cleveland and Akron, the Bike and Hike Trail passes alongside beautiful natural areas, including the 65-foot Brandywine Falls, a stunning cascading waterfall. With its first section opening in 1972, the pathway was one of the first rail-trail conversions in the country. The 34-mile route follows the corridor of two former railway lines, the Lake Erie & Pittsburg Railway, which later became part of the New York Central Railroad, and the old Akron, Bedford & Cleveland Railroad (AB&C), often referred to as the Alphabet Railroad.

The Bike and Hike Trail is a rambling route peppered with bridge crossings and neighborhood roads in both rural and suburban settings. Unlike most rail-trails, which are fairly flat, this route has delightful dips and rises. Playgrounds and restroom facilities are ample, though you may want to stock up on drinking water and snacks before striking out for the day.

On the southern loop of the trail, an observation deck overlooks the Cuyahoga River in Munroe Falls.

Counties
Cuyahoga, Portage, Summit

Endpoints
Alexander Road, 0.25 mile west of Dunham Road (Northfield), to Judson Road and Hudson Road (Kent)

Mileage
34.2

Type
Rail-Trail

Roughness Index
1

Surface
Asphalt

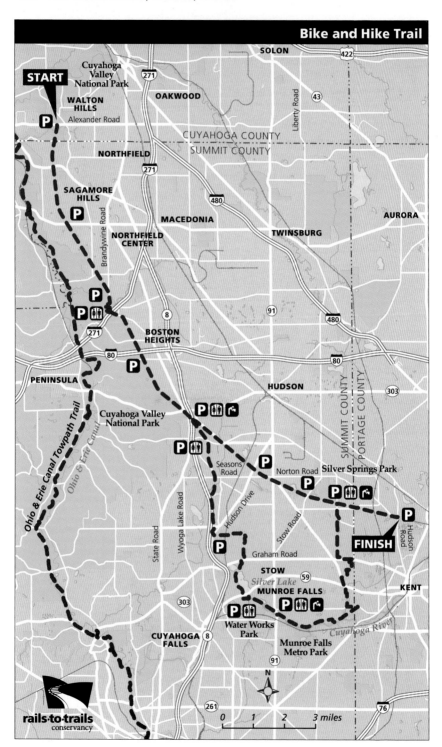

Starting at the northern end on Alexander Road, experience a beautiful, mostly secluded, multiuse, paved trail, much of which borders Cuyahoga Valley National Park. If you wish to explore the park, travel 1.6 miles west from the Alexander Road trailhead to reach the Ohio & Erie Canal Towpath Trail (see page 194), which traverses the park and spans a whopping 81 miles.

As the trail winds south, it passes through rural neighborhoods and wooded areas. With an early enough start, you might see some deer grazing at the path's edge. The trail's southern loop has some on-road sections; look for the green trail signs to guide you along the route. In Munroe Falls, an observation deck on the Cuyahoga River offers lovely scenery, as well as an opportunity for fishing.

Once you complete the southern loop, you can finish the trail by heading back to the northern trailhead. If you still have energy to burn after the return trip north, complete your day's adventure by exploring Cuyahoga Valley National Park. With miles of hiking trails, breathtaking views, and wildlife—ranging from bald eagles to coyotes—the national park is the perfect complement to the northeast Ohio nature that this rail-trail serves up.

CONTACT: www.summitmetroparks.org/bike-and-hike-trail.aspx

DIRECTIONS

To reach the northern trailhead on Alexander Road in Northfield: From I-271 N, take Exit 23. Turn left onto Broadway Ave., and in 0.1 mile turn left onto Oak Leaf Road. From I-271 S, take Exit 23 for OH 14 W. As you exit the interstate, you merge with Oak Leaf Road. In 1 mile turn right onto Alexander Road (a sign at the intersection indicates that this is toward Walton Hills). Drive 2.7 miles west on Alexander Road to the trailhead and parking lot.

To reach the southern trailhead in Munroe Falls: From I-76, take Exit 27 for OH 91N. Continue north 0.3 mile to OH 91 and turn right (north). Follow OH 91N for 5.3 miles (it becomes Main St. north of Tallmadge) to the parking lot and the trailhead, located on the right immediately after crossing the Cuyahoga River.

Additional parking waypoints are available; see the map for locations.

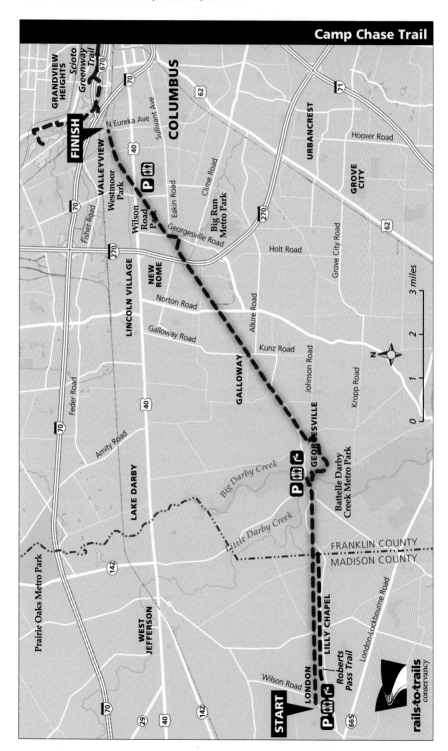

The Camp Chase Trail plays a role in two of Ohio's most exciting trail projects: it is a key piece of the cross-state Ohio to Erie Trail (see page 198) and an integral part of the Central Ohio Greenways network around the greater Columbus region. The trail takes its name from the railroad that shares the corridor with it; it's a shining example of a well-constructed rail-with-trail.

The route begins in rural Madison County, just north of the city of London at the Wilson Road trailhead. The first mile and a half offers a peaceful trail experience through Ohio farm country; you'll see fields of soybeans and corn, in addition to well-maintained homes and barns. The crossroads at Lilly Chapel are notable due to the grain elevator operation located close to the trail. If you're lucky, you may see a train being loaded with the bounty of the fields you just crossed. Once past the elevator, fields again predominate the landscape.

As you approach Columbus, take this stunning trail bridge over I-270.

Counties
Franklin, Madison

Endpoints
Wilson Road SE, 1 mile north of OH 665/London-Lockbourne Road (London), to N. Eureka Ave., 300 feet south of Valleyview Dr. (Columbus)

Mileage
15.9

Type
Rail-Trail/Rail-with-Trail

Roughness Index
1

Surface
Asphalt

Georgesville appears in another 3.2 miles. The trail weaves through town, and you head downhill to the Darby Creek Bridge. Crossing the bridge takes you into Battelle Darby Creek Metro Park. The path is now off the rail corridor for the only time in its entire length. You'll have a great experience getting close to the creek, crossing under the very tall rail trestle bridge, and then meandering up the hill through the forest. The trail eventually takes you to the park entrance road, and you travel on that road for a short distance back to the rail corridor.

The small town of Galloway greets you just 4 miles past the park. Not far from Galloway the ambience takes on a different character as you enter the first outlying neighborhoods of greater Columbus. Another 2.5 miles from Galloway and almost at the end of the trail, you get a nice treat. In 2015 a new trail bridge was built next to the active railroad bridge and across the very wide and busy I-270 loop. Crossing this bridge means that you're almost at trail's end in Columbus's Hilltop neighborhood. If you're up for more riding, a short gap of on-road riding will take you to the Scioto Greenway Trail (see page 216), which follows the Scioto River through downtown Columbus.

CONTACT: centralohiogreenways.com/index.php/site/full_trail/39

DIRECTIONS

To reach the Wilson Road trailhead on the west end of the trail: From I-70, take Exit 85 for OH 142 (to Plain City). Head south on OH 142/NE Plain City–Georgesville Road, and go 2.3 miles. Turn right onto US 40/National Pike, and travel west 0.8 mile. In the town of West Jefferson, turn left (south) onto Walnut St.; at Garrette Park, the road veers right and continues as Fellows Ave. In 0.3 mile take a left onto Garfield Ave., then an immediate right onto Lilly Chapel Road. Head west on Lilly Chapel 0.2 mile, and make a slight left onto W. Jefferson Kiousville Road SE. Travel 1.6 miles and, at the fork, turn right onto Wilson Road. Go 2.6 miles as the road heads south; the trailhead parking lot will appear on your right (on the west side of the road).

To reach the Battelle Darby Creek Metro Park trailhead: From I-270, take Exit 5 for Georgesville Road, and head west 1.3 miles. Turn left onto Norton Road, and travel south 0.7 mile. Turn right onto Bausch Road, and travel west 0.9 mile; it becomes Alkire Road. Continue another 3 miles (you'll be heading southwest); the trailhead and parking lot will be on your left (on the south side of Alkire Road).

To reach the trailhead at Wilson Road Park in Columbus, take I-270 to Exit 7A, and head east on US 40/W. Broad St. In 1.3 miles turn right onto S. Wilson Road, and go 0.5 mile. Turn right onto Wilson Park Way to reach the trailhead parking. Camp Chase Trail is at the north end of the park.

Once the corridor of the Wheeling and Lake Erie Railway, today the 11.2-mile Conotton Creek Trail offers complete immersion in a bucolic setting in northeastern Ohio. Situated in the rolling Appalachian foothills, the route has a significant coal-mining past.

At one time, the line was used to transport iron ore from Great Lakes ports to the steel mills of the Ohio River Valley, and haul coal mined from Harrison County to markets in all directions. Today, one of the rail lines is still used, carrying coal, raw materials, and manufactured goods.

The Conotton Creek Trail models the rustic beauty of its surroundings, and its careworn surface covers a paved, albeit bumpy in sections, undulating route. Several particularly rough spots may bounce you around a bit, but the rest of this trail lulls you into a state of relaxation and delivers a serene setting rich in wildlife.

Conotton Creek runs adjacent to the trail for its entire length.

County
Harrison

Endpoints
Broadway St. at OH 151/
Boyce Dr. (Bowerston)
to Cadiz St. at Water St.
(Jewett)

Mileage
11.2

Type
Rail-Trail

Roughness Index
1

Surface
Asphalt

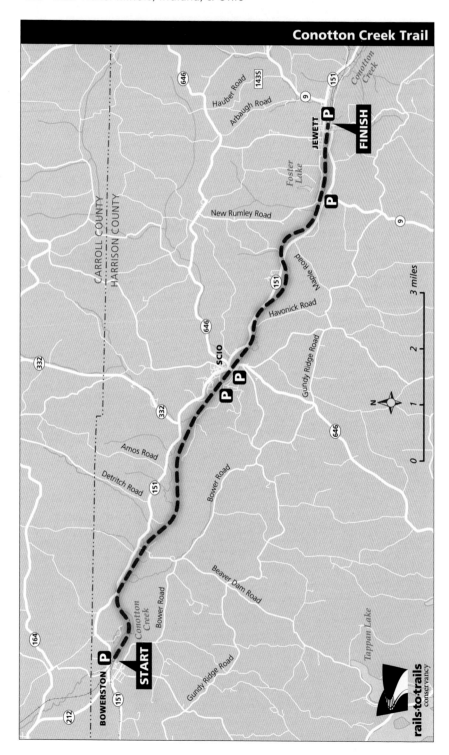

Riding from quaint Bowerston east to Jewett makes your return trip slightly downhill. The ponds east of Bowerston provide a wonderful environment for birding, as do the berried bushes along the route and more than 40 birdhouses. A colorful palette of wildflowers and pastoral landscapes dotted with horses and cattle completes the picturesque backdrop.

A highlight of the experience is passage through the trail's five covered bridges crossing Conotton Creek. The waters below the bridges eventually feed into the Ohio River, as well as into the Mississippi River more than 500 miles away.

The final few miles into the town of Jewett are just as calming and refreshing as those from Bowerston to the trail's midpoint at Scio. Jewett, similar to Bowerston, has fewer than 1,000 people, but the town was an important cog in the wheel of this region's development. Jewett was not only an important stop on the railroad, like the other towns you pass, but was also once home to a streetcar manufacturer and an opera house.

CONTACT: harrisoncountyohio.org/trails

DIRECTIONS

To reach the trailhead in Bowerston: From I-77, take Exit 65 for US 36. Head east on US 36, and go 14.2 miles. Continue straight on US 250 another 1.3 miles. Turn left to stay on US 250, and go 4.5 miles. Turn left onto OH 151, and go 5.3 miles northeast toward Bowerston. Just past downtown Bowerston, find signs directing you to the trailhead on the right (south) side of OH 151.

To reach the trailhead in Jewett: Follow the directions above to OH 151. Once on OH 151, go 16.8 miles to Jewett. Turn left onto Cadiz St., and in 0.1 mile turn right onto Water St. Look for the well-marked trailhead on the right.

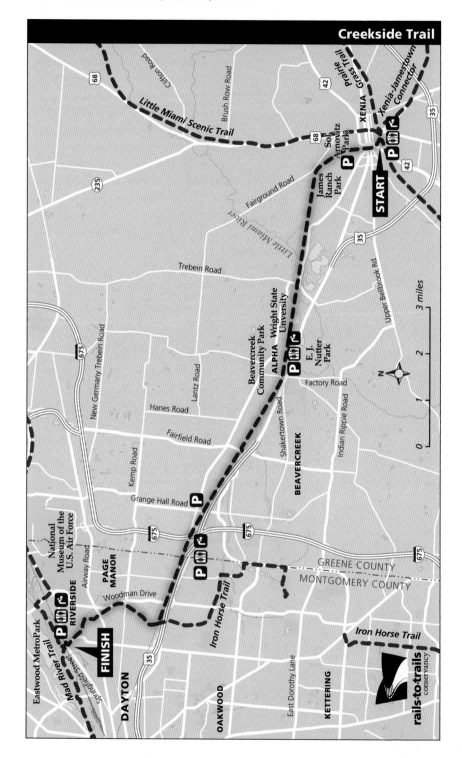

The 15-mile Creekside Trail is part of a network of more than 340 miles of trails that travel throughout Ohio's scenic Miami Valley. The route follows a nature-filled corridor offering many opportunities for side exploration, and because the trail parallels two streams much of the way, there are also spots to cool off on hot summer days. The Creekside Trail is one of several trails that radiate from Xenia Station, allowing for connections to the Xenia-Jamestown Connector (see page 247), the Little Miami Scenic Trail (see page 178), and the Prairie Grass Trail (see page 207), the latter two of which are also part of the cross-state Ohio to Erie Trail (see page 198).

Begin in Xenia to travel toward Dayton. Here, you'll find a replica railroad depot with a museum dedicated to the town's railroad history, as well as restrooms and water fountains. Head north, crossing Cincinnati Avenue, Second Street, and Main Street; the latter is very busy, so use

A charming mill adorns the Creekside Trail in Beavercreek.

Counties
Greene, Montgomery

Endpoints
Xenia Station at N. Miami Ave. and S. West St. (Xenia) to Springfield St. at N. Smithville Road (Dayton)

Mileage
15.2

Type
Rail-Trail

Roughness Index
1

Surface
Asphalt, Concrete

caution. Shortly afterward, the trail takes on a much different tone and enters more natural surroundings. Find shade trees, wetland areas, and streams. Keep alert for the abundant and diverse wildlife that lives in the area.

On the east side of Towler Road, you'll find the entrance to Sol Arnovitz Park, which has parking as well as hiking trails and a disc golf course. Across the street, you can pick up the James Ranch Connecting Spur, a short paved pathway that leads to James Ranch Park, which features a 19th-century farmhouse and beautiful gardens. Soon afterward is the entrance to the Kil-Kare Raceway; on race days, it's loud and the smell of hot rubber fills the air.

Continuing west you reach the William Maxwell Rest Area, which has a covered picnic table. Cross over the Little Miami River and stop at overlooks at each end of the bridge for beautiful views of the river and its banks. At mile 6, a spur leads to Beavercreek Community Park, which has restrooms, water, and parking facilities. Staying on the trail, find nearby E. J. Nutter Park, which is home to baseball diamonds, as well as more restrooms, water, parking, and concession stands (open during games only). Farther along, just after passing under Fairfield Road, arrive at Beavercreek Station, which offers amenities and features Miami Valley's September 11th Memorial.

At about mile 10, the route passes Fifth Third Gateway Park before crossing I-675 via an impressive 465-foot restored railroad overpass. At the T-junction turn right to continue to the trail's end in Eastwood MetroPark; left leads to the Iron Horse Trail. Cross Burkhardt Road and then busy Airway Road, where you will see the huge, shining, silver hangars of the National Museum of the U.S. Air Force. As you enter the park, you'll see the trailhead for the Mad River Trail, which travels to downtown Dayton. Be sure to plan time to explore this popular urban park, which presents endless opportunities for recreation, including boating, fishing, hiking, paddling, and much more, in addition to providing typical amenities.

CONTACT: gcparkstrails.com/216/Creekside-Trail

DIRECTIONS

To reach the Xenia Station trailhead on the east end of the trail: From I-675, take Exit 13A and head east on US 35. In 9.1 miles exit onto US 42. Head north 1.2 miles, and turn right onto S. Miami Ave. Look for the restored depot on the left in 0.4 mile.

To reach the Eastwood MetroPark trailhead in Dayton: From I-675, take Exit 15 for Colonel Glenn Hwy. At the end of the mile-long exit ramp, turn right (west) onto Colonel Glenn Hwy., and go 1.8 miles as the road becomes Airway Road. Turn right onto Harshman Ave., and go 1.5 miles. Look for Eastwood MetroPark on the left.

The Great Miami River Trail is the backbone of one of the nation's largest paved trail networks, spanning 340 miles throughout Ohio's Miami Valley. The route connects beautiful natural areas, small towns, and large cities across four Ohio counties. Beginning in Piqua, the trail has a wonderfully maintained asphalt surface for its entire length of more than 86 miles. The majority of the trail keeps you close to the river, creating a prime opportunity to observe wildlife along the way. Riding along the river, you quickly see that the impressive levee system built to keep the river out of town has allowed the space for a trail to be built.

Leaving Piqua on your way south to Troy, you'll be delighted with the Robert J. Shook Memorial Bikeway Bridge over the river. Entering Troy, you'll experience some impressive routing through the city that allows you

Counties
Butler, Miami, Montgomery, Warren

Endpoints
Roadside Park at OH 66, 0.15 mile south of County Road 110 (Piqua), to Baxter Dr., 0.1 mile north of OH 73 (Franklin); N. Verity Pkwy., 0.1 mile east of N. Breiel Blvd. (Middletown) to Oxford State Road, 0.2 mile east of Radabaugh Road (Trenton); and Rentschler Forest MetroPark at Reigart Road, 0.9 mile north of OH 4 (Hamilton), to Waterworks Park at Groh Ln. and Ponderosa Dr. (Fairfield)

Mileage
86.2

Type
Greenway/Non-Rail-Trail

Roughness Index
1

Surface
Asphalt

The north end of the trail hugs the river in Piqua.

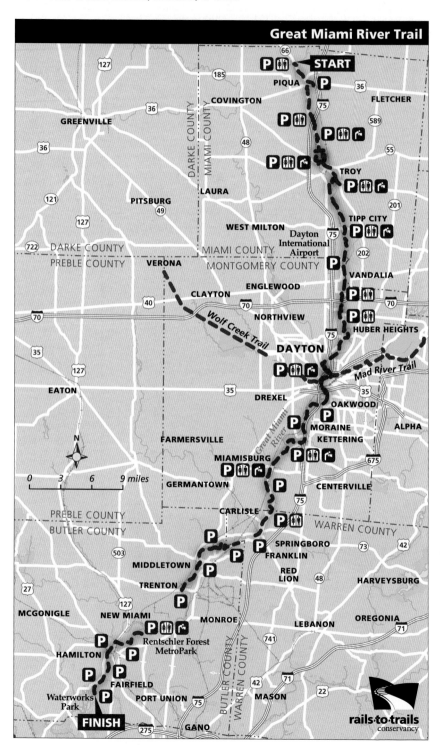

Great Miami River Trail

to maintain a trail experience in some tight space situations. As you regain the river, you're greeted with an impressive city park along the waterfront.

Heading south, you will welcome the shaded tree canopy. Tipp City offers many amenities for trail users, including some of the best way-finding signage you can hope to see along a trail. The next stretch of trail is amazingly scenic and quiet as you ride through forests and a metro park before crossing the river again and continuing underneath I-70.

The trail entrance into Dayton proper is a great experience. You pass through five different parks and one island and cross two trail bridges! The path hugs the river through the city, with ample chances to turn off and enjoy amenities. The trail continues through small towns, including Miamisburg, which boasts many trail-friendly places to visit and helpful signage telling you how to get to them. The end of this long stretch of connected trail is just south of Franklin, 57.6 miles from Piqua.

After a short gap, the trail picks up again just southwest of Franklin and continues uninterrupted through the city of Middletown. After another gap, the final completed section of the path begins at Rentschler Forest MetroPark north of Hamilton. The trail travels through the city to its terminus at Waterworks Park just south of Hamilton.

CONTACT: miamivalleytrails.org/trails/great-miami-river-trail

DIRECTIONS

The Great Miami River Trail has numerous trailheads across its 86-mile length; below you'll find directions to some of the key trailheads. Use the link above or TrailLink.com to find others.

To reach the northern trailhead in Piqua's Roadside Park: From I-75, take Exit 83 for County Road 25A to Piqua. Travel west on CR 25A/Sidney Road 1.5 miles. Turn right onto Riverside Dr. Go 0.6 mile and continue onto OH 66/N. Broadway St. Travel 1.2 miles to Roadside Park, which will be on the right.

To reach the trail's midpoint in Dayton at Deeds Point MetroPark: From I-75, take Exit 54B for OH 4 N to Springfield. Follow signs for Webster St. and turn south. At the end of the exit ramp, make an immediate right onto Deeds Park Dr. The trailhead is at the dead end at 510 Webster St.

To reach the southern trailhead at Fairfield's Waterworks Park: From I-275, take Exit 36 for US 127/Hamilton Ave. Head 3.5 miles north on US 127, and turn left onto Nilles Road, which becomes River Road. In 1.3 miles turn right onto Groh Ln.; Waterworks Park (5133 Groh Ln.) will be on the left.

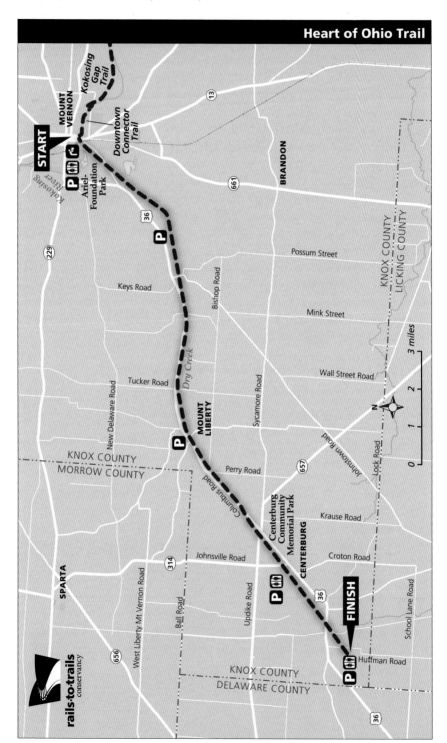

Heart of Ohio Trail

True to its name, the Heart of Ohio Trail lies in the central part of the state, extending from Mount Vernon southwest to the Knox-Licking County line just south of Centerburg. Along its nearly 16 miles, the trail highlights picturesque landscapes of woodlands, farm fields, and wetlands. The vast majority of the path is paved, with only a short section awaiting asphalt; that stretch spans just over a mile from Huffman Road in Centerburg south to the county line.

In Mount Vernon, the Heart of Ohio Trail begins at the beautifully restored Cleveland, Akron & Columbus (CA&C) Railroad Depot, which dates back to 1907. The trail is built on the railbed that once carried trains in and out of the station. From here, you could hop on the Downtown Connector Trail, which runs a mile across town to meet up with the Kokosing Gap Trail (see page 175) on

The Heart of Ohio Trail ends in Centerburg, the geographic center of Ohio.

County
Knox

Endpoints
S. Main St./OH 13 at County Road 80 (Mount Vernon) to Huffman Road, 0.5 mile south of US 36 (Centerburg)

Mileage
15.7

Type
Rail-Trail

Roughness Index
1–2

Surface
Asphalt, Ballast

Mount Vernon's east side. All three trails are part of the Ohio to Erie Trail, a planned 320-mile trail network that will eventually span Ohio from the shores of Lake Erie in Cleveland to the Ohio River in Cincinnati (see page 198).

Another worthwhile side excursion while you're in Mount Vernon is the Ariel-Foundation Park. Like many rail-trails, its grounds have an industrial past. Once the site of a glass manufacturing plant, the 250-acre park houses unique sculptures (including a glass "stream") and a labyrinth, in addition to a towering smokestack with a staircase spiraling around the outside that you can climb for a breathtaking view of the countryside.

Head southwest from Mount Vernon to travel on the Heart of Ohio Trail. Soon, you'll be loosely paralleling Dry Creek, which gets quite close to the path at some points. Several bridges on the route take you over the creek. From spring through fall, wildflowers add to the trail's beauty.

The trail ends in Centerburg, which is the geographic center of Ohio, hence the town's name. A large boulder with a mounted plaque marks the central spot in the community park. The bustling small town also provides restaurants and shopping downtown.

CONTACT: knoxcountyparks.org/trails/bike-trails/heart-of-ohio-bike-trail

DIRECTIONS

On the trail's northern end, parking is available at the William A. Stroud Welcome Center, located in the Cleveland, Akron & Columbus Railroad Depot (501 S. Main St., Mount Vernon). From I-71, take Exit 131 for US 36/OH 37. Go east 3.7 miles, and turn left to remain on US 36. In 21.9 miles, turn right onto County Road 80/Columbus Road. In 1.7 miles, the road meets S. Main St., and the depot will be on your left.

On the trail's southern end, parking is available at Memorial Park (59 Johnsville Road, Centerburg) and the path's terminus (2750 Huffman Road, Centerburg). To reach Memorial Park, from I-71, take Exit 131 for US 36/OH 37. Go east 3.7 miles, and turn left to remain on US 36. In 10.6 miles turn left onto Johnsville Road, which is also OH 314 N; the park is 0.1 mile ahead on your left. To reach the parking area on Huffman Road, from I-71, take Exit 131 for US 36/OH 37. Go east 3.7 miles, and turn left to remain on US 36. In 8.1 miles turn right onto Huffman Road. Go 0.5 mile, and the parking area will be on your left.

The Hockhocking Adena Bikeway is one of southeast Ohio's hidden trail gems. Tucked into the foothills of Appalachia, this 20-mile trail gives a sampling of the best the Buckeye State has to offer: from college town amenities and atmosphere to scenic natural features and idyllic Midwest farmland.

The trail quietly begins in Ohio's quintessential college town, Athens, home of Ohio University. Riding on a smooth asphalt surface, which will be enjoyed the entire length, you start behind a busy section of town with numerous businesses situated along State Street. After a few miles, you will pass the Athens Community Center and pool, then travel upon the levee of the Hocking River. Ohio University's campus comes along the north side of the trail and creates a pleasant atmosphere, including close passage by the imposing Bob Wren Stadium, home of the Ohio Bobcats baseball team. The route continues through the west side of Athens about another 2 miles, passing West State Street Park with its impressive community gardens.

The paved path crosses the Hocking River twice.

County
Athens

Endpoints
E. State St. at US 50/OH 32 (Athens) to Myers St., 0.1 mile west of Monroe St. (Nelsonville)

Mileage
20.4

Type
Rail-Trail/Rail-with-Trail

Roughness Index
1

Surface
Asphalt

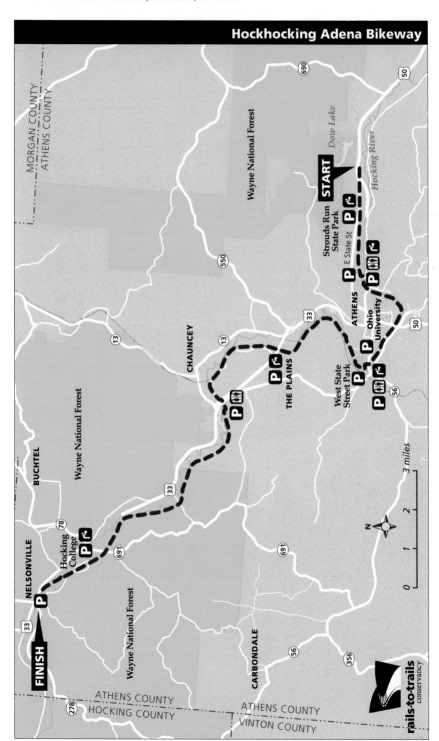

Hockhocking Adena Bikeway

After you cross the bridge over the Hocking River, there is a noticeable shift from an in-town feeling to the solitude of quiet forest. Lush tree cover creates a tunnel-like effect for the vast remainder of the path, a pleasant respite on a hot summer day. As you meander in and out of the dense forest, openings in the trees frame classic farm field vistas, which, combined with rock outcrops, make this stretch of trail an absolute joy to experience. Common sights along the trail include deer, herons, snakes, and many more species. Adding visual interest to the experience, active railroad tracks are in close proximity to the trail the majority of the way, though train traffic is not frequent.

The very rural, natural setting is finally broken when you emerge onto the small campus of Hocking College outside Nelsonville. A couple of miles past the college, you will enter the town of Nelsonville itself. The path ends behind the Rocky Boots factory (founded in 1932) at a dedicated trailhead. Whether you begin or end your ride in Nelsonville, a visit to the historical town square, just a block from the trailhead, is highly recommended.

Plans are in the works to extend the trail another 1.5 miles east from its current southern endpoint. The new section, anticipated for completion in 2018, would continue the trail along the south side of US 50 to Canaan Road in Athens.

CONTACT: athensohio.com/wheretoplay/hockhocking-adena-bikeway-2

DIRECTIONS

To reach the southeastern trailhead in Athens: From I-77, take Exit 176 for US 50. Head west 10.2 miles on US 50, and use the left lane to merge onto OH 32/OH 7/US 50. In 11.5 miles, keep right to stay on US 50. In 16.4 miles take the exit for E. State St. Head west 1 mile on State St. to find the trailhead on the left.

To reach the West State Street Park trailhead: Follow the directions above to OH 32/OH 7/US 50. Go 20.6 miles, and take Exit 17 for OH 682 and head north. In 0.4 mile turn right onto Richland Ave. In 0.2 mile turn left onto Shafer St. Go 1 mile and turn left onto W. State St. West State Street Park will appear in about a mile at the end of the road.

To reach the northern trailhead in Nelsonville: From I-70, take Exit 132 for OH 13. Head south on OH 13, and go 7.7 miles. Turn right onto OH 256, and go 1.7 miles. Turn left onto OH 664. In 10.8 miles, turn right to stay on OH 664, and go 11.3 miles. At the second traffic circle, take the third exit (essentially turning left) for US 33 eastbound. In 11.4 miles take the exit for John Lloyd Evans Memorial Dr. Turn right onto John Lloyd Evans Memorial Dr., and go 0.5 mile. At the traffic circle, take the second exit (turning left) for W. Washington St., which becomes W. Canal St., then Old US 33 in the heart of Nelsonville. In 1.1 miles take a right onto Hocking St. (Myers St.); the trailhead is on the right in the parking lot behind the large Rocky Boots factory.

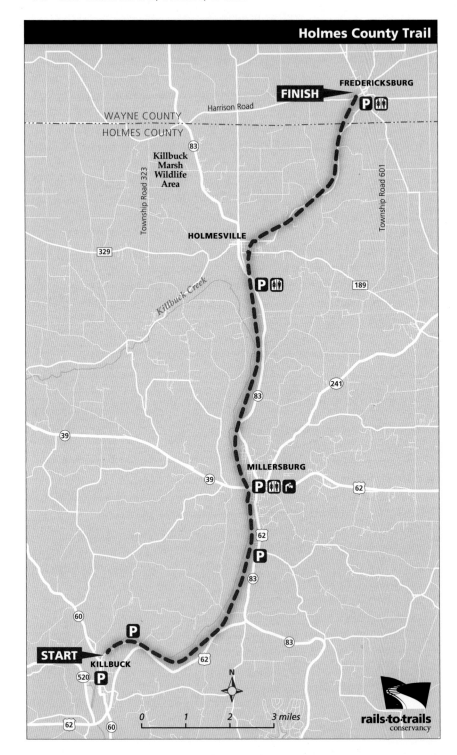

Holmes County Trail

Holmes County, located in northeastern Ohio, is the heart of the state's Amish country. Visitors to this rural enclave will find meandering country roads and bucolic natural areas, as well as the 15.7-mile Holmes County Trail. The path was the first recreational trail in the country designed to accommodate Amish buggies, and throughout much of the route it is just as common to pass a horse-drawn buggy as it is to pass a cyclist or walker.

Plans are in place to extend the trail 7.5 miles south, and work could be completed by late 2017, but until then start at the southern trailhead in Killbuck. Here you will find picnic tables and benches at the trail entrance. The paved route has an adjacent path for equestrians. Be sure to review the etiquette rules posted at the trailhead so you can share the trail safely with its myriad users.

As you travel north, follow the Killbuck Creek as the path traverses wetlands and long cutoff channels of the creek. Immerse yourself in the tranquil surroundings before reaching Hipp Station in Millersburg. Here you will find a beautifully restored historical train depot, which serves as

The Hipp Station trailhead in Millersburg features a historical depot with trail information and amenities.

Counties
Holmes, Wayne

Endpoints
N. Main St. near S. Railroad St. (Killbuck) to W. Clay St. near Water St. (Fredericksburg)

Mileage
15.7

Type
Rail-Trail

Roughness Index
1

Surface
Asphalt

the trail's headquarters with a visitor center featuring wildlife displays, trail information, restrooms, vending machines, a covered picnic area, and a playground.

The trail meanders north out of Millersburg at a very easy, even grade. The corridor passes picturesque swamplands for long stretches, and wildlife abounds among the water and trees. You will likely see turtles, snakes, and birds, including cardinals, doves, and hawks. Given the trail's wet terrain, there are numerous stream crossings, including a couple over restored railroad bridges.

A well-designed square tunnel takes you underneath OH 83 at mile 6 just before the small town of Holmesville. When you enter Holmesville, you will follow quiet community streets about 1 mile until the rail corridor picks up again. The bypass is very well marked, and the streets are little used and easy to navigate. Once through Holmesville, the trail continues another 4 miles along a wonderful mixture of farm fields and tree-lined streams to the Fredericksburg trailhead and the trail's north end, where you will find restrooms.

The trail began its life as a spur of one of Ohio's earliest railroads, the Cleveland and Pittsburgh, and the tracks reached Millersburg in 1854. A catastrophic flood in 1969 washed out sections of railbed, leading to the end of the line's use. Fortunately, with the conversion of the railway to a rail-trail, which opened in 2005, a new generation of users—bicyclists, walkers, in-line skaters, and horse and buggy riders—can now roll along this picturesque corridor.

The Holmes County Trail is also a vital component of the Ohio to Erie Trail, a developing 320-mile route, which will eventually span Ohio from the shores of Lake Erie in Cleveland to the Ohio River in Cincinnati (see page 198).

CONTACT: holmestrail.com

DIRECTIONS

To reach the southern trailhead in Killbuck: From I-77, take Exit 65, and head west on US 36. In 18.2 miles, turn right to remain on US 36. In 6.3 miles, turn right onto OH 60. Go 14.3 miles, and turn left then right onto Amish Country Byway, which becomes Main St. and County Road 622. In 1 mile, find the trailhead on your left next to a former train depot. Parking is available in downtown Killbuck on Front St., Water St., Main St., and north of the depot on CR 622.

To reach the Millersburg trailhead at Hipp Station: From I-77, take Exit 83 and head west on OH 39, which merges with US 62 and Jackson St. In 25.4 miles, turn right onto N. Grant St., follow it 0.1 mile, and then head west on W. Clinton St., which dead-ends at the Hipp Station trailhead.

To reach the Fredericksburg trailhead, from I-77, take Exit 87 and head northwest on US 250. In 3.2 miles, turn left to remain on US 250. In 10 miles turn left onto Harrison Road, which becomes Clay St. in town, and go 9.2 miles. Find the parking lot just past the elementary school next to the bridge and pavilion.

The Kokosing Gap Trail delights visitors with its rich railroad history, which is on display throughout the 13-mile paved route. Once the corridor of the Pennsylvania Railroad, the rail-trail now connects the towns of Mount Vernon, Gambier, Howard, and Danville, each just a few short miles apart. Enjoy a landscape of ravines and farmland as you cross the Kokosing River twice along railroad bridges more than 250 feet long, and appreciate a moment's respite from summer sun while traveling through the Howard Tunnel. Also stop to marvel at an old locomotive and a bright-red wood caboose, both of which were fully restored with funds raised in the local community. The trail has a smooth asphalt surface and park benches about every 0.5 mile.

Starting at the trailhead in Mount Vernon, the first part of the trip takes you along the sunken valley of the Kokosing River. You'll head east, passing one of several overlooks of the river and the surrounding valley, and cross two former railroad trestles. The bridges have been meticulously restored and are well worth a stop to admire the handiwork. Shortly after crossing the first bridge, you'll reach the Brown Family Environmental Center at

County
Knox

Endpoints
Phillips Park at Liberty St., 0.15 mile south of Pennsylvania Ave. (Mount Vernon), to S. Richards St. just north of W. Washington St. (Danville)

Mileage
13.5

Type
Rail-Trail

Roughness Index
1

Surface
Asphalt

The Gambier trailhead features a train engine and a few cars.

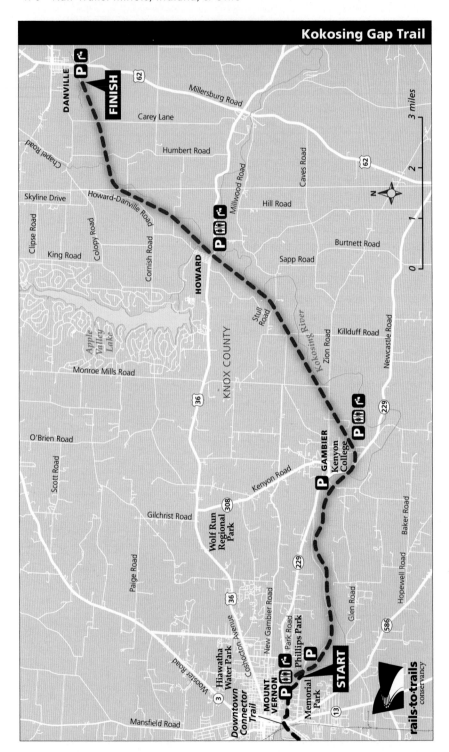

Kenyon College. A visitor center and a butterfly garden beckon you to take a break and come in for a self-guided tour through the garden. Where the trail intersects busy OH 229 and enters Gambier, pay close attention for a safe crossing. After passing the campus of Kenyon College, find the Gambier trailhead and its impeccably restored train cars. In early morning and twilight hours, vintagelike streetlamps shed light on your journey near the Gambier trailhead.

Howard, like the rest of the towns along the Kokosing Gap Trail, provides notable diversions. The trailhead has a parking lot, restroom, and a playground donated by the Rotary Club. Just after an arched stone passage under US 36, an incredible historical mill towers over the trail. Another bridge provides views of a smaller tributary that flows into the Kokosing River, and the trail soon opens up again onto farm fields and pastures. After about a mile more, you are back among trees, with periodic glimpses through the gaps in the forest of farm fields in the distance. Enjoy a quiet final 3.5 miles until the trail's end in Danville.

For a longer ride, you can easily extend your journey on other trails. From its west end in Mount Vernon, you can connect with the Heart of Ohio Trail (see page 166) via the Downtown Connector Trail. And on its east end, there's a short gap across Danville, but then you can pick up the Mohican Valley Trail. These trails, in addition to the Kokosing Gap, are a crucial link in the Ohio to Erie Trail through Knox County (see page 198). The planned 320-mile route (which includes both trail and on-road segments) will eventually span Ohio from the shores of Lake Erie in Cleveland to the Ohio River in Cincinnati.

CONTACT: kokosinggaptrail.org

DIRECTIONS

All of the towns along the route provide trailheads with parking and seasonal facilities. See the link above or use TrailLink.com to learn more.

The Mount Vernon trailhead is on Mount Vernon Ave. From I-71, take Exit 131, and head east on US 36/OH 37. In 3.7 miles, turn left to remain on US 36, and go 21.9 miles. Turn right onto Columbus Road/County Road 80, and in 0.8 mile, turn right onto Parrot Road/CR 83. In 0.6 mile, turn left onto S. Main St., which in 0.7 mile veers right to become Mount Vernon Avenue. In 0.9 mile the trailhead is on the right (south) after Cougar Dr.

To reach the Danville trailhead: From I-71, take Exit 151, and head east on OH 95, which eventually becomes Sandusky St. and then Mount Vernon Ave. In 10.5 miles, turn left onto Montgomery Road, and go 2.8 miles. Turn right onto Old Mansfield Road, and in 0.3 mile, turn left onto Lower Fredericktown Amity Road/County Road 66, which becomes Danville Amity Road/CR 14 after crossing OH 3. In 12 miles, turn right onto S. Richards St. In 0.5 mile the trailhead will be on the right.

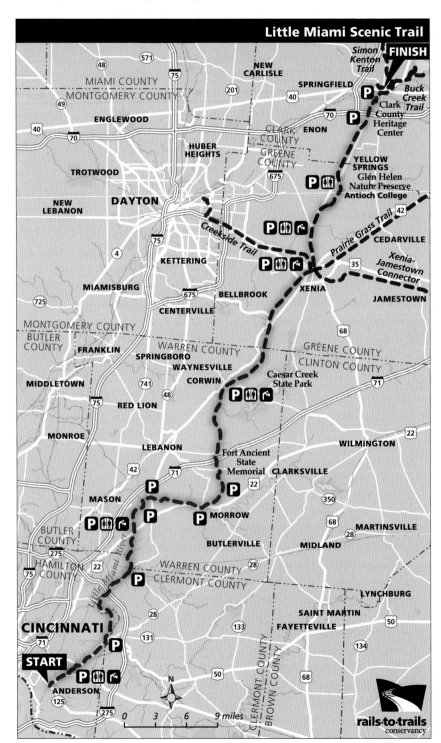

Little Miami Scenic Trail

The Little Miami Scenic Trail (LM) is a jewel in the crown of Ohio rail-trails, and a recent extension makes this popular route even more spectacular. Now just over 78 miles long—winding its way from the outskirts of Cincinnati to Springfield over historical bridges and through tranquil state parks, charming small towns, and stunning natural habitats—the Little Miami offers a long, uninterrupted route through a beautiful southwestern Ohio landscape. The trail is the longest section of a vast network of more than 340 miles of off-road trails that travel throughout Ohio's Miami Valley. It is also a significant section of the cross-state Ohio to Erie Trail (see page 198), which travels from the Ohio River in Cincinnati to Lake Erie in Cleveland on more than 270 miles of off-road trails. For the adventurous, it is possible to embark from the Little Miami on a multiday cycling exploration of the Buckeye State.

Numerous bridges dot the rail-trail.

Counties
Clark, Clermont, Greene, Hamilton, Warren

Endpoints
OH 32 and Beechmont Ave. (Anderson) to W. Jefferson and S. Center Sts. (Springfield)

Mileage
78.1

Type
Rail-Trail

Roughness Index
1

Surface
Asphalt, Concrete

The Yellow Springs Bridge is one of many charming sights along the way.

The LM is often thought of in terms of its southern and northern sections, with the dividing line being the town of Xenia. The southern section begins just outside downtown Cincinnati and runs alongside the Little Miami River much of the way, traveling through quiet countryside, forests, and fields on a shaded route that passes through several small towns with shops and restaurants. Along the way, you will see a former railway depot and iron trestle in Morrow; you can stop to visit the American Indian archaeological site of Fort Ancient in Lebanon.

Farther along, you will reach Xenia (where mileage markers start over at 0). The replica rail depot at Xenia Station is the hub of three other rail-trails—the Creekside Trail, Xenia-Jamestown Connector, and Prairie Grass Trail (see pages 160, 247, and 207, respectively)—and the beginning of the northern portion of the LM. Past Xenia, the trail leaves the river behind and skirts alongside beautiful wooded areas, including Glen Helen Nature Preserve, located across the street from Antioch College in Yellow Springs. Here, you can stop to wander this tranquil oasis or stroll the small downtown, which has a number of quirky shops and restaurants. In town, see a reminder of the LM's railroad past: Yellow Springs Railroad Station now houses the chamber of commerce.

It's about 7 more miles, with a gradual uphill, to the trail's end in Springfield. The route once traveled on roads through the heart of the city, but in September 2016 a new section of the trail opened, allowing trail users to stay on dedicated pathway through Springfield to the trail's end at the Clark County Heritage Center. From here, you can connect with the 35.5-mile Simon Kenton Trail (see page 219), which travels north, and, slightly farther along, to the 6-mile Buck Creek Trail, which goes through town.

CONTACT: miamivalleytrails.org/trails/little-miami-scenic-trail

DIRECTIONS

To reach the southern trailhead: From I-275, take Exit 65 for Beechmont Ave./OH 125 W. Head west on OH 125, and go 6.7 miles. Exit at OH 32 N and look for the parking lot on your immediate left at the Ohio Department of Natural Resources River Access.

The Xenia Station trailhead is located on S. Detroit St./OH 380 in Xenia, 1 mile south of the US 35 and US 68 intersection. To reach Xenia Station from I-675, take Exit 13A, and head east on US 35. In 6.6 miles, veer right to remain on US 35 E toward Washington Court House. Continue 2.5 miles, and exit onto US 42. Head north on US 42, and go 1.2 miles. Turn right onto S. Miami Ave., and turn left into the station parking lot in 0.4 mile.

At the northern end of the trail, the Heritage Center (117 S. Fountain Ave.) in Springfield has parking and trail facilities. From I-70, take Exit 54 and head north on OH 72/S. Limestone St. Travel 1.9 miles north (note that to stay on Limestone you need to bear left at the intersection with Selma Road) and turn left onto E. Pleasant St. Take the first right onto S. Fountain Ave. In 0.3 mile, turn left onto High St. to reach the parking lot. From the parking lot, reach the trail by heading two blocks south to W. Jefferson St.

For directions to other trailheads, see miamivalleytrails.org/trails/little-miami-scenic-trail or TrailLink.com.

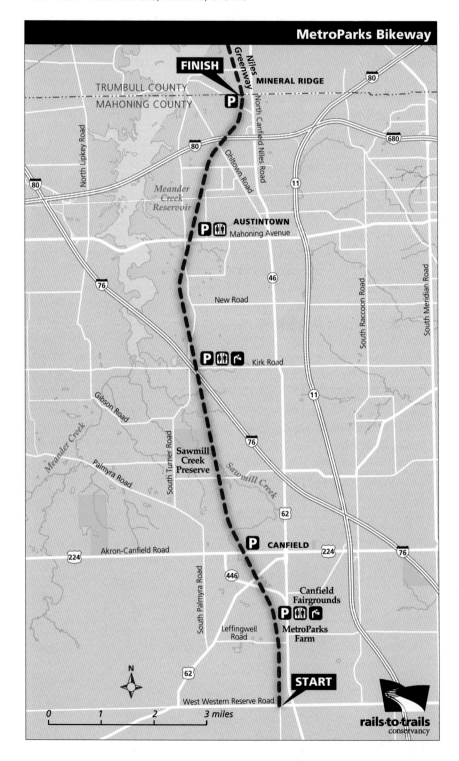

MetroParks Bikeway

The nearly 11-mile MetroParks Bikeway provides a scenic and well-designed link to communities and natural sites in this northeast region of Ohio. The rail-trail follows a corridor between Canfield and Austintown townships that was originally built in the 1860s as a portion of the Cleveland and Mahoning Valley Railroad. This rail line provided an important link between Cleveland and Pittsburgh, while also offering passenger service to towns along the way. Though rail service here is long since gone, today the rail-trail connects several of the communities that were once served by the railroad. For visitors and locals alike, the route provides an ideal way to discover the charms of this tranquil region of the state.

The paved MetroParks Bikeway passes through both suburbs and countryside. Traveling north from the trail's beginning at West Western Reserve Road, find the MetroParks Farm. This 400-acre working farm sprawls along both sides of the trail and presents educational programs,

At the Kirk Road trailhead, you'll find a sandstone structure built in 1938.

County
Mahoning

Endpoints
West Western Reserve Road and Washingtonville Road (Canfield) to Salt Springs Road just west of OH 46 (Mineral Ridge)

Mileage
10.6

Type
Rail-Trail

Roughness Index
1

Surface
Asphalt

tours, and agricultural displays seasonally. On the east side of the trail, the Canfield Fairgrounds holds one of Ohio's largest fairs every year.

Farther along, you'll travel alongside Sawmill Creek Preserve, a 154-acre forested area with trees and shrubs that prevents sediments from entering Sawmill Creek. This is a tributary of Meander Creek Reservoir, the major source of drinking water for the region. Keep your eyes open for diverse species of birds and other wildlife that live in the preserve.

Enjoy a break at one of the jewels of the trail: the Kirk Road trailhead. This award-winning, depot-themed facility provides trailside basics, such as a picnic pavilion, drinking fountains, and restrooms, and also hosts educational and trailside activities. Housed in a historical 1938 Works Progress Administration–built sandstone structure at the trailhead is a bicycle rental and repair shop. Spend time at the shop exploring both the interior and exterior of the site. Later, travel over the Mahoning Avenue overpass, and see additional nods to the route's railroad past in this unique structure, designed to resemble a historical trestle.

The trail ends at County Line Road, where you can make a seamless transition to the 4.5-mile Niles Greenway.

CONTACT: millcreekmetroparks.org/visit/places/metroparks-bikeway

DIRECTIONS

There is no parking at the southernmost end of the trail; the closest parking is at MetroParks Farm. From I-80, take Exit 224A. Take OH 11 south 6.2 miles to Exit 34. Turn right onto US 224 and go 1 mile; then turn left onto OH 46, which becomes S. Broad St. In 0.8 mile, turn left to remain on OH 46. The bikeway parking lot is immediately on your right after turning.

To reach the Kirk Road trailhead from I-80, take Exit 223, and head south on OH 46 N/Canfield Niles Road. In 3.8 miles, turn right onto Kirk Road, and go 1.4 miles. The trailhead and parking lot are on the left, just before you go under the I-76 overpass.

To reach the Mahoning Ave. overpass from I-80, take Exit 224A. Head south on OH 11, and go 1.4 miles to Exit 39. Turn right onto Mahoning Ave./County Road 18, and go 1.9 miles. Immediately after traveling under the overpass, turn right onto Harold St. to reach a small trailhead with a gravel parking lot on the left. This access point is approximately 2.5 miles from the northern end of the MetroParks Bikeway.

The North Coast Inland Trail is a series of trails across multiple northern Ohio counties that, as they expand and connect, are emerging as an impressive long-distance trail between Cleveland and Toledo. Within Huron County, two segments are open that total 15.6 miles.

The first segment goes 10.3 miles from the east side of Bellevue to the county seat of Norwalk. This crushed-stone path is well maintained, but the loose stone can make it tough at times for skinny tires and some wheelchairs. The views consist of classic Midwestern farm fields stretching to the horizon. Much of this route runs alongside an active rail corridor, creating excellent train-watching opportunities. The agriculture landscape continues to the town of Monroeville, where a fabulously restored train depot

Much of the route parallels an active railroad and has expansive views of farm fields.

County
Huron

Endpoints
Prairie Road/County Road 22 at US 20 (Bellevue) to State St. and Ohio St. (Norwalk); and Laylin Road and Gibbs Road (Norwalk) to Derussey Road at Collins Road (Collins)

Mileage
15.6

Type
Rail-Trail/Rail-with-Trail

Roughness Index
1–2

Surface
Crushed Stone

North Coast Inland Trail (Huron County)

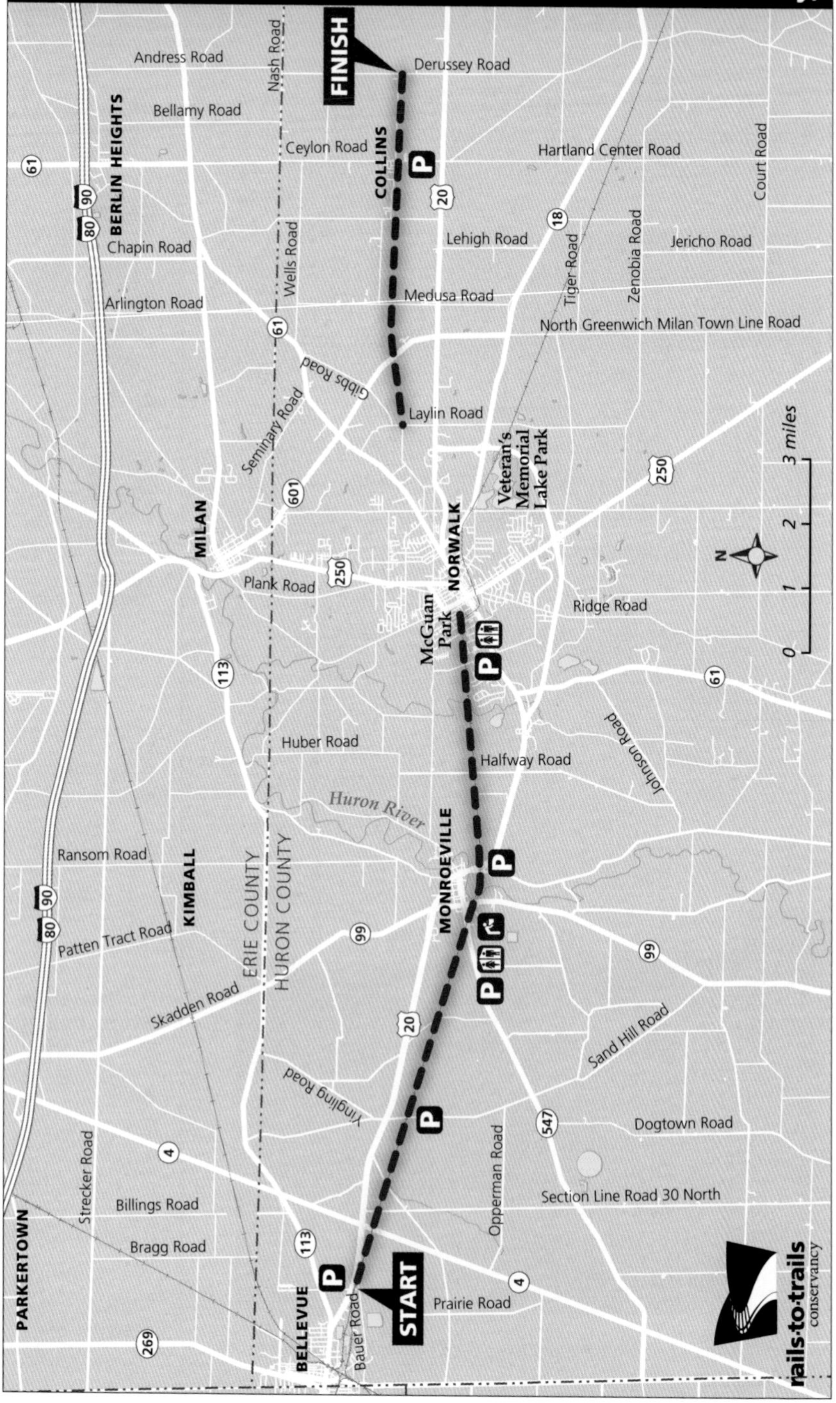

FINISH

Andress Road
Nash Road
Derussey Road
BERLIN HEIGHTS
Bellamy Road
Ceylon Road
Hartland Center Road
Court Road
COLLINS
P
61
80 90
Chapin Road
Wells Road
Lehigh Road
18
Zenobia Road
Jericho Road
Tiger Road
20
Arlington Road
Medusa Road
61
North Greenwich Milan Town Line Road
Gibbs Road
Seminary Road
Laylin Road
Veteran's Memorial Lake Park
250
3 miles
601
MILAN
NORWALK
N
250
Plank Road
McGuan Park
Ridge Road
113
P
61
Huber Road
Halfway Road
Huron River
ERIE COUNTY
HURON COUNTY
Johnson Road
Ransom Road
KIMBALL
MONROEVILLE
P
Patten Tract Road
80 90
99
P
99
Skadden Road
20
Sand Hill Road
Yingling Road
P
547
Dogtown Road
Strecker Road
4
Billings Road
Opperman Road
Section Line Road 30 North
PARKERTOWN
Bragg Road
113
P
START
Prairie Road
4
BELLEVUE
Bauer Road
269

rails·to·trails
conservancy

(dating back to 1863) awaits. The depot and surrounding area host drinking water, a picnic shelter, restrooms, and—if you're lucky—some great company from a local volunteer!

About 3 miles after leaving the depot, you arrive at a beautiful historical bridge over the East Branch of the Huron River. The 1871 stone double-arch bridge is a sight to behold, and wonderfully built observation platforms allow a great view of it. Moving a few short miles along the tree-lined trail brings you into the city of Norwalk and the terminus of this section.

It's about a 3-mile gap before the next section of trail begins. You can reach it by taking surface streets through Norwalk, but only if you're comfortable riding in traffic. The crushed-stone path picks up east of Norwalk and stretches just over 5 miles. Pleasant vistas of more farmland are plentiful along this section, though the tree cover is also heavier, which offers a good respite if riding on a sunny day.

In Collins, a horse trailer parking lot is adjacent to the trail. The Huron County section of trail ends at Derussey Road; there is no formal parking or a trailhead here, so plan on backtracking a short distance to Collins.

CONTACT: firelandsrailstotrails.org

DIRECTIONS

To reach the westernmost trailhead (located just outside of Bellevue): From the Ohio Turnpike (I-80/I-90), take Exit 110 toward OH 4 (Sandusky/Bellevue) and go south. Travel 4.8 miles and take a left onto Beckstein Road. Go 0.9 mile, and turn left onto US 20 E. Go 1 mile, and take a right onto Sand Hill Road; the trailhead will be on the left in 0.3 mile. The end of the trail is 2.7 miles west.

To reach the Monroeville trailhead: From the Ohio Turnpike (I-80/I-90), take Exit 110 toward OH 4 (Sandusky/Bellevue) and go south 0.4 mile. Take a left onto Harris Road. After 0.7 mile, take a right onto OH 99 S. Travel 7.3 miles through the town of Monroeville; the train depot trailhead will be on the right shortly after passing Monroe St.

To reach the Collins trailhead at the east end of the trail: From the Ohio Turnpike (I-80/I-90), take Exit 118 for US 250 S and continue south 2.3 miles. In the town of Milan, take a left onto Williams St. and then in 0.2 mile a right onto S. Main St./OH 601 S. Travel 4.7 miles and then take a left onto US 20 E. Go 2.6 miles and take a left onto Heartland Center Road. Go another 0.7 mile, and the trailhead is on the right. The end of the trail is 1.3 miles east.

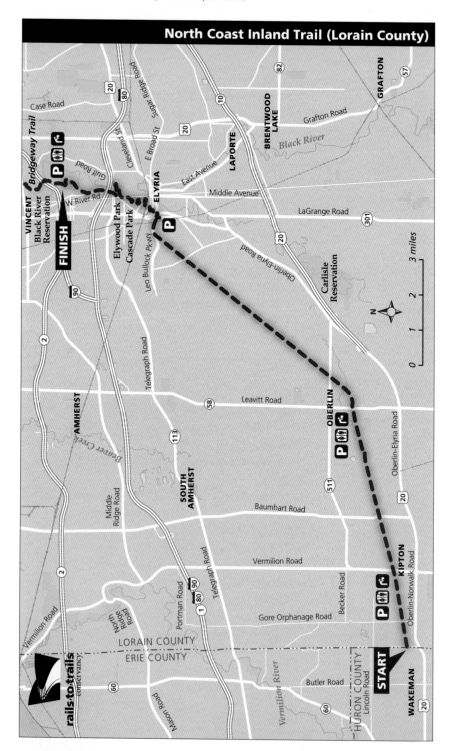

North Coast Inland Trail (Lorain County)

The North Coast Inland Trail will one day stretch across northern Ohio from Indiana to Pennsylvania on a network of connecting off-road trails. Today, large sections of the trail, especially from the Indiana border to Lorain County, Ohio, are well defined. One of these segments, a 19.3-mile route from Wakeman to Elyria, formerly known as the Oberlin Bike Path, is a popular and well-used trail. It follows the corridor of the former Toledo, Norwalk and Cleveland Railroad along a primarily paved pathway that offers a classic rail-trail experience: flat and mostly straight. Only the trail's western tip, from Wakeman to Kipton, is crushed stone.

The route begins at County Line Road (also called Green Street) at the Huron County border in Wakeman. Enjoy a quiet ride through farmland for about 2 miles before reaching Kipton's downtown community park.

The popular, well-used trail offers a mixture of wooded and bucolic views.

County
Lorain

Endpoints
County Line Road, 0.35 mile north of US 20 (Wakeman), to Ford Road, 0.3 mile northeast of Midway Blvd. (Elyria)

Mileage
19.3

Type
Rail-Trail

Roughness Index
1

Surface
Asphalt, Crushed Stone

Just past the park, you will find a plaque commemorating the Great Kipton Train Wreck. It was here in 1891 that two trains collided head on, resulting in eight deaths. The wreck was blamed on a train conductor's watch, which was slow by 4 minutes and caused him to delay moving one of the trains to a separate track. Railroad officials hired prominent Cleveland jeweler Webb Ball to investigate railroad timekeeping and institute standards to avoid such accidents. Locals credit Ball's capable work with the origin of the much-used idiom "on the ball."

Heading toward Oberlin, you'll pass rural homes and enjoy sweeping views of a community golf course. Before entering Oberlin, the route turns off the rail corridor and onto country roads for less than 1 mile. The on-road bike lanes are well defined, traffic is light, and the course is easy to negotiate. The rail-trail picks up again in the beautiful college town of Oberlin. The path travels through the town's central park, which has drinking fountains and a playground, and passes Oberlin's restored train depot. Here you will also find numerous restaurants and shops along nearby Main Street.

Past Oberlin, the vista becomes rolling farmland, with herds of cattle and roaming horses, as well as rural homesteads. Birdlife along the way includes cardinals, turkey vultures, bluebirds, warblers, and vireos. This end of the trail has recently been extended and now continues to the Black River Reservation in Elyria. This trailhead provides restrooms and water fountains, as well as a connection to the Bridgeway Trail.

CONTACT: metroparks.cc/north_coast_inland_trail.php

DIRECTIONS

There is no parking at the western end of the trail. The Kipton trailhead has the closest available parking and is easy to reach. From the Ohio Turnpike (I-80/I-90), take Exit 135, and head south on Baumhart Road/County Road 51. In 1.3 miles turn right onto OH 113. In 1.4 miles turn left onto Vermilion Road, which becomes OH 511. Go 5.2 miles, and turn right onto Rosa St. Park on the right in Kipton Community Park. The end of the trail is 2 miles west.

To reach the Oberlin trailhead from the Ohio Turnpike (I-80/I-90), take Exit 140. Head south on OH 58 to downtown Oberlin. Go 6.4 miles to reach the parking lot on the right at the Oberlin Depot (240 S. Main St.).

To reach the northern end of the trail: From I-90, take Exit 148 for OH 254 toward Sheffield/Avon. Follow OH 254 west 1.6 miles, then turn left onto W. River Road. In 1.5 miles turn left onto Midway Blvd., and continue straight (veering left) onto Ford Road. In 0.5 mile turn left into the Black River Reservation and the High Meadows Picnic Area parking lots.

The North Coast Inland Trail (NCIT) represents a regional collaboration among park districts across the Buckeye State to connect trails linking Ohio to Indiana and Pennsylvania.

Begin this section of the NCIT in Ottawa County's village of Elmore, which has a trailside bike shop as well as a downtown featuring antiques stores and a few small eateries. A restored railroad depot greets visitors, highlighting the history of Penn Central Railroad's Norwalk Branch that served local industries and passengers.

From there, the route heads southeast for nearly a dozen miles to Fremont, entering Sandusky County and transporting trail users through charming small towns,

From the path, you'll have a view of this covered bridge on the grounds of the Sugar Creek Golf Course in Elmore.

Counties
Ottawa, Sandusky

Endpoints
Witty Road, 0.5 mile west of OH 51 (Elmore), to County Road 177 at CR 296 (Bellevue)

Mileage
28.0

Type
Rail-Trail/Rail-with-Trail

Roughness Index
1

Surface
Asphalt

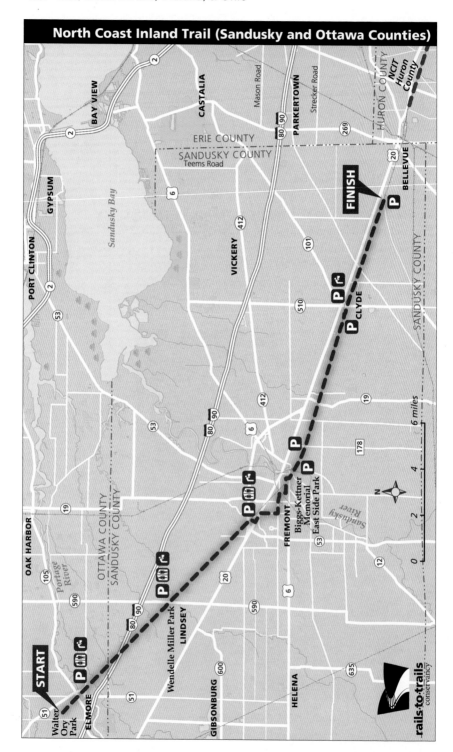

North Coast Inland Trail (Sandusky and Ottawa Counties)

lovely parks, and pristine rural areas. Midway, you'll travel through Lindsey, where you'll find Wendelle Miller Park, which provides public restrooms and drinking water.

At the Walter Avenue trailhead in Fremont, a gap in the trail begins, requiring travel via a low-trafficked, marked on-road route across town. While in town, a notable stop is the Rutherford B. Hayes Presidential Library & Museums, about 0.5 mile from the bike route.

At Hayes Avenue, you can pick up the trail again. As you pedal out of town, you'll cross the spectacular bicycle and pedestrian bridge over the Sandusky River. The path continues just over 12 more miles through Clyde to the western edge of Bellevue, ending at County Road 177. Most of this segment is rail-with-trail and provides proximity to such icons as the world's largest washing-machine factory. You'll also have ample opportunity to take in the Ohio countryside.

On the eastern side of Bellevue, the unpaved Huron County corridor of the NCIT begins and continues eastward (see page 185).

CONTACT: lovemyparks.com/parks/north_coast_inland_trail

DIRECTIONS

On the west end of the trail in Elmore, parking and restrooms are available at Walter Ory Park. From the Ohio Turnpike (I-80/I-90), take Exit 81 for OH 51. At the T-intersection, turn right onto OH 51, and go north 1.3 miles. Entering Elmore, the route becomes Rice St. Cross Ottawa Street and immediately see the park and public parking lot on your right. The trail runs through the park and ends 1.2 miles northwest.

On the east end of the trail in Bellevue, parking is available at County Road 292/Riddle Road. From the Ohio Turnpike (I-80/I-90, take Exit 110 for OH 4. Head south on OH 4, and go 5.6 miles. Turn right onto US 20, and travel 5.7 miles to Riddle Road. Turn left onto Riddle Road, and travel 0.3 mile south to the trail parking lot, which will be on your left. The trail's end is just 0.5 mile east.

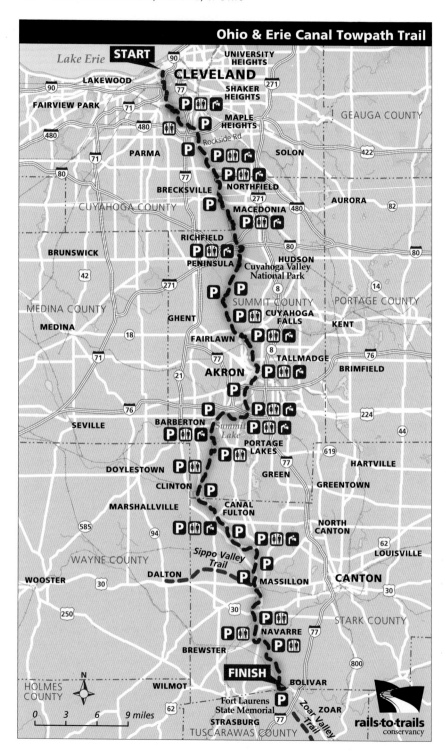

Ohio & Erie Canal Towpath Trail

The Ohio & Erie Canal Towpath Trail is an amazing trail journey that takes users from the heart of this country's industrial might in cities like Cleveland and Akron, to some of the most beautiful places in this part of the world, like Cuyahoga Valley National Park. This more than 80-mile route boasts a little of everything; whether you're looking for a long-distance trail adventure or just a short jaunt, the towpath can deliver in ways few other trails can.

Start in the industrial valley, looking up at downtown Cleveland. Here, a couple of small sections of completed trail will soon be connected to the Harvard Road trailhead, where the majority of the connected trail starts. A well-maintained asphalt surface heads south out of the city. Wonderful trailside exhibits tell the story of the adjacent

The trail runs adjacent to the canal in downtown Akron.

Counties
Cuyahoga, Stark, Summit, Tuscarawas

Endpoints
Scranton Flats at Scranton Road and Carter Road (Cleveland) to OH 212 and Shepler Church Ave. SW (Bolivar)

Mileage
81.1

Type
Canal/Rail-with-Trail

Roughness Index
1

Surface
Asphalt, Crushed Stone, Boardwalk

The Towpath Trail winds through scenic Cuyahoga Valley National Park.

canal's past and present. Remnants of the old canal itself are an almost constant companion, and wildlife sightings are frequent even in the urban environment.

Two world-class trail bridges take users over busy intersections as you meander south to Rockside Road. At this point, the path transitions into a crushed limestone surface as it enters Cuyahoga Valley National Park. The trail—and the park—don't disappoint. The stone surface is firm, even under road tires, and the beautiful scenery of one of the most-visited national parks in the country is hard to just roll by. Constant stops are a must and there are ample opportunities. Quaint historical towns, historical sites, and pure beauty make this section of trail exquisite.

A bustling stop along the route is the community of Peninsula, once a hub of canal activity and now a station on the popular Cuyahoga Valley Scenic Railroad, which features tourist excursions within the park. Many visitors like to bike the Towpath Trail one way and take the train back (only available April–October). In the charming village, travelers will find restaurants, art and antiques shops, an old-fashioned candy shop, and historical homes.

Farther south, you will enter the city of Akron. The trail becomes paved again here and some on-road riding is needed, but the route is not too hard to follow. Akron offers some great historical stops and refreshment opportunities as well.

Moving south, the path becomes boardwalk as it floats across scenic Summit Lake on a buoyed bridge. The trail transitions back to crushed stone with Clinton and Canal Fulton as the next stops; don't miss the seasonal canalboat rides in the latter. The quiet, shaded experience persists all the way to the next city of Massillon. Here, trail users again have a short on-road route to navigate. While not difficult, it does have a couple of short stretches along busier streets.

The path is again beautifully quiet and wild until it comes to the southern trailhead at OH 212 just west of the village of Bolivar. On the south end of Bolivar, the Zoar Valley Trail is accessible at Fort Laurens, though it's a rougher ride best suited for hybrids or mountain bikes.

The Ohio & Erie Canal Towpath Trail is also a major component of the Ohio to Erie Trail (see page 198). The growing 320-mile trail network will eventually span Ohio from the shores of Lake Erie in Cleveland to the Ohio River in Cincinnati.

CONTACT: ohioanderiecanalway.com/Main/Pages/The_Towpath_Trail_56.aspx and **nps.gov/cuva/planyourvisit/ohio-and-erie-canal-towpath-trail.htm**

DIRECTIONS

There are several places to park and access the trail along its more than 80-mile route; below are directions to a few of its main trailheads. Visit the links above or TrailLink.com for more information.

To reach the northern trailhead: From I-71, take Exit 246 for OH 176 S to Parma. Head south on OH 176, and in 0.1 mile, take the Steelyard Dr. exit toward Jennings Road. Take a right onto Steelyard Dr., which becomes Jennings Road. Go 0.5 mile and take a left onto Harvard Ave.; the trailhead is on the right in 0.3 mile.

To reach the Peninsula trailhead within Cuyahoga Valley National Park: From I-77, take Exit 146, and head south on OH 21/Brecksville Road. Go 0.5 mile, and turn left onto Boston Mills Road. In 1.1 miles, take a right onto Black Road. In 1.2 miles, take a left onto OH 303/Streetsboro Road. Travel 3.3 miles into the town of Peninsula, and take a left onto Locust St., then in 0.1 mile another left onto Mill St.; the trailhead is on the left.

To reach the Bolivar trailhead at the southern end of the trail: From I-77, take Exit 93 for OH 212 and go west on OH 212. Go one block, and take a right onto OH 212/Park Ave.; go 0.5 mile. Take a left onto OH 212/Poplar St. Travel 1 mile and find the trailhead on the right.

The Ohio to Erie Trail links dozens of communities from Cleveland to Cincinnati.

The Ohio to Erie Trail is a colossal project, not just for the state of Ohio but also nationally. Dreamed up more than 25 years ago, this route will eventually connect the Ohio River in Cincinnati to Lake Erie in Cleveland. Of its planned 320 miles, more than 270 miles of trail are complete as of early 2017. Trail lovers the world over can now come to the Buckeye State and enjoy either the entire route (with some on-road connectors) or choose from the myriad of completed trails that make up this corridor. Below you'll find a brief overview of the route; learn more about the individual trails that make up the network on TrailLink.com.

Starting in Cleveland, the **Ohio & Erie Canal Towpath Trail** stretches more than 80 miles from the city, through beautiful Cuyahoga Valley National Park and the vibrant city of Akron, south to the village of Bolivar (learn more

continued on page 202

Views of the Columbus skyline are a highlight of the Ohio to Erie Trail experience.

Counties
Clark, Clermont, Cuyahoga, Delaware, Franklin, Greene, Hamilton, Holmes, Knox, Madison, Stark, Summit, Warren, Wayne

Endpoints
Scranton Flats at Scranton Road and Carter Road (Cleveland) to Elm St. and US 52 (Cincinnati)

Mileage
271.9

Type
Rail-Trail/Rail-with-Trail

Roughness Index
1–2

Surface
Asphalt, Concrete, Crushed Stone

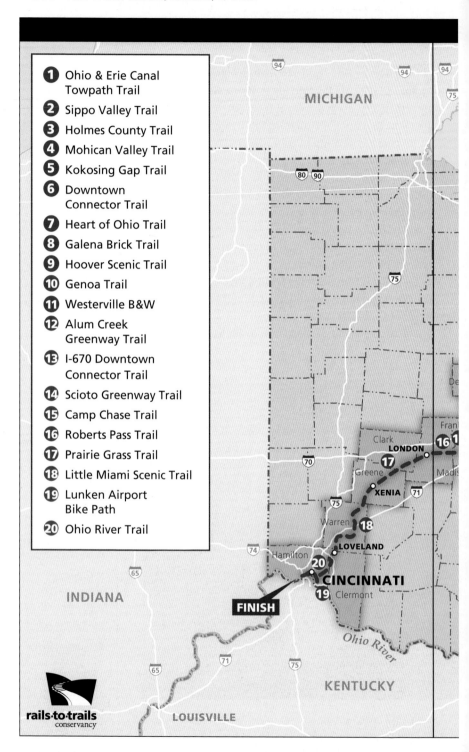

1 Ohio & Erie Canal Towpath Trail
2 Sippo Valley Trail
3 Holmes County Trail
4 Mohican Valley Trail
5 Kokosing Gap Trail
6 Downtown Connector Trail
7 Heart of Ohio Trail
8 Galena Brick Trail
9 Hoover Scenic Trail
10 Genoa Trail
11 Westerville B&W
12 Alum Creek Greenway Trail
13 I-670 Downtown Connector Trail
14 Scioto Greenway Trail
15 Camp Chase Trail
16 Roberts Pass Trail
17 Prairie Grass Trail
18 Little Miami Scenic Trail
19 Lunken Airport Bike Path
20 Ohio River Trail

rails·to·trails
conservancy

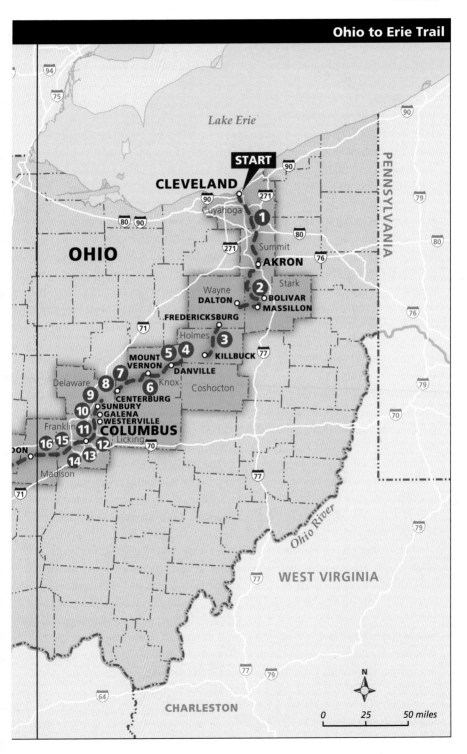

continued from page 199

about the towpath on page 194). As it approaches its southern end, the Towpath Trail connects to the **Sippo Valley Trail** (see page 223) in Massillon. From there, the Sippo Valley Trail heads west into Wayne County and ends in Dalton.

Between Dalton and Fredericksburg, about 17 miles of on-road riding is required, but once in Fredericksburg, you can pick up the **Holmes County Trail** (see page 172), notable for its adjacent Amish buggy path, which creates a unique shared-corridor experience for everyone. Holmes County boasts one of the largest communities of Amish in North America.

From Holmes County, you will enter Knox County and encounter the Bridge of Dreams, Ohio's second-longest covered bridge and quite the trail experience. The **Mohican Valley Trail** includes the bridge and some breathtaking vistas before its end in Danville. Just on the other side of town, you will come upon the crowd favorite **Kokosing Gap Trail** (see page 175), which takes you through the Knox County seat of Mount Vernon. Though short (just a mile long), the **Downtown Connector Trail**, which runs through the heart of Mount Vernon, makes a crucial link to the **Heart of Ohio Trail** (see page 166), a newly emerging route that continues to connect many small towns on its way into suburban Columbus.

The Heart of Ohio Trail whisks travelers to the border of Delaware County. From there, it's about 10 miles of on-road riding to the **Galena Brick Trail**, a mile-long pathway named after the town's historical Galena Shale Tile and Brick Company dating back to the 1890s. On the south side of Galena, you can join the **Hoover Scenic Trail**, a beautiful short paved path with great views of the Hoover Reservoir. The route ends at Plumb Road, where you can connect to the **Genoa Trail**, just on the other side of the roadway. This 4-mile paved path weaves through many landscapes, including some wonderful residential neighborhoods, ending at the border of Westerville. The town offers an exceptional trail system—the **Westerville B&W**—and as you pedal through town, you will be entering Franklin County.

The **Alum Creek Greenway Trail** (see page 148) begins at Westerville's Main Street; heads south, passing under I-270; and travels through Columbus as it follows a lush riparian corridor dotted with parks. At I-670, a short but important connector, the **I-670 Downtown Connector Trail**, takes travelers into the city center. The Scioto River winds right through downtown, and the **Scioto Greenway Trail** (see page 216) hugs its banks, crossing the waterway via an amazing bridge to get into the Hilltop neighborhood. Once in this neighborhood, you can connect to the **Camp Chase Trail** (see page 154) after a short gap. The Camp Chase Trail goes over I-270 and back into the country.

Seamlessly blending together, the **Roberts Pass Trail** picks up where Camp Chase ends in Madison County. Beautiful farmland and wetlands take you into

Natural beauty abounds throughout the trail network, like this wooded section of the Holmes County Trail.

the county seat of London, where you meet the **Prairie Grass Trail** (see page 207) on the other side of town (there's a short gap through town). This paved, 29-mile route crosses classic Ohio farm country with quaint small towns sprinkled all the way to Xenia in Greene County. Xenia Station is the terminus of this trail and the nexus of three other major regional trails, a truly unique place to visit.

Ohio to Erie Trail travelers will take the **Little Miami Scenic Trail** (see page 178) south from here. This Hall of Fame rail-trail begins the final leg of the journey, extending more than 50 miles from Xenia to just outside Cincinnati. A few short miles of on-street riding and a quick hop on a portion of the **Lunken Airport Bike Path** take you to the **Ohio River Trail** in Cincinnati, which allows you to touch the Ohio River and thus end an epic trail adventure.

CONTACT: ohiotoerietrail.org

DIRECTIONS

With such an extensive trail network, there are numerous points at which to park and access the Ohio to Erie Trail system. Please visit the pages referenced above for some of the individual trails within the network, as well as TrailLink.com and ohiotoerietrail.org for interactive maps.

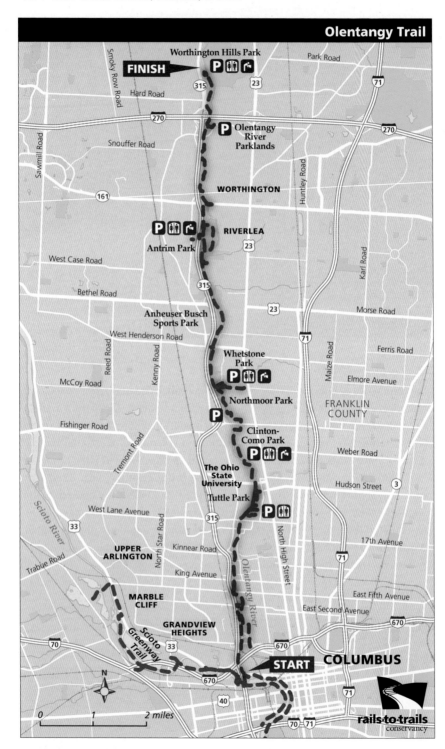

For visitors and locals alike, the Olentangy Trail is the ideal way to explore Columbus, the dynamic capital of Ohio, as well as the surrounding communities. Named after the eponymous river it follows for much of its 17.5 miles, the trail serves as an important link between neighborhoods. Along the route, you can explore natural areas, pass through the heart of The Ohio State University campus, and use the trail as a base from which to travel onward to many of the city's significant historical and cultural sites.

The Olentangy Trail begins west of downtown Columbus at a connection with the Scioto Greenway Trail (see page 216) on the south side of US 33; head north from there, using the well-marked crosswalk at the busy road. Once across the road, the route continues north on the west side of the Olentangy River. At some points, the path is very close to the river and flood warnings are posted.

Enjoy views of the Olentangy River and Columbus skyline along the route.

County
Franklin

Endpoints
US 33/W. Spring St. at OH 315 to Worthington Hills Park at Olentangy River Road/OH 315, just south of Clubview Blvd. S. (Columbus)

Mileage
17.5

Type
Greenway/Non-Rail-Trail

Roughness Index
1

Surface
Asphalt, Concrete

After passing under several highways, the trail becomes quieter, meandering along the riverbank under light tree cover. The sound of flowing water drowns out some of the city noise.

At Third Avenue, a bridge takes you to the east side of the river. At Fifth Avenue, find an upper and a lower route; keep left and follow the lower route to continue north. The upper trail provides access to nearby neighborhoods at Fifth Avenue and King Avenue and features an overlook with a large concrete deck jutting over the river. This vantage point provides a good view of a restoration area created after the removal of the Fifth Avenue dam.

As you traverse The Ohio State University campus—roughly 1 mile—you may want to dismount and walk if traveling by bike. Along the way, spot many trail connectors that provide access to the campus. A local landmark rises on the right side: Ohio Stadium, or the Horseshoe as locals call it, home of the Ohio State Buckeyes football team. The trail then passes under the Lane Avenue Bridge, a striking structure with an amazing cable-stayed design.

Unmarked neighborhood paths periodically feed into the Olentangy Trail, and near mile 4, the university's wetland research area flanks the west side of the route. Stop to take a self-guided tour of the native plants and wetland habitat. Just north of Clinton-Como Park, follow a short stretch on a well-marked route over city streets before rejoining the off-road trail again at Northmoor Park (near the corner of Olentangy Boulevard and Northmoor Place). Farther along, Whetstone Park offers restrooms and a drinking fountain at the Park of Roses, a 13-acre park within a park with more than 12,000 roses and other flora.

At Henderson Road, turn left and follow a wide sidewalk across the bridge to join the trail on the river's west bank. Continue north to a loop around Antrim Lake; you can also cross under Olentangy Freeway (OH 315) to reach Antrim Park, where restrooms are available. After crossing under I-270, it's about 0.8 mile to the trail's end in Worthington Hills Park, where you will find benches, a picnic shelter, and access to parking.

CONTACT: columbus.gov/recreationandparks/trails/Olentangy-Trail and centralohiogreenways.com/index.php/site/full_trail/12

DIRECTIONS

To reach the northern trailhead in Worthington Hills Park, take I-270 to Exit 22, and head north on OH 315. In 0.5 mile, find the Olentangy Valley Center on your right. The trailhead and parking are located in the southeast corner of the shopping center.

Though no designated trail parking lots are on the south end of the trail, its northern half has numerous parking spots in the parks that line the route. Use the links above or visit TrailLink.com for details.

The 29-mile Prairie Grass Trail is one of four rail-trails that radiate from Xenia Station, the hub of a vast, paved trail network in southwestern Ohio. The site is a former Baltimore & Ohio (B&O) freight yard and includes a local history museum that features information about the three railroads that once ran through the town: the B&O Wellston Subdivision and two lines of the Pennsylvania Railroad (the Little Miami branch and the Pittsburgh to St. Louis Main Line).

Today, rail-trails pass through Xenia Station on the converted rail corridors, traveling throughout the scenic Miami River Valley, as well as connecting to the cross-state Ohio to Erie Trail (see page 198). This route, which includes the Prairie Grass Trail, will span 320 miles of trail from the Ohio River in Cincinnati to Lake Erie in Cleveland, allowing for endless exploration.

The paved Prairie Grass Trail travels between Xenia and London, generally following US 42. If you are interested

An artistic sign greets visitors at the trailhead in London.

Counties
Clark, Greene, Madison

Endpoints
Midway St./OH 38 at US 42/High St. (London) to Xenia Station at N. Miami Ave. and S. West St. (Xenia)

Mileage
29.2

Type
Rail-Trail

Roughness Index
1

Surface
Asphalt

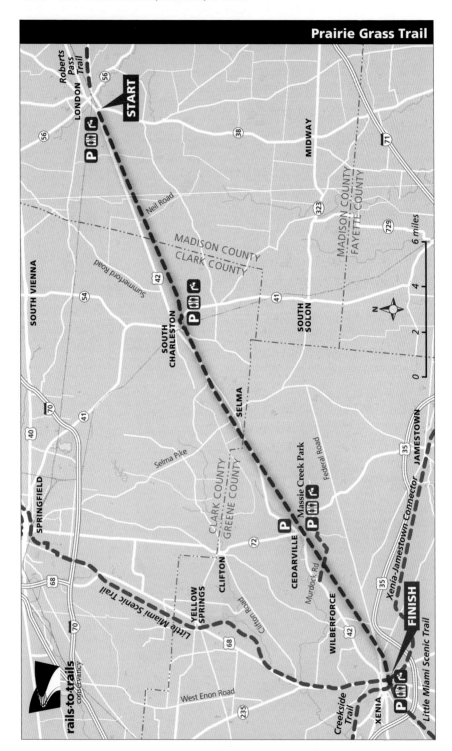

Prairie Grass Trail

in connecting to additional trails in Xenia, begin at the northern trailhead in London, located behind the senior center. Here, you'll find a picnic pavilion, restroom, and a newly added camping area with a shelter house. The trailhead is located across town from the Roberts Pass Trail, which heads east toward Columbus.

Leaving London behind, the path becomes quite rural. You'll find a corridor planted with natural prairie grasses and surrounded by flat, open farmland. In keeping with the prairie grass landscape, there are few trees, which makes it important to keep your water bottles full and sunscreen handy.

After 10.4 miles, you'll reach South Charleston. As the route passes through town, it diverts onto sidewalks for 0.5 mile. A restored train depot highlights the South Charleston trailhead, which also offers picnic tables, water, and restrooms.

Almost 10 miles lie between South Charleston and Cedarville, and vast fields of corn and soybeans dominate the landscape. The route travels close to US 42 for much of the way and also shares the corridor with power lines owned by Dayton Power and Light (which allowed an easement on the corridor that made the path possible).

In Cedarville, the trail travels beside Massie Creek Park, which has parking, water, and portable restrooms. From here, the Prairie Grass Trail runs another 9 miles to its endpoint in Xenia. Just before the crossing at Murdock Road, 1.7 miles out of Cedarville, a couple of benches and a nice overlook provide a relaxing rest stop and views of a small creek and farmland. Also keep an eye out for monarch butterflies, which are prevalent in the area.

As you approach the town of Xenia, there is a busy crossing of Old US 35. The final mile or so has many road crossings; follow the well-placed signs. From the trail's endpoint at Xenia Station, you can head west to Dayton on the Creekside Trail (see page 160), east to Jamestown and beyond on the Xenia-Jamestown Connector (see page 247), and south to Cincinnati or north to Springfield on the Little Miami Scenic Trail (see page 178).

CONTACT: fmcpt.com

DIRECTIONS

The trailhead in London, on the northeast end of the trail, is located behind a senior center, which allows overflow parking in its lot. From I-70, take Exit 72. Head south on OH 56/Urbana-London Road. In 4.7 miles turn right onto W. High St., then in 0.6 mile turn left onto Midway St. The trailhead is on the right. The senior center is 0.1 mile past Midway on US 42/High St.

To reach the Xenia Station trailhead on the southwestern end of the trail: From I-675, take Exit 13A and head east on US 35. In 9.1 miles exit onto US 42. Head north 1.2 miles, and turn right onto S. Miami Ave. Look for the restored depot on the left in 0.4 mile.

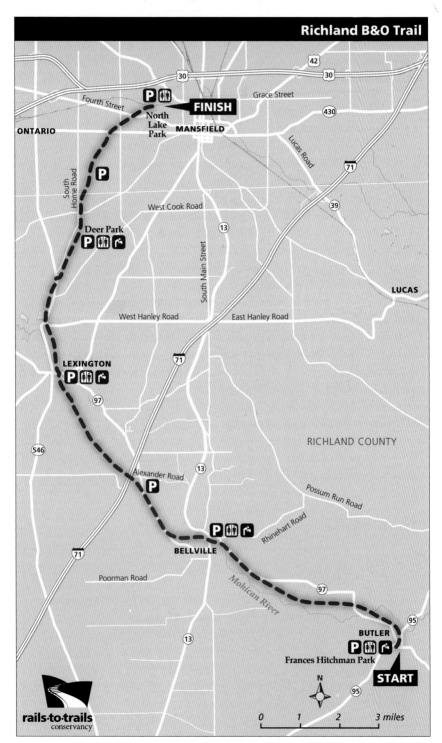

Richland B&O Trail

Traveling just over 18 miles through some of the most scenic areas of the Buckeye State, the Richland B&O Trail is an ideal way to immerse yourself in the region. Built partially as a result of the National Trails System Act amended in 1983, the path follows the disused line of the Baltimore & Ohio Railroad along a semicircular route between Butler and Mansfield in north-central Ohio. In addition to presenting stunning views and abundant wildlife, the trail passes through quaint towns with shops and restaurants.

Begin at Frances Hitchman Park in Butler, where commemorative benches depict the history of the railroad that operated along the corridor. Head northwest as the trail zigzags across several roads and weaves in and out of rural landscapes. Just outside of town, you'll cross a fork of the Mohican River and enjoy beautiful views of the valley from the bridge. On the far side of

This towering structure sits trailside near Bellville.

County
Richland

Endpoints
Simmons St., just southeast of OH 95/Newville St. (Butler), to North Lake Park at Hope Road and Helen Ave. (Mansfield)

Mileage
18.5

Type
Rail-Trail

Roughness Index
1

Surface
Asphalt

the slow-moving river, the trail takes you into quiet rural fields. At the next crossing of OH 97, note that trail users have a stop sign and that motorists have only a warning sign, so use caution.

Cross the river again on a unique curved-deck iron trestle bridge that leads into Bellville, about 5 miles from the start. Just over the bridge, the Bellville trailhead is located in a railroad depot that's a replica of the one built in 1906. The depot offers restrooms, parking, and some interesting information about area history. Several more road crossings are ahead, as is a view south toward downtown Bellville with its classic small-town Main Street shopping district.

After crossing OH 97 again, the path reaches Alexander Road. Here, you'll find many restaurants; just take a right at this crossroads. Continuing on, you'll pass underneath I-71 and then experience a serene journey for the next 2-plus miles, with only one rural road crossing and a few farm fields breaking up the pleasant forested environment.

Coming out of the forest, the trail parallels South Mill Street for about 1 mile and passes a water treatment plant just before arriving in Lexington. The Lexington Senior Civic Center (a former depot) on the left side of the trail provides a restroom and a place to fill your water bottle, the last opportunity for a pit stop for nearly 7 miles.

At mile 15, you'll arrive at Deer Park, which supplies basic trailhead amenities, before arriving at Home Road Marsh. Here, you may see an abundance of bird species, from swallows to hawks, as well as an assortment of other animals, including turtles, snakes, deer, and raccoons. Rest on one of the many benches and observe wildlife. Afterward, reach Mansfield and the tranquil northern end of the trail at North Lake Park.

CONTACT: mansfieldtourism.com/what-to-do/richland-bando-trail-and-mansfield-city-bike-loop

DIRECTIONS

The southern trailhead in Butler is located in Hitchman Park. From I-71, take Exit 165. Head southeast on OH 97 toward Bellville. In 3 miles, turn left onto Main St./OH 97, and go 0.3 mile. Turn right to remain on OH 97, and in 3.9 miles, turn right again onto OH 97. Go 1.8 miles; OH 97 becomes Main St. in Butler. At Elm St., turn right and immediately look for Frances Hitchman Park on your left behind Butler Town Hall.

The northern trailhead in Mansfield is located in North Lake Park. From I-71, take Exit 176 for US 30 W. Travel westbound on US 30 6.7 miles, and take the exit for OH 39 S/Springmill St. Head south on OH 39 into Mansfield; turn right onto Bowman St. in 0.9 mile, then take another right at the first cross street (0.3 mile) onto W. Sixth St. In 0.5 mile, turn right onto Rowland Ave. and continue 0.3 mile into North Lake Park; a parking lot is available on the west side of the lake.

The Rocky River Reservation All Purpose Trail parallels Valley Parkway through several western suburbs of Cleveland, but this is no traditional suburban side path. Instead, the winding trail through the Rocky River Reservation contributes spectacular views, dozens of trailside spots to relax or play, and the perfect shade for a hot summer trail trek. Like many of the trails within Cleveland's impressive Metroparks system, this trail is located close to Ohio's second-largest city, making it immensely popular with both commuters and recreational users every day of the week.

Begin your journey in Berea at the intersection of West Bagley Road and Valley Parkway, where a trailhead

The all-purpose trail offers a wooded escape in the Cleveland suburbs.

County
Cuyahoga

Endpoints
W. Bagley Road and Valley Pkwy. (Berea) to Detroit Road and Valley Pkwy. (Lakewood)

Mileage
13.5

Type
Greenway/Non-Rail-Trail

Roughness Index
1

Surface
Asphalt

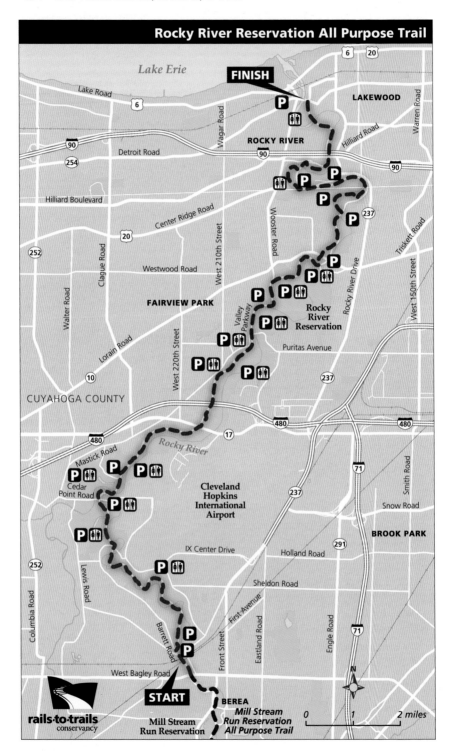

accommodates a handful of vehicles. Be sure to head north from this point; the route that heads south—also worth a trip—moves farther away from Cleveland through the Mill Stream Run Reservation.

After a brief descent, the trail enters the river valley floor, where it remains until it makes a quick ascent to the street network in Lakewood at the opposite endpoint. Shade quickly envelops the path, and it is easy to forget about the nearby road as you enjoy the scenery. The only interruption along this stretch is the frequent roar of low-flying planes as they make their way into and out of Cleveland Hopkins International Airport, whose runway is out of sight due to the dense tree cover.

Those accustomed to trails lacking amenities will be shocked by the number of small parking lots, picnic areas, and recreational fields encountered along the way. The park does its best to accommodate all users, as evidenced by the parallel bridle path that gives horses and their riders a separate winding experience, though it ends near Puritas Avenue, a couple miles south of the main path's northern endpoint. In fact, the trail's only fault may be that it's too skinny to comfortably accommodate the horde of users who want to enjoy it every day.

Be sure to keep your eyes on the path to avoid running into other trail users, but pause to admire the steep shale cliffs in the near distance, as well as closer views of the Rocky River below, near the trail's northern end. Upon the final approach to Detroit Road, you'll encounter a short, steep climb before you emerge on the edge of Lakewood's charming downtown.

CONTACT: clevelandmetroparks.com/parks/visit/parks/rocky-river-reservation

DIRECTIONS

To reach the southern trailhead in Berea, take I-71 to Exit 235, and head west on Bagley Road. Travel 1.9 miles to Valley Pkwy., and turn left. A small parking lot is located on the left shortly after the intersection. Be sure to turn left onto the trail from the parking lot to access the All Purpose Trail; a right will take you onto a trail through the Mill Stream Run Reservation.

To access any of several other parking lots throughout the Rocky River Reservation, follow the same directions above, but instead of turning left onto Valley Pkwy., turn right onto Barrett Road. After 0.3 mile, bear right onto Valley Pkwy. The trail closely follows the road, so park at any parking lot you see and hop right on the path to begin your journey.

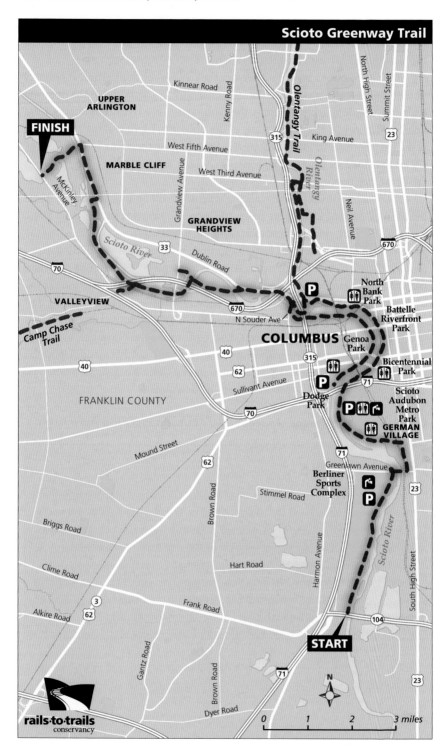

Scioto Greenway Trail

The Scioto Greenway Trail is an urban greenway at its best. A segment of the Central Ohio Greenways trail network that covers more than 120 miles throughout the state, the 12.2-mile multiuse trail hugs the banks of the Scioto River, connecting several parks and presenting fabulous views of downtown Columbus.

The route starts just north of OH 104 and follows the west side of the Scioto River. Parking and access to the trail can be found at Berliner Sports Complex, across the river from German Village. From the park, you can travel north or south on the rail-trail. Southbound, the trail travels through lush forest all the way to the endpoint near OH 104. North takes you to downtown Columbus.

The start of the northbound route is densely forested, making it easy to forget that you are traveling in a large city. At Greenlawn Avenue, ride or walk straight across the street, or descend a steep slope below it to get to the

County
Franklin

Endpoints
OH 104 at I-71 to McKinley Ave. and W. Fifth Ave. (Columbus)

Mileage
12.2

Type
Rail-Trail

Roughness Index
1

Surface
Asphalt, Concrete

The path closely follows the Scioto River.

other side. From there, you'll cross the Scioto River on the Greenlawn Avenue bridge's bike- and pedestrian-friendly path. The next 0.3 mile along Front Street alternates between brick and concrete sidewalk, but note that the route here is unmarked. Turn left, heading west on Whittier Street, to rejoin the paved rail-trail route. The trail curves along the river and passes Scioto Audubon Metro Park, which features a nature center, restrooms, and drinking fountains.

I-70/I-71 roars overhead near mile 3, followed by a breathtaking view of the Columbus skyline. First Bicentennial Park and then Battelle Riverfront Park provide vantage points overlooking the river and the newly transformed riverfront. At North Bank Park, a good stopping point, enjoy the million-dollar view of downtown Columbus from an observation deck over the river.

A short 0.5-mile ride takes you across the river to where the Scioto and Olentangy Rivers meet. Here, the Scioto Greenway Trail connects with the Olentangy Trail (see page 204). Both routes provide access to the urban heart of the city, as well as its many natural areas, vibrant neighborhoods, and important cultural and historical sites.

From North Bank Park, the path travels another 4.5 miles northwest, paralleling city streets. At North Souder Avenue, you have the option of crossing the river and following a trail spur south to Dodge Park. Continuing on the northbound route, you'll travel underneath Grandview Avenue and, shortly thereafter, have the option of crossing the Hilltop Connector bridge over the river to the Hilltop neighborhood and the village of Valleyview, where you can pedal on residential streets for about 0.5 mile to reach the beginning of the Camp Chase Trail (see page 154) at North Eureka Avenue. The Camp Chase Trail continues more than 15 miles southwest, providing access to Battelle Darby Creek Metro Park, a recreational gem of prairies and forests. Both trails are part of the Ohio to Erie Trail network (see page 198), which stretches more than 270 miles across the state.

The Scioto Trail ends at McKinley Avenue, after one final crossing of the river.

CONTACT: columbus.gov/recreationandparks/trails/Scioto-Trail or
centralohiogreenways.com/index.php/site/full_trail/11

DIRECTIONS

Berliner Sports Park is the best southern trail access point. From I-71, take Exit 105, and head east on Greenlawn Ave. for just under 0.25 mile. Turn right onto Deckenbauch Road. The park is on the left. Travel east from the parking lot to access the trail.

Though no designated trail parking lots are on the north end of the trail, a cluster of them is located in the middle of the route, where several parks line the waterfront. Visit the website above or TrailLink.com for directions to those parks.

Seamlessly spanning the 35.5-mile distance between the Ohio communities of Bellefontaine and Springfield, the Simon Kenton Trail presents visitors with ample opportunities for recreation and wildlife sighting throughout its entire length. In reality, though, the uninterrupted trail—named for the famous frontiersman who once lived nearby—is composed of two very distinct experiences with the metaphorical dividing lining at Urbana. North of the city, the trail is crushed stone and rural; from Urbana southward, you'll experience a busier, paved pathway.

From Bellefontaine to Urbana, the trail runs immediately adjacent to a still-active rail line.

Counties
Champaign, Clark, Logan

Endpoints
Carter Ave., 0.1 mile west of Detroit St. (Bellefontaine), to W. Washington St. and S. Center St. (Springfield)

Mileage
35.5

Type
Rail-Trail/Rail-with-Trail

Roughness Index
1–2

Surface
Asphalt, Crushed Stone

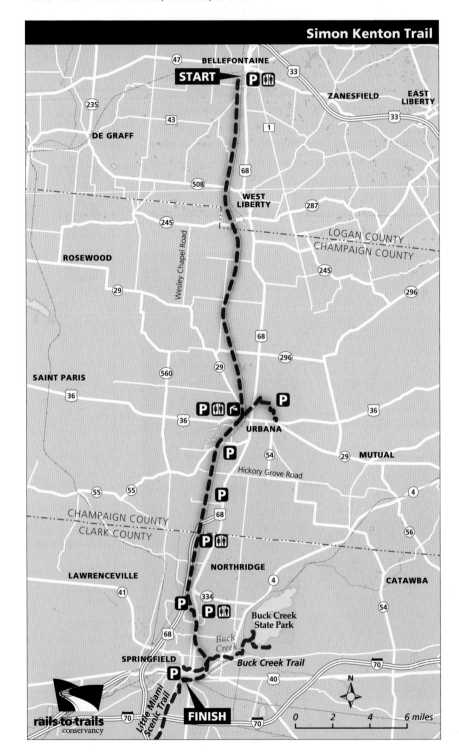

The trail's north end begins in Bellefontaine, a small city where Ohio's highest point can be found. Those accustomed to mountains may be left unimpressed by Ohio's flat peak, and like all rail-trails, the Simon Kenton Trail slopes only gradually, as the corridor once had to accommodate the needs of the many freight and passenger trains that ran through here. In fact, the 16 miles from Bellefontaine to Urbana run immediately adjacent to a still-active rail line.

On this northern 16-mile stretch, farmland reaches out as far as the eye can see. The crushed-stone surface is looser in some spots than others, so even those accustomed to long rail-trail treks will likely work up a sweat in the direct Ohio sun. Amenities are limited, so be prepared with ample amounts of water. The small town of West Liberty offers an opportunity for a rest or bite to eat; turn left onto Runkle Street to access the charming community's downtown.

Entering Urbana, the trail's surface turns to smooth pavement and trees begin to envelop the corridor, providing much welcomed shade. Near the center of town, the Depot Coffee House, in a restored train station adjacent to the trail, serves a wide selection of refreshments, as well as a publicly available parking lot, restrooms, drinking fountains, and a fix-it station for quick bike repairs. From here, a spur trail heads northwest to provide access to local parks and the city's YMCA.

Proceeding south from Urbana, you'll be pedaling on a gradual downhill slope. As you approach Springfield, homes, businesses, and schools begin to line the route, though the corridor's surrounding tree cover is maintained for nearly the entire length. The larger population is noticeable here, as this section sees much heavier traffic than the northern portion. Nearing the city center, you'll cross Buck Creek, where you can pick up the scenic Buck Creek Trail on the far side of the bridge. The trail spans just over 6 miles and heads both east and west along the eponymous waterway.

The Simon Kenton Trail ends in downtown Springfield in front of the Heritage Center, a gorgeous building that once served as both city hall and a marketplace and is now home to a charming café and the Clark County Historical Society. Stop in at the end of your trek to view both the impressive architecture and vast collection. From here, the Little Miami Scenic Trail (see page 178) is just a block away; turn left at South Center Street to reach it. Spanning almost 80 miles, the trail provides access to the artistic community of Yellow Springs, the trail hub of Xenia, and the suburbs of Cincinnati.

CONTACT: miamivalleytrails.org/trails/simon-kenton-trail

DIRECTIONS

To reach the northern endpoint in Bellefontaine from I-75, take Exit 110. Head east on US 33, and go 11.6 miles. Turn right to remain on US 33, and go 12.9 miles to the exit for County Road 37. Turn right onto CR 37, and in 0.1 mile, turn left onto CR 130. In 4.8 miles, turn right onto Troy Road, and go 1 mile. Turn left onto Plumvalley St., and in 0.3 mile, turn right onto Carter Ave. The trailhead is located on the right, 0.2 mile ahead.

To reach the halfway point in Urbana from I-75, take Exit 82. Head 24.8 miles east on US 36 into downtown Urbana. A large trailhead and parking lot are located adjacent to the Depot Coffee House between Glenn Ave. and Washington St.

The southern endpoint is located at the Heritage Center in downtown Springfield, but parking there is limited. Instead, park at the trailhead on Villa Road north of downtown. To reach the trailhead, take I-70 to Exit 52B. Head north on US 68, and go 7 miles to the exit for OH 334. Turn right onto OH 334, stay in the right lane, and in 0.2 mile take the first ramp onto OH 72, heading south. After 1 mile, turn left onto Villa Road. Parking is located on the right after 0.3 mile.

Following a portion of the former Wheeling & Lake Erie Railroad corridor, the Sippo Valley Trail spans 10 miles between Dalton and Massillon in northwestern Ohio, presenting a mix of rolling farmland, forests, and small towns. The trail takes its name from Sippo Creek, which cascades along the side of the path for nearly its entire length. There are numerous small bridge crossings, as well as 12 road crossings. All road crossings are well marked for both trail and road traffic and are easily navigated.

The rail-trail begins in Dalton at Village Green Park, where open green space (bordered by ball fields and a playground) and amenities are plentiful. Heading north out of the park, you'll be traveling a short distance on a marked on-road bike route. Once out of town, though, you'll be on a paved, wooded path.

The path provides a mix of rolling farmland, forests, and small Midwestern towns.

Counties
Stark, Wayne

Endpoints
Village Green Park at Freet St., just south of US 30 Alt./Main St. (Dalton), to Tremont Ave. SW and Fifth St. SW (Massillon)

Mileage
10.0

Type
Rail-Trail

Roughness Index
1–2

Surface
Asphalt, Crushed Stone

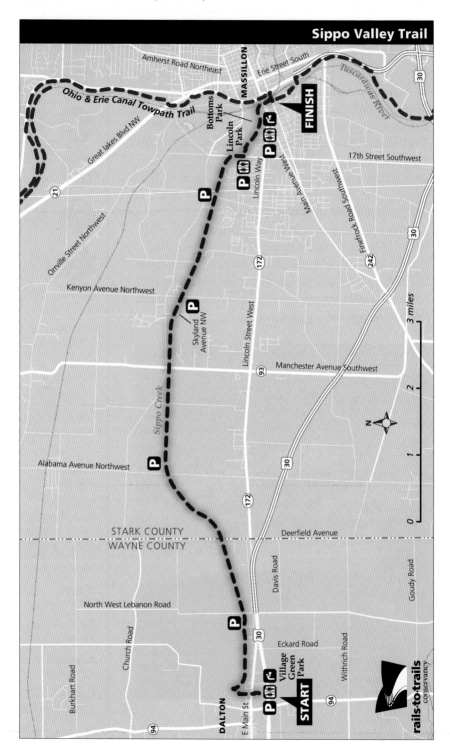

You will come upon numerous small bridge crossings along the trail.

At Deerfield Avenue, which marks the line between Wayne and Stark Counties, you'll begin a 3-mile section that has a crushed-stone surface. In dry weather, the trail here is easily passable; in wet conditions, the stone surface gets slick and may be difficult for road bikers and wheelchair users. Pockets of forest create pleasant shade along the corridor.

The rural feel of the trail begins to change around mile 9 as you enter Massillon. While the path is mostly flat, here you will encounter a short but significant ascent to 17th Street and a steep descent into Lincoln Park. The route ends at Tremont Avenue, where you can pick up the Ohio & Erie Canal Towpath Trail (see page 194), which travels more than 80 miles, including passage through the incredibly scenic Cuyahoga Valley National Park. Both trails are part of the Ohio to Erie Trail (see page 198), a cross-state route stretching from the shores of Lake Erie in Cleveland to the Ohio River in Cincinnati.

CONTACT: starkparks.com/parks/sippo-valley-trail and **waynecountytrails.org**

DIRECTIONS

The Dalton trailhead can be reached by taking I-77 to Exit 104. Head west on US 30/US 62, and go 16.1 miles. Turn right onto US 30 Alt./Main St., and in 0.8 mile, turn left onto Freet St., which dead-ends at Village Green Park.

The Massillon trailhead can be reached by taking I-77 to Exit 104. Head west on US 30/US 62, and go 6.7 miles to OH 21/Great Lakes Blvd. Head north 2.6 miles on OH 21. Exit onto Lillian Gish Blvd., and in 0.1 mile turn left onto Lincoln Way W/OH 172. In 0.2 mile, take a right onto Sixth St. NW and go one block. Take the first left and head west on Water Ave. NW, which dead-ends at Bottoms Park. This is the closest parking to the east end of the trail.

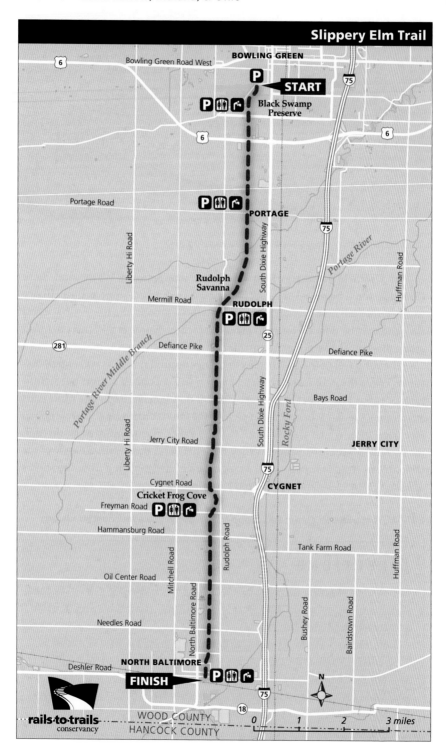

Slippery

In 1875 the Bowling Green Railroad Company operated its first train from its namesake city in Ohio south to Tontogany on rails made from the wood of the local slippery elm tree. The trees were ubiquitous in the Great Black Swamp of northwest Ohio, which was a barrier for the development of farmland and roads in the area due to the expense of draining it. Selling the slippery elm wood to the railroad produced an opportunity to finance the draining. With this lucrative partnership in place, a corridor was cleared for the railroad and farmland was gained. By 1890 the route had been extended to North Baltimore, providing access to a rich gas and oil belt in southern Wood County. For 103 years, the railroad operated along this corridor, until eventually discontinuing service in 1978.

Today, the 13-mile Slippery Elm Trail follows the route of the former rail corridor, running south from

Experience a peaceful ride through rural northwestern Ohio.

County
Wood

Endpoints
Sand Ridge Road and Ontario St. (Bowling Green) to E. Broadway St. near Rhodes Ave. (North Baltimore)

Mileage
13.1

Type
Rail-Trail

Roughness Index
1

Surface
Asphalt

Bowling Green through the small town of Rudolph and ending in North Baltimore. Its half-marathon length is ideal for runners in training, and the smooth, flat surface is a joy for cyclists and in-line skaters. Between Rudolph and the southern endpoint, expansive agricultural landscapes impart the quiet charm visitors have come to expect from this area of the country.

Start in Bowling Green, taking time to explore this vibrant college town, which is brimming with great little shops, restaurants, and cafés. The Sand Ridge Road trailhead is on the south end of town; from there, you'll head south on the paved trail. At 0.5 mile, pass through the Black Swamp Preserve, where restrooms are available.

After 1 mile, the trail ducks under US 6. When you emerge on the other side, the urban surroundings melt away and the countryside takes over. With a keen eye, you may catch sight of red-tailed hawks, white-tailed deer, red squirrels, or the many birds found here. Be sure to take note of the unique terrain: as far as the eye can see, the land here—as in much of northern Ohio—is as flat as a pancake, thanks to the glaciers that moved south through Ohio, leveling everything in their path. This area used to be the Great Black Swamp, leaving behind the rich, fertile farmland that now yields corn, soybeans, and livestock.

In Portage, you'll find a bike repair station, water fountain, and portable restrooms. Continuing south, admire the native plants and pollinator gardens that line the route. If you're here in July, keep your eyes open for blackberries and mulberries, which you are free to pick if you're lucky enough to find them!

Approaching the small, charming community of Rudolph, you'll pass the Rudolph Savanna, a beautiful natural oasis, where you'll find wildflowers, tall prairie grasses, and sand dunes. On your way through town, you'll encounter arguably one of the best signs you will ever see on a rail-trail: "Welcome to Rudolph, the Deerest Little Village in Wood County." There are restrooms and a trailhead in the village.

After Rudolph, you're about halfway along the trail. The southern half is extremely rural and quiet. At Freyman Road, you can take a side excursion by turning right onto the country road and pedaling 0.5 mile to Cricket Frog Cove, a wildlife habitat with hiking trails.

From Freyman Road, it's 3.5 miles to the trail's end in North Baltimore, where you'll find a small park, drinking water, and restrooms.

CONTACT: woodcountyparkdistrict.org

DIRECTIONS

Access the northern trailhead in Bowling Green by taking I-75 to Exit 179. Head 2.2 miles west on US 6, and turn right onto Rudolph Road/County Road 133. Go 0.7 mile, and turn right onto Sand Ridge Road. Trail access and parking is located 0.9 mile ahead on the right at the Montessori School of Bowling Green.

To reach the southern trailhead in North Baltimore, take I-75 S to Exit 168. Turn left onto Insley Road, and in 0.3 mile, turn right onto Eagleville Road, which becomes E. Broadway St. Go 1.2 miles; the parking lot is on the right just after Beecher St. From I-75 N, take Exit 168, and turn right onto Grant Road. In 0.1 mile turn right onto Eagleville Road, and follow the directions above. This trailhead has parking and restroom facilities.

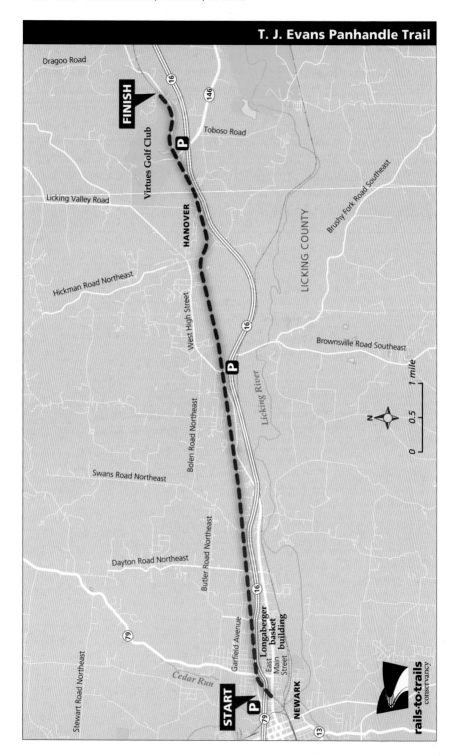

T. J. Evans Panhandle Trail

Cruising along on the nearly 10-mile T. J. Evans Panhandle Trail (known locally as the Panhandle Trail), you might be surprised to encounter a massive basket seemingly plunked down by a giant. In fact, this quirky piece of Americana is the former home of the Longaberger Company, maker of handcrafted baskets. The seven-story building is a replica of the company's iconic Medium Market Basket, and its majestic appearance near the trail adds a surreal spirit to a route that is otherwise imbibed with a friendly neighborhood feel.

Beginning just east of downtown Newark, the T. J. Evans Panhandle Trail runs parallel to active tracks of the Ohio Central Railroad, making this a nice example of a rail-with-trail. Built and funded by the T. J. Evans Foundation, the path is primarily used as a recreational corridor by families who live nearby. Its first few miles

The tree-lined path is especially beautiful in autumn.

County
Licking

Endpoints
E. Main St. at N. Morris St. (Newark) to Felumlee Road/Township Hwy. 193, just north of Marne Road (Hanover)

Mileage
9.8

Type
Rail-Trail/Rail-with-Trail

Roughness Index
1

Surface
Asphalt

are tucked behind neighborhoods and businesses and run along OH 16 and the rail line, illustrating how much urban activity and transportation can fit along a single corridor.

Looking south around mile 3.5, find the larger-than-life Longaberger basket building. Longaberger employees conceptualized the picnic-basket exterior and interior and constructed the majority of the building's cherry woodwork. If you are interested in Longaberger baskets, the town of Frazeysburg, about 10 miles from the trail's end in Hanover, is the site of the Longaberger Homestead. Here you can learn about basketmaking on the weaving floor, visit the shop, or even try your hand at making one of the signature baskets.

For the next handful of miles, the path winds through the rural landscape of eastern Licking County. Here in Amish country, horse and buggy caution signs are as prevalent as cornfields. You sail past grazing cows and hear frogs croaking in marshy areas along the trail. Summer days find turtles sunning on logs and creekbanks. American sycamores, slippery elms, and bittersweet grow in the surrounding woods, and white-tailed deer visit isolated ponds along the route. The best time to experience this trail is early October, when the leaves are bright and the air is crisp. The last 2 miles of the Panhandle Trail mark the southern border of the Virtues Golf Club property, the top-ranked public course in the state; the club also has a nice restaurant.

Back in Newark, you'll find the Panhandle Trail's sister route, the 14-mile T. J. Evans Trail (see page 233) on the west side of town. With Newark's growing trail system, there are less than 2 miles of on-road riding between them.

CONTACT: lickingparkdistrict.com/bike-paths

DIRECTIONS

To reach the trail's west end in Newark, from I-70, take Exit 132. Head north on OH 13, which becomes W. National Dr., and go 7.5 miles. Turn right to stay on W. National Dr., and go 0.3 mile. Turn left onto S. Third St. In 0.4 mile at the traffic circle, take the first exit (right) onto S. Park Pl., and go 0.1 mile. At the next traffic circle, take the second exit (left) onto S. Second St., and go one block. Take a right onto E. Main St. In 0.5 mile, turn left onto N. Morris St. After crossing the railroad tracks, veer right and turn left into the parking lot.

To reach the eastern endpoint in Hanover, from I-70, take exit 129 or 129A. Head north on OH 79, and go 9.4 miles. Turn right onto OH 16 E, and go 10.5 miles to the OH 146/Nashport Road exit. Turn left onto OH 146/Nashport Road, and go 0.3 mile. Turn right onto County Road 585/Marne Road. Go 1 mile to Felumlee Road and turn left. Go across the railroad tracks; the end of the trail will be on your left.

L ocated in central Ohio, the 14-mile T. J. Evans Trail is a popular route, attracting both locals and visitors. With its tree-covered canopy that provides respite from the sun on hot summer days, interludes in charming small towns, and a smooth paved surface, the path offers an ideal day trip with multiple opportunities for side exploration. The corridor was once used by Penn Central Railroad, and railroad enthusiasts will enjoy learning more about this rail line at historical markers along the route.

Begin at the southern trailhead at West Main Street in Newark and head west on the T. J. Evans Trail. As you continue along, you'll head into a beautifully shaded ravine area and hear the rapids of Raccoon Creek on the trail's east side. After passing under OH 16, fields dotted with cows extend from both sides of the path.

A couple of scenic bridges cross over creeks along the rail-trail.

County
Licking

Endpoints
W. Main St. at Coffman Road (Newark) to E. Jersey St. at Track St. (Johnstown)

Mileage
14.3

Type
Rail-Trail

Roughness Index
1

Surface
Asphalt

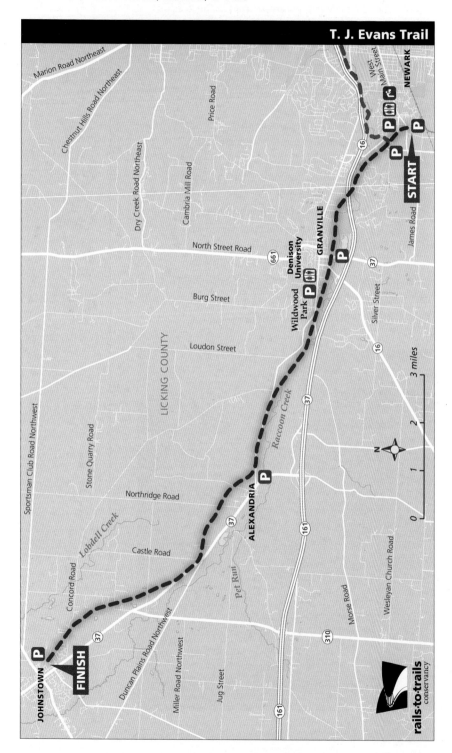

At about 4 miles, you will come to Granville. If you're interested in a side trip, visit Alligator Mound, located less than a mile off the trail, by turning right onto Fairview Drive and heading north. Overlooking Raccoon Creek, this is one of two local animal effigy mounds built by prehistoric people; it is listed on the National Register of Historic Places. Continuing along the trail, follow the signage for a short climb to the beautiful New England–style downtown, where you can find many restaurants, shops, and lodging options, as well as Denison University.

If you remain on the trail, a pedestrian crossing guides you over OH 661 at the former Granville railroad station, which now houses a real estate agent's office. Stop for a break at Wildwood Park, which features open fields and an incredible, wooden castle-shaped play area. Later, arrive at the ruins of Clemons Station. Several bridges span small creeks between here and Alexandria, about 2 miles northwest.

When you cross Raccoon Valley Road, you are in the village of Alexandria. The remaining 6.3 miles of trail to Johnstown pass alternately through woods, ravines, and farm fields. The setting is remote and relaxing, but the many rural road crossings require caution.

The Jersey Street trailhead in Johnstown signals the route's end. The beautiful T. J. Evans rail-trail only gets better on the return trip, as a slight grade gives you a downhill advantage.

Once back in Newark, you can pick up the T. J. Evans Panhandle Trail (see page 230) on the east side of town. Near the Cherry Valley Road parking lot where you started your adventure, you can take a spur trail north under Reddington Road, which then shortly thereafter heads east, paralleling OH 16 toward downtown and leading to a shopping area, Flory Park, and the local YMCA. From there, it's less than a 2-mile on-road ride to connect to the T. J. Evans Panhandle Trail.

CONTACT: lickingparkdistrict.com/bike-paths

DIRECTIONS

To start the trail in Newark, take I-70 to 129A, and head north on OH 79. Go 6.1 miles, and turn left onto Irving Wick Dr. Go west 1.7 miles, then turn right onto Thornwood Dr. SW. In 1 mile turn right onto W. Main St. In 0.5 mile look for the trail parking area on the right.

To reach the Jersey St. trailhead in Johnstown: From I-270 on the northeast side of Columbus, take Exit 33 toward Easton. Keep left to continue to Exit 30 for OH 161. Once on OH 161, go 4.5 miles east to US 62/Johnstown Road. Turn left here and head northeast 7.9 miles. Turn right onto OH 37, and go 0.3 mile. Take a left onto Jersey St. Jersey St. dead-ends at the trailhead parking lot in 0.25 mile.

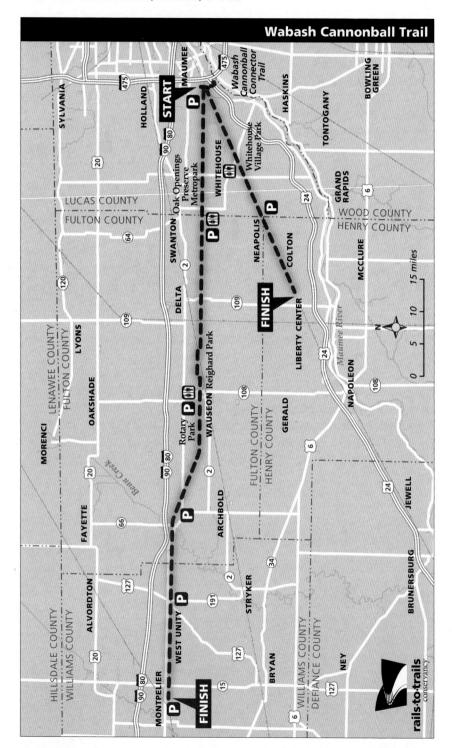

Wabash Cannonball Trail

The Wabash Cannonball Trail in northwest Ohio is actually two trails in one: its North Fork runs east–west for 46 miles and its South Fork makes up the balance of this nearly 63-mile trail. The forks converge in the eastern city of Maumee and then jackknife away on their separate routes.

The Wabash Cannonball, one of the state's longest rail-trails, traverses four counties along the former corridor of two rail lines established by the Wabash Railroad. The South Fork was built in 1855 and the North Fork circa 1900. See vestiges of the Wabash as you travel through the small towns that were once bustling with railroad activity. Spot an original depot, travel over railroad bridges, and browse railroad memorabilia at the historical museum in nearby downtown Montpelier.

Also enjoy spectacular wildlife-viewing opportunities. Portions of the trail are segments of the North

Counties
Fulton, Henry, Lucas, Williams

Endpoints
Jerome Road, 0.1 mile south of Monclova Road (Maumee), to Airport Road and Magda Dr. (Montpelier) and County Road 6C, 0.5 mile north of CR T (Liberty Center)

Mileage
62.9

Type
Rail-Trail/Rail-with-Trail

Roughness Index
2

Surface
Asphalt, Crushed Stone

The trail traverses four counties in the rural northwestern corner of Ohio.

The North Fork of the trail crosses several bridges over small creeks, marshy wetlands, and deeper ravines.

Country National Scenic Trail, a 4,600-mile-long hiking trail that will eventually connect the Lewis & Clark National Historic Trail in western North Dakota with the Appalachian Trail in Vermont.

Begin in Maumee on the east end of the trail, where both sections of the route begin at Jerome Road within sight of The Shops at Fallen Timbers. Don't be confused by the sign labeled WABASH CANNONBALL TRAIL—NORTH FORK; just 0.25 mile west, the South Fork breaks off to the left while the North Fork continues straight.

It's worth noting that a side excursion to the Fallen Timbers Battlefield and Fallen Timbers State Memorial (recognizing the 1794 battle that helped open the Northwest Territory) is within easy reach; simply take a paved trail spur south along Jerome Road for 1.6 miles, passing over US 24 on a bicycle and pedestrian bridge. Side Cut Metropark is also accessible on the south side of the US 24 bridge. The park gets its name from an offshoot of the Miami and Erie Canal and provides a great place to learn about Ohio's canal history or enjoy beautiful views of the Maumee River.

Traveling west from Jerome Road, the first 9.5 miles of the North Fork are nicely paved. Travel across several bridges over small creeks, marshy wetlands, and deeper ravines before the pavement ends and the smooth paved trail gives way to crushed stone, grass, and dirt for the remainder of its length, with the exception of 2 paved miles in the town of Wauseon.

Along this first paved stretch, you'll traverse the scenic Oak Openings Preserve Metropark. More than 50 miles of trail, a few of which intersect with the Wabash Cannonball Trail, exist within the park, so you'll have the option to take one of these into the park to explore the range of habitats found within its almost 5,000 acres.

Approaching Wauseon, the trail follows a short on-road section at County Road 11. To navigate this, take a right onto CR 11, traveling north 0.2 mile, and then turn left onto CR F, traveling west 2 miles, before turning left onto CR 13 another 0.2 mile south. The trail appears again on the right.

Back on the path, you come to the town of Wauseon. Rotary Park, on the right side of the trail, offers parking, restrooms, and plenty of shade. Continue to the trail's end in Montpelier.

The beautiful South Fork route travels through western Lucas County for about 17 miles. The first 10.5 miles are paved and deliver a fun, flat, and fast ride. The final miles are similar to the unpaved section on the North Fork; the crushed-stone section is best suited to walkers, equestrians, and hybrid or fat-tire bikes.

As you traverse the charming community of Whitehouse, you'll pass Whitehouse Village Park, where you can find restrooms and picnic tables. A little farther on, you'll spot a red caboose circa 1927 sitting trailside. Just before the caboose, you'll cross Providence Street, a major thoroughfare in town; turn right onto the street if you want to reach restaurants. You'll pass through two more small communities, Neapolis and then Colton, before reaching the trail's end on the rural outskirts of Liberty Center.

CONTACT: wabashcannonballtrail.org

DIRECTIONS

The main trailhead is at Jerome Road in Maumee. From I-475 on Toledo's west side, take Exit 4 or 4A for US 24, and head east 0.75 mile to Monclova Road. Turn left onto Monclova, and travel 1.3 miles before turning left onto Jerome Road. The trailhead and parking are on the right in 0.1 mile.

To reach the North Fork's Montpelier trailhead: From I-80/I-90, take Exit 13 to merge onto OH 15 S/US 20 Alt. S. Find the parking lot on your right in 2 miles, just past the trail and near Magda Dr.

The best trailhead for the South Fork is in Whitehouse. From I-475, take Exit 4, and head west on US 24. In 5.4 miles, take Exit 63. Turn right onto OH 64, and go 2.5 miles. Turn right onto Gilead St. or Providence St., and park at Whitehouse Village Park, which is adjacent to the trail on St. Louis Ave.

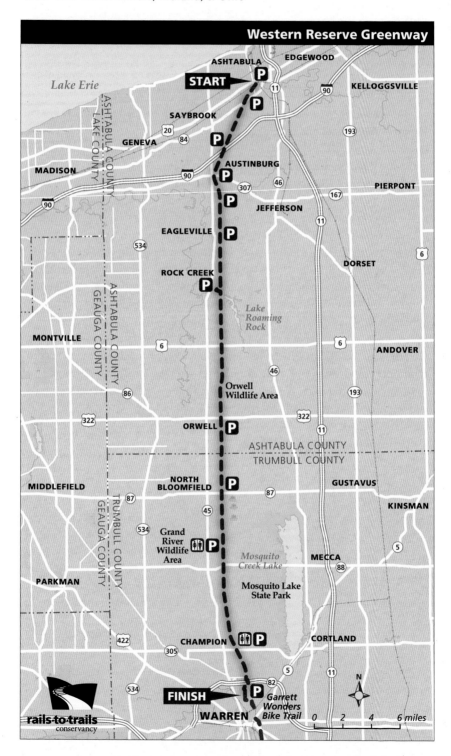

The Western Reserve Greenway travels 43 miles through a scenic, mostly rural area, cutting a north–south course from Ashtabula to Warren in northeastern Ohio. The route follows much of the Pennsylvania Railroad's former branch line, extending to the shores of Lake Erie at Ashtabula. This rail line once transported iron ore to the steel mills of eastern Ohio and western Pennsylvania. Today, the trail is the longest section of the planned 110-mile Great Ohio Lake-to-River Greenway that will begin on the shores of Lake Erie and travel south to the banks of the Ohio River in East Liverpool.

The Western Reserve Greenway begins only a few miles from Lake Erie, and a planned extension will bring it right to the shoreline. For now, you can start at Herzog Rotary Park (off Woodman Avenue), where you will find the first of 12 interpretive signs detailing the importance

Fall is a spectacular time to visit the tree-shaded path.

Counties
Ashtabula, Trumbull

Endpoints
W. 52nd St. and Madison Ave. (Ashtabula) to N. River Road NW, 0.1 mile west of Sferra Ave. NW (Warren)

Mileage
43.0

Type
Rail-Trail

Roughness Index
1

Surface
Asphalt

Heading north of Warren, the trail dives into more trees.

of northeast Ohio in the Underground Railroad. The greenway is used year-round, but note that snowmobiling is allowed only in Ashtabula County (the northern half of the trail).

Heading south, cross the historical King Bridge, a steel trestle built in 1897 that now spans Clay Street. Ahead is Austinburg, with a trailhead and plenty of options for food and drink. South of town, reenter the trail's rural surroundings and enjoy the company of deer, beavers, and a multitude of birds, including wild turkeys and waterfowl.

As you pass through the small town of Rock Creek, you will have a short section of on-road riding. Upon leaving the community, you'll cross a trestle spanning the eponymous watercourse. The bridge features bump-outs that give a bird's-eye view of the creek and scenery below. When the path picks up again, you sail beneath sheltering trees and past the tiny village of Orwell, with a trailhead located below a water tower off Oak Street.

A stone arch bridge over Baughman Creek in Trumbull County is a true highlight of the Western Reserve Greenway (see note on the next page).

Back on the trail, you will come to the Sunside trailhead at OH 305, where you'll find a large parking lot and restrooms. The rail-trail continues beyond here to North River Road in Warren, where you can connect to the Garrett Wonders Bike Trail heading south into town.

Closure Notice: A portion of the Western Reserve Greenway between Mahan Denman Road and Hyde-Oakfield Road near the southern end of the trail (about a mile northeast of Bristolville) is closed until further notice. A sandstone arch bridge over Baughman Creek, dating back to the mid-1800s, is awaiting repair. To detour around the closure, take Mahan Denman Road west to Oakfield North Road, head south to Hyde-Oakfield Road, and then head east to return to the trail. For more information, please visit trumbullmetroparks.org.

CONTACT: ashtabulametroparks.com/western-reserve-greenway-trail and trumbullmetroparks.org/parks-and-trails/western-reserve-greenway

DIRECTIONS

At the northern end of the trail, there are two places to park in Ashtabula. The first is at H. L. Morrison Station on W. Ave. Take I-90 to Exit 223, and head north on OH 45. In 0.2 mile turn right onto Austinburg Road, and go 5.3 miles. Turn right onto OH 84, and go 0.3 mile. Turn left onto West Ave. The station is 0.5 mile ahead on the right. The other place to park is at the Herzog Rotary Park trailhead, located on the west side of Woodman Ave. To reach it, follow the directions above to OH 84. Turn left onto OH 84, and in 0.1 mile turn right onto Woodman Ave. The trailhead will be on the left in 0.2 mile.

The trailhead in Austinburg can be reached from I-90 by taking Exit 223 for OH 45. Head south on OH 45, and go 1 mile. Turn left onto OH 307 and go 0.1 mile. The trailhead is on the left at the edge of town. A large parking area and trailhead are available at Jefferson-Eagleville Road along the eastern side of the trail. To reach that trailhead, take I-90 to Exit 223, and head south on OH 45. In 5.1 miles, turn left onto Jefferson-Eagleville Road. The lot is on the right in 0.4 mile.

To reach the Sunside trailhead in Warren, take I-80 to Exit 209. Head east on OH 5, and go 7.6 miles. Take the exit for OH 45, and turn left. Go 2.4 miles, and turn right onto OH 305. Go 0.8 mile, and look for the trailhead on your left.

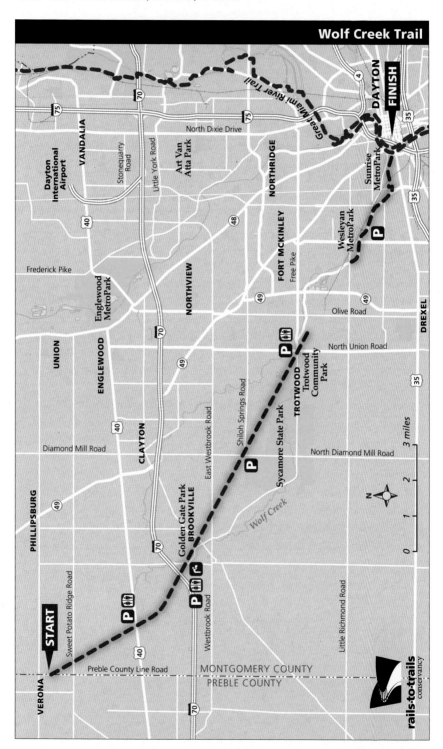

Wolf Creek Trail

DAYTON

FINISH

Great Miami River Trail

4

35

75

North Dixie Drive

75

Sunrise MetroPark

VANDALIA

Stonequarry Road

Little York Road

Art Van Atta Park

NORTHRIDGE

Wesleyan MetroPark

P

35

Dayton International Airport

40

48

FORT MCKINLEY

Free Pike

Frederick Pike

49

Olive Road

49

DREXEL

NORTHVIEW

Englewood MetroPark

70

North Union Road

UNION

Trotwood Community Park

P

35

ENGLEWOOD

49

TROTWOOD

Shiloh Springs Road

Diamond Mill Road

40

North Diamond Mill Road

CLAYTON

East Westbrook Road

Sycamore State Park

3 miles

PHILLIPSBURG

49

P

N

2

Golden Gate Park

BROOKVILLE

Wolf Creek

1

70

0

Sweet Potato Ridge Road

START

P

P

Little Richmond Road

Westbrook Road

VERONA

40

Preble County Line Road

MONTGOMERY COUNTY

PREBLE COUNTY

70

rails-to-trails
conservancy

Ohio's Miami River Valley, with 340 miles of off-road trails, is home to one of the nation's largest paved trail networks. The trails connect cities and small towns; link to cultural, educational, and natural sites; and provide a safe, car-free route to explore the beautiful southwest corner of the state. Heading northwest from Dayton, the 16.2-mile Wolf Creek Trail is one piece of this important resource.

The well-maintained asphalt route is currently open in two disconnected segments. The longest section of the trail begins in Verona at the Preble County line and heads southeast 13 miles to end in Trotwood in Montgomery County, with a shorter, slightly over 3-mile segment radiating from Dayton's Sunrise MetroPark.

The northern segment follows the former corridor of the Dayton and Greenville Railroad. The railway was built in 1852 and went through many mergers over the years before finally ending service in the 1980s.

The rail-trail heads northwest out of Dayton through a wooded river corridor.

Counties
Montgomery

Endpoints
Preble County Line Road at Hemlock St. (Verona) to Vickwood Ln., 0.1 mile south of Wolf Creek Pike (Trotwood); and N. James H. McGee Blvd., 350 feet south of Little Richmond Road, to Sunrise MetroPark at W. Third St. and N. Edwin C. Moses Blvd. (Dayton)

Mileage
16.2

Type
Rail-Trail

Roughness Index
1

Surface
Asphalt

Starting at the western end, near Sweet Potato Ridge Road, the trail's first 5 miles pass through spacious expanses of farm fields. At US 40, you'll reach a trailhead; the busy crossing is unmarked for motorists, so take care. Shortly thereafter, an underpass for I-70 provides safe passage from heavy traffic. On the other side, enter Brookville, a sleepy town of 5,800. A real gem here is Golden Gate Park, which features a kids' playground that resembles a scaled-down castle and even hosts local theater productions. Also find restrooms, water fountains, and picnic shelters.

At Snyder Road, you will come upon an entrance to Sycamore State Park, which has miles of hiking and bridle trails under canopies of giant sycamore trees. Farther on, the Olde Town Depot in Trotwood, with historical exhibits, an information kiosk, and restored railroad cabooses, is an ideal spot for a break. A bus stop in front of this old railroad station provides a convenience for bike and bus commuters. The trail continues less than a mile from here, crossing Wolf Creek before the first segment ends.

After a short gap, the shorter section of the trail begins farther east and follows Wolf Creek for most of its journey toward downtown Dayton. While it is possible to bridge the 3.5-mile gap on-road, the route is very busy and not recommended. Pick up the trail at Little Richmond Road and James H. McGee Boulevard, and travel about 3 miles to end in Sunrise MetroPark, where the Wolf Creek Trail meets the Great Miami River. In the park, the path connects with the Great Miami River Trail (see page 163), which stretches more than 80 miles between Piqua and Fairfield.

CONTACT: metroparks.org/places-to-go/paved-trails/#wolf-creek-trail

DIRECTIONS

To reach the Verona trailhead on the northwestern end: From I-70 W, take Exit 24 toward OH 49. Continue north on OH 49, and go 1.3 miles to Wengerlawn Road. Turn left onto Wengerlawn and look for the trailhead just past Number 9 Road, after 4.5 miles. From I-70 E, take Exit 14, and head north on OH 503. In 1.3 miles, turn right onto US 40, and go 2.9 miles. Turn left onto Preble County Line Road, and in 0.9 mile turn right onto Wengerlawn Road. Go 1 mile to the trailhead.

The Olde Town Depot trailhead in Trotwood is located at the intersection of Wolf Creek Pike/Main St. and Broadway. From I-70 W, take Exit 26, and head south on Hole road. Go 0.3 mile and turn left onto OH 49. Follow the directions below from OH 49. From I-70 E, take Exit 26, and head southeast on OH 49. In 3.5 miles, turn right to remain on OH 49, and continue 1.6 miles. Turn right onto E. Main St. toward Trotwood and look for the depot after 1.6 miles.

To access the shorter trail segment on Dayton's west end, park in Wesleyan MetroPark (2222 N. James H. McGee Blvd.). From I-75, take Exit 52 for US 35 W. Head 0.1 mile west on US 35 and take the exit for James H. McGee Blvd. Take a right onto the boulevard and follow it north 2.1 miles to the park; the parking lot will appear on your right.

The Xenia–Jamestown Connector links these two eponymous communities and travels east beyond Jamestown to the Greene–Fayette County line at Rosemoor Road. It's part of Ohio's Miami River Valley trail system, one of the nation's largest networks of paved, off-street trails. From its starting point in Xenia, the path is less than 0.5 mile from the trail hub at Xenia Station, where you can pick up the Little Miami Scenic Trail, the Creekside Trail, and the Prairie Grass Trail (see pages 178, 160, and 207, respectively).

A thick canopy of deciduous trees shades the trail corridor.

County
Greene

Endpoints
Washington St., 0.1 mile east of US 68 (Xenia), to Rosemoor Road, 0.75 mile south of Old US 35 (Silvercreek)

Mileage
15.7

Type
Rail-Trail

Roughness Index
1

Surface
Asphalt

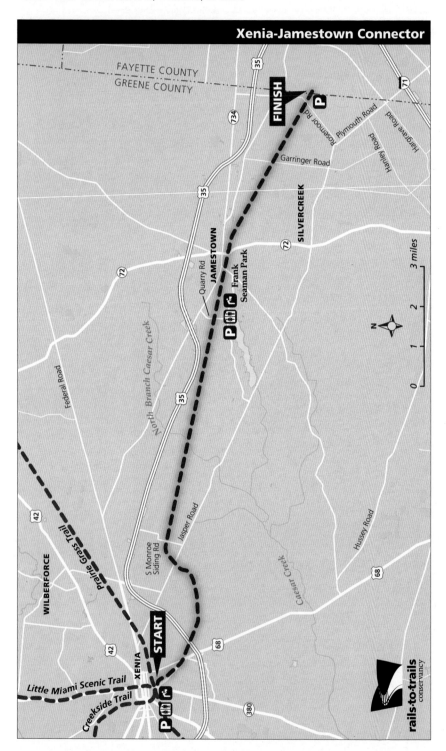

From Washington Street in Xenia, you'll pedal southeast out of town, largely under a thick canopy of trees. You'll pass under US 35 and continue through a mixture of forests and vast farm fields that dominate this part of central Ohio. From the underpass, it's 2.7 miles to South Monroe Siding Road. As you approach the roadway, look to your left and you'll see a small airfield for Skydive Greene County, which offers skydiving opportunities; on a nice day, you may see airplanes taking off and landing, and parachutists in the sky.

After another 2.4 miles, the path crosses the North Branch of Caesar Creek. The bridge has a nicely built concrete deck and scenic views both up and down the meandering waterway. With lush vegetation clinging to the banks, it is well worth a stop.

From the creek, it's 3 miles of rural riding before you reach a well-marked crossing of Quarry Road. About 0.5 mile farther and you'll come to a spur on your right leading south into Frank Seaman Park. The park supplies ample amenities, including restrooms, water, parking, and a picnic area, as well as ample green space to unwind.

From the park, you enter Jamestown. The trail experience here becomes busier, with a mix of residential and commercial areas close at hand. As you leave town, the last 4 miles of the route become rural once again to the trail's end at Rosemoor Road.

CONTACT: gcparkstrails.com/243/Xenia-Jamestown-Connector

DIRECTIONS

To reach Xenia Station, near the north end of the trail, from I-675, take Exit 13A, and head east on US 35. In 6.6 miles, veer right to remain on US 35 E toward Washington C H. Continue 2.5 miles, and exit onto US 42. Head north on US 42, and go 1.2 miles. Turn right onto S. Miami Ave., and turn left into the station parking lot in 0.4 mile.

For the southern end of the trail, the best parking can be found in Frank Seaman Park. To reach the park from I-71, take Exit 58. Head north on OH 72, and go 5 miles. Turn left onto Jasper Road, and go 2.3 miles. Turn right onto Waynesville Jamestown Road, and go 1.8 miles. Turn left onto Cottonville Road. Just 0.8 mile down the road, look for Greenview High School on the right. Access Frank Seaman Park by going through the high school parking lot and turning right.

A

B

C

Presented by

rails·to·trails
conservancy

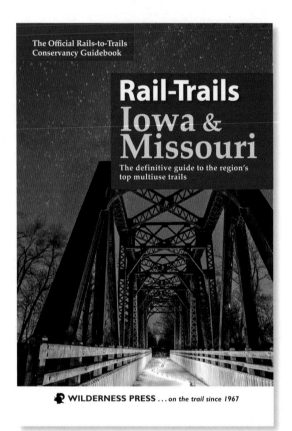

The Official Rails-to-Trails
Conservancy Guidebook

Rail-Trails
Iowa &
Missouri
The definitive guide to the region's
top multiuse trails

🐾 **WILDERNESS PRESS** ... *on the trail since 1967*

Rail-Trails: Iowa & Missouri

ISBN: 978-0-89997-846-8   176 pages, full-color
$16.95, 1st Edition   maps and photos

Explore 44 of the best rail-trails and multiuse pathways across two
states. Enjoy one of the most well-known trail art installations in the
country along Iowa's High Trestle Trail, or visit some of Missouri's
most welcoming communities on the nearly 240-mile Katy Trail.
You'll love the variety in this collection of Midwestern multiuse
trails—from beautiful waterways and scenic areas to the hustle and
bustle of the states' urban centers.

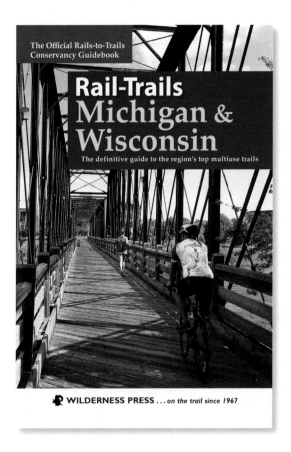

Rail-Trails: Michigan & Wisconsin

ISBN: 978-0-89997-873-4   264 pages, full-color
$18.95, 1st Edition   maps and photos

Explore 63 of the best rail-trails and multiuse pathways across two states. Discover Wisconsin's iconic Elroy-Sparta State Trail—widely acknowledged to be the oldest rail-trail in America—or Lake Michigan Pathway, which features beaches and marinas that will keep you in close touch with its namesake. You'll love the variety in this collection of Midwestern multiuse trails—from beautiful waterways and scenic areas to the hustle and bustle of the states' urban centers.

Page iii: Ronald P. Ziolkowski Jr.; *page x:* courtesy of the Sweetser Park Board; *page 7:* Ryan Cree; *page 9:* Tom Roach; *page 11:* Aurie Barnes; *page 15:* Ken Bryan; *page 19:* Katie McKinney Guerin; *page 21:* Liz Thorstensen; *page 23:* Liz Thorstensen; *page 25:* S. Haberstroh; *page 29:* Ken Bryan; *page 33:* Rick Pawela; *page 35:* Ryan Cree; *page 37:* Ryan Cree; *page 41:* Viana Oliver; *page 45:* courtesy of the Springfield-Sangamon County Regional Planning Commission; *page 47:* Frank L. Masterman; *page 51:* Ken Bryan; *page 53:* Tracy L. Doyle; *page 57:* Ken Kogler; *page 59:* John Zurbriggen; *page 63:* Katie McKinney Guerin; *page 65:* Molly McKinney; *page 69:* John Junker; *page 71:* Steve Blackburn; *page 75:* courtesy of the Rails-to-Trails Conservancy; *page 79:* Ryan Cree; *page 81:* Jennifer Davis; *page 85:* Katie McKinney Guerin; *page 89:* Brad Wallace; *page 90:* Debbie Innis; *page 93:* Paul Procaccio; *page 95:* John Tierney; *page 99:* Tom Roach; *page 101:* courtesy of the Rails-to-Trails Conservancy; *page 103:* courtesy of Cardinal Greenway, Inc.; *page 107:* Adam Moss; *page 111:* Tom Roach; *page 113:* Cindy Dickerson; *page 117:* courtesy of Indy Parks & Recreation; *page 118:* courtesy of Indy Parks & Recreation; *page 121:* Cindy Dickerson; *page 123:* Tom Roach; *page 127:* Cindy Dickerson; *page 129:* Rich Dominiak; *page 133:* Cindy Dickerson; *page 135:* Cindy Dickerson; *page 137:* Cindy Dickerson; *page 139:* courtesy of the Sweetser Park Board; *page 143:* Cindy Dickerson; *page 147:* Ryan Simmons; *page 149:* Brian Housh; *page 151:* Rob Blair; *page 155:* Brian Housh; *page 157:* Matthew J. Gilson; *page 161:* Tom Bilcze; *page 163:* Eli Griffen; *page 167:* Chuck Gulker; *page 169:* Eric Oberg; *page 173:* Calvin Holderbaum; *page 175:* Tom Bilcze; *page 179:* Abigail Holloran/courtesy of Greene County Parks & Trails; *page 180:* courtesy of Greene County Parks & Trails; *page 183:* courtesy of Mill Creek MetroParks; *page 185:* Eric Oberg; *page 189:* courtesy of Lorain County Metro Parks; *page 191:* Eli Griffen; *page 195:* Bruce S. Ford/courtesy of Summit Metro Parks; *page 196:* Rob Blair; *page 198:* Richard T. "Tom" Bower; *page 199:* Susan Sharpless Smith; *page 203:* Calvin Holderbaum; *page 205:* Adam Schweigert; *page 207:* courtesy of Friends of Madison County Parks & Trails; *page 211:* Tom Bilcze; *page 213:* Eric Oberg; *page 217:* Susan Sharpless Smith; *page 219:* Eli Griffen; *page 223:* Denny Williams/courtesy of Stark Parks; *page 225:* Denny Williams/courtesy of Stark Parks; *page 227:* Jared M. McCool; *page 231:* Brian Spain; *page 233:* Paul Black; *page 237:* Christine Heflinger; *page 238:* Christine Heflinger; *page 241:* Tom Bilcze; *page 242:* Tom Bilcze; *page 245:* Amy Forsthoefel/courtesy of Five Rivers MetroParks; *page 247:* Eric Oberg.

The nation's leader in helping communities transform unused rail lines and connecting corridors into multiuse trails, Rails-to-Trails Conservancy (RTC) depends on the support of its members and donors to create access to healthy outdoor experiences.

Your donation will help support programs and services that have helped put more than 22,000 rail-trail miles on the ground. Every day, RTC provides vital assistance to communities to develop and maintain trails throughout the country. In addition, RTC advocates for trail-friendly policies, promotes the benefits of rail-trails, and defends rail-trail laws in the courts.

Join online at railstotrails.org, or mail your donation to Rails-to-Trails Conservancy, 2121 Ward Court NW, Fifth Floor, Washington, D.C. 20037.

Rails-to-Trails Conservancy is a 501(c)(3) nonprofit organization, and contributions are tax deductible.